HARVARD ECONOMIC STUDIES, Volume 146

Awarded the David A. Wells Prize for the year 1973–74
and published from the income of the David A. Wells fund.

The studies in this series are published under the
direction of the Department of Economics of
Harvard University. The Department does not
assume responsibility for the views expressed.

# Interbrand Choice, Strategy, and Bilateral Market Power

Michael E. Porter

Harvard University Press
Cambridge, Massachusetts
and London, England 1976

Copyright © 1976 by the President and Fellows of Harvard College
All rights reserved
Printed in the United States of America
Library of Congress Cataloging in Publication Data

Porter, Michael E        1947–
   Interbrand choice, strategy, and bilateral market power.

   (Harvard economic studies ; v. 146)
   Bibliography: p.
   Includes index.
   1.  Industrial organization.  2.  Marketing.  3.  Con-
sumers.  4.  Supply and demand.  5.  Corporate planning.
I.  Title.  II.  Series.
HD31.P646        658.4        76–7612
ISBN 0–674–45820–6

# Contents

## FIGURES

# *Preface*

This book lies at the intersection between the mainstream economic research in industrial organization and the preoccupation of research in business administration with the problems of the manager. It has grown out of my work in the Business Economics Program at Harvard, which reflects the vision of its chairman, John Lintner, that innovative research and teaching in both economics and administration will benefit greatly from exposure to the other's territory. This is a view which I strongly share. To advance, applied microeconomics needs to capture the richness and complexity of decision making in individual firms, investigate relations among vertical stages of economic units, and model the pervasive information constraints under which economic agents act. Movement in such directions would make microeconomics appear a great deal more relevant and useful from the point of view of the business manager. Conversely, research in administration, in combination with the case study approach that has characterized much of it, needs to recognize the structural context within which individual firms make major decisions, and to look at firm decision making more generally and more rigorously. If research in administration did so, economists would sit up and take notice. This book, which combines the two perpsectives, aims to illustrate the benefits.

As a study that ranges widely in industrial organization, this book leads into further research that is still underway. Chapters 2, 4, 6, and 7 reflect ideas that I had largely developed earlier. Chapters 3 and

5 have been greatly modified from my previous work and extended in the course of my teaching and research in industrial organization. This growth has paralleled research on extensions and related ideas. "Consumer Behavior, Retailer Power, and Market Performance in Consumer Goods Industries," published in the *Review of Economics and Statistics,* November 1974, summarized a portion of the theory in Chapter 2 and some of the results in Chapter 6. "From Entry Barriers to Mobility Barriers," with Richard E. Caves, extends the theory in Chapter 4 and will appear in the *Quarterly Journal of Economics.* "The Structure within Industries and Market Performance" presents empirical tests of the differences in rates of return among firms within industries resting on the model of corporate strategy in Chapter 4. "Interbrand Choice, Media Mix and Market Performance," published in the *American Economic Review,* May 1976, extends the analysis of advertising and market power to show that the advertising media differ in their significance for market competition. And other research is in progress.

The study has benefited from support in many forms. The General Electric Foundation and the Division of Research at the Harvard Business School provided financial support. Very able editorial, typing and research assistance came from Cheryl Suchors, Deborah Kauer Harrity, Jane Arnold, Margaret Bennett, and Emily Fuedo. C. Roland Christensen inspired my interest in the practical and administrative problems of setting firm strategy that are central to the individual firm manager. John Lintner, as intellectual father of the Business Economics Program, provided the conceptually fertile environment from which this study sprouted. Thomas A. Wilson and Jesse W. Markham provided numerous helpful comments and, perhaps even more important, the encouragement to undertake a work of such broad scope. Joseph L. Bower, Robert D. Buzzell, John Lintner, and Howard H. Newman provided very helpful comments at various points in the study. And A. Michael Spence read and commented perceptively on the entire manuscript.

But it is to Richard E. Caves that I owe my greatest intellectual debt. My exposure to the field of industrial organization came under his tutelege. He patiently nudged youthful enthusiasm toward the care and technical standards necessary to yield a scholarly product. As a colleague he has made innumerable contributions to the study, including detailed criticism of the final manuscript.

# Interbrand Choice, Strategy, and Bilateral Market Power

# 1

# *Introduction*

## Industrial Organization: Its Structure and Limitations

The field of industrial organization has developed out of the study of how firms and industries behave. The essence of the structuralist tradition in industrial organization lies in identifying displacements of the supply of goods from the norm of perfect competition, associating these imperfections with the behavior of firms and industries, and hypothesizing theoretical links between market power and the structural environment. Indeed, the structure-performance paradigm has provided the major framework for empirical research in the field as well as the central set of policy conclusions.

The problem of determining the most economically meaningful unit of analysis has been fundamental to the historical development of industrial organizations. The field as we know it today had its beginnings in the controversy over this question. Drawing on contemporary developments in the theory of imperfect competition, Edward S. Mason and his followers advanced the view that the industry could be a powerful unit for the explanation of economic performance.[1] Applied research up to Mason's time had emphasized the uniqueness of the large firm and despaired of generalizations beyond the firm to its market environment. The particular history, organization, and competitive strategy of the individual firm were posited to dominate its behavior and performance,

1. For a discussion, see Bain, "Comparative Stability of Market Structure Elements," in Bain (1972).

overshadowing the influence of the markets in which it sells. This view has been nurtured and developed right up to the present in the literature on business management and may in part explain the surprisingly slight interaction between managerial and economic research on the large industrial firm.

Mason and his followers transferred the focus from the firm to the industry in which it competes. They took up the industry study as the primary vehicle for analyzing the behavior of the firm in its market context. The early industry studies displayed breadth and artful organization of much relevant detail. However, they lacked horsepower in underlying deductive theory; and they proved somewhat resistant to inductive generalization, as their rich detail tended to obscure some vital forces common to the situations of many industries and posed difficulties for empirical testing.

Under J. S. Bain's leadership, however, the structure-performance paradigm began to take shape. Bain pioneered the approach of identifying a very few critical structural traits of industries and relating these to their market performance. Bain contributed not only the structural approach but also the seminal concept of entry barriers. That concept systematized the influence of many industry characteristics that theretofore had appeared diverse, provided a potent stimulus for further theoretical development, and performed powerfully in empirical tests. The structure-performance paradigm allowed the measurement of a few structural traits across broad samples of industries and the testing of their hypothesized influence on the industries' performance, measured chiefly by profitability. Some considerable success has been achieved in explaining variations in economic performance across industries. Indeed, a rich variety of cross-section statistical studies have provided the cutting edge for research in industrial organization during the past 20 years.[2]

Reviewing the progress in the field, we can identify three major assumptions that have characterized its development to date. First, the pursuit of the economically important elements of industry structure has been concentrated among the conditions of supply. The major elements of industry structure hypothesized to affect performance have thus included seller concentration, entry barriers, and industry growth rates. The influence of product differentiation has been analyzed and tested but only in the context of its contribution to entry barriers. Furthermore, product differentiation has been measured by and associated with the industry's level of advertising, and a given rate of advertising outlay

2. For a survey see Weiss (1972).

has implicitly been assumed equally influential in every industry. Thus the conditions of demand have largely been ignored.[3] The consumer's process of choice among brands of a product, his strategy for gaining product information to make that choice, and the seller's decision to take part in supplying information have not been explored for their market-power implications.

The second assumption to characterize the development of industrial organization has been that the manufacturing industries can be given nearly exclusive attention. In part this concentration testifies to the greater ease of securing and interpreting information here than in the extractive or services sectors. But it also rests on a substantive belief that vertical market relations between manufacturing and the other sectors—in particular, retail distribution—could be ignored.

Finally, economically relevant intra-industry differences in firm strategies, characteristics, and market power have been neglected or assumed away. Market power has been assumed to be an intangible private asset shared by firms in an industry in proportion to their sales. This assumption allows an industry to be characterized by a single level of product differentiation (level of advertising), condition of entry, growth rate, and so on, and under it profits of firms would diverge from their industry's average only by a random component.

What have been the consequences of these assumptions? In my view the limits they place on the scope and development of structure-performance analysis have been straitening. The emerging stream of new research has by and large devoted itself to identifying new imperfections in supply (lack of import competition, risk, absolute firm size, and the like), obtaining only modest improvements in ability to explain industry performance. Further, there is an element of circularity. The relevant unit of analysis, the traditional industry, has been defined in terms of the hypotheses themselves. The relevant industry has become that group of firms for which, for example, the concentration-rivalry-profits hypothesis makes sense. This centripetal tendency has limited the attention of new research to hypotheses relevant only within the context of the traditional industry. Finally, important possibilities for integrating knowledge gained from the large body of research on the management of

---

3. That "consumer ignorance" can contribute to poor performance at the manufacturing stage was noted by Scitovsky (1950) and Markham (1958). Markham noted that buyer ignorance among farmers purchasing fertilizers led firms in the industry to compete in terms of the uninformed criteria used by the farmers. Some interesting recent literature links consumer ignorance to product variety and quality (Spence 1974). The focus of this study is primarily on allocative performance.

individual firms with the structural-performance paradigm have been blocked.

The fact that previous research has avoided demand characteristics, vertical relations, and structural and behavioral differences among firms within industries is perhaps not surprising. The problems of estimating demand functions for many sorts of markets are well known. More fundamentally, however, demand theory has been occupied with a limited number of parameters of the buyer's choice (essentially the parameters of choice among different products) to the exclusion of parameters that are important to understanding an industry's behavior—factors affecting the buyer's choice among brands of a given product and variations of this process across products. Theoretical and empirical problems are introduced by adding the complexity of intra-industry heterogeneity, including product variety, to the list of important structural factors. Finally, the highly formal focus of economists' training in the last decade may have tended to minimize their exposure to the richness of detail in actual firm policies, marketing behavior, retailing, and so on.

This study is based on the proposition that refinement of industrial organization research within the framework of these fundamental assumptions has reached the point of diminishing return. It therefore challenges all three of the assumptions by showing that in their absence we can still derive and successfully test structuralist hypotheses about the determinants of market performance. I will argue that the characteristics of final buyers' demand exert a fundamental impact on an industry's performance. Differing processes of interbrand choice, reflecting differences among products in the consumer's strategy for gathering information about brands, fundamentally influence the payoffs to various strategies of product differentiation by the manufacturer and, through these, industry performance. I will furthermore advance and test the hypothesis that the structure of the retailing market as a buyer of the manufacturer's product is an important determinant of the manufacturing industry's performance. I will show how the retail stage departs from the competitive organization that has been implicitly assumed in previous work. The sources of these departures will be shown to provide the retail stage with monopsony power against the manufacturing industry. Furthermore, I will argue that the structure and operation of retailing varies among products in ways that reflect traits of consumers' demand and that these variations provide an operational way to test hypotheses about the influence of demand characteristics. This link between retailer structure and buyer demand will be shown to yield an important source of monopsony power for the retail stage.

Finally I will relax the assumption of intra-industry homogeneity of firms. I will develop a model of the effect of intra-industry heterogeneity on industry profitability. Then I will show that intra-industry heterogeneity is partially explicable in terms of diverse adjustments to consumer demand traits and retail structure by firms selling consumer goods. Thus the characteristics of demand by final buyers and of the retailing sector interact with intra-industry heterogeneity in an important way.

This study, then, parts company with the principal line of research development in industrial organization. Though my belief in the soundness of the basic structure-performance paradigm is reaffirmed, I will propose an expansion in its scope both within the traditionally defined industry and outside of it. That this approach leads to a major improvement in our understanding of industry performance, both theoretically and empirically, and opens up new areas of future research is what I hope to demonstrate in the chapters which follow.

## Outline of the Study

The flow of product from manufacturer to ultimate buyer differs greatly between consumer and producer good industries. The producer good is sold directly to its buyer, and hence the vertical relations between manufacturer and buyer take on the character of a standard bilateral market structure. The consumer good, however, is generally sold to an independent retail sector that resells it to the ultimate buyer. The bargaining relations between manufacturer and retailer are greatly different from the conventional analysis of bilateral market power. These relations are the subject of Chapter 2.

Chapter 2 models the interaction between the manufacturing and retail stages in consumer goods. Market power in the retail stage is seen to derive from two important sources, which vary systematically across consumer-goods industries. First, the structure of the retail stage diverges from the competitive structure along a number of dimensions. Second, the buyer's process of choice among brands of a product gives the retailer power to influence a brand's differentiation through the retailer's unique ability to provide information. The power of the retailer to influence product differentiation varies markedly among consumer-goods industries, corresponding to variations in the buyer's process of interbrand choice. Visible characteristics of the retailing sector reveal its influence in product differentiation and also register important aspects of the buyer's process of choice. The influence of these visible characteristics can be tested statistically. The results aid our understanding of the sources of market power, but they also point beyond the present study to operational characteristics of consumer choice under uncertain and costly information that could and should receive further study.

Recognizing the power of the retailer to influence the sale of the product allows a better understanding of the process by which the consumer-good manufacturer differentiates his product. It gives the manufacturer alternative sales-promotion strategies, on the one hand to persuade the ultimate buyer to purchase the product, and on the other hand to persuade retailers to promote its sale; these alternative strategies affect the bargaining relationship between manufacturer and retailer. The retailer's unique situation for providing information about products and power to influence their sale yields implications for product innovation, the manufacturer's process of gaining access to distribution channels, and the manufacturer's marginal cost of increasing his market share.

Thus the model implies that the determinants of the market power of consumer-goods manufacturers extend far beyond the conditions of supply. Profits in a manufacturing industry should depend on: the market structure of manufacturing as traditionally defined; the structure of the retail sectors distributing the product (number of firms, firm sizes, number of establishments, breadth of retail product line and variety of types of retail outlets selling the product); the manufacturer's sales-promotion strategies in relation to the influence of the retailer in differentiating the product.

The model of interaction between manufacturer and retailer developed in Chapter 2 will be extended in Chapter 3 to yield a number of implications for optimizing behavior by manufacturer and retailer, for the observed structure of the distributive sector, and for public policy towards relations between manufacturers and retailers. I will use the model to derive predictions about where multi-unit or chain retailers will be present, where products will sell under the retailer's brand name rather than the manufacturer's (private-label brands), and what economic consequences flow from vertical contractual relations between manufacturer and retailer. Understanding how manufacturers and retailers interact will aid in understanding the terms of contractual relations between them and in interpreting these for purposes of developing antitrust policies toward them. I will also discuss John Kenneth Galbraith's countervailing-power hypothesis in the context of manufacturer-retailer relations.

Chapter 4 treats the economic consequences of differences among firms within an industry. The power of the retailer in promoting a product and the resulting possibility of alternative manufacturer selling mechanisms carry with them another important implication for the structure-performance link. The manufacturer's choice of selling mechanisms can vary not only among industries, but also within industries. Different manufacturers in a given industry may choose to place differing emphases on promoting sales directly to the ultimate buyer versus persuading the retailer to promote their products. Beyond these variations, the concept of the buyer's process of choice among brands (introduced in Chapter 2) will be extended to show that a product's buyers are not homogeneous in the way they evaluate it: some are most interested in price, others in other attributes of the product. These differences among buyers of a product, contributing to what we will term market segmentation, offer another source of variation in manufacturers' selling strategies within industries.

This variation is but one instance of economically significant differences among the manufacturers in an industry other than in their size. In Chapter 4 I will examine the implications of these variations for the industry's profitability. The concept of the firm's strategy will be introduced as a way of characterizing the vector of key decisions the firm makes about its competitive position in its industry. I will show that the firm's strategy is constrained but not determined by the structure of its industry, and that firms' strategies within an industry differ in economically important ways. While the model is presented generally and applies to strategy variations in any class of industries, I will defend and develop it primarily in the context of variations in manufacturers' selling strategy within industries manufacturing consumer goods. The analysis of the manufacturer-retailer interaction presented in earlier chapters will be applied to show that the characteristics of the retail distribution system for a product are an important determinant of how the assortment of sales-promotion strategies available to sellers varies from industry to industry.

Chapter 5 will extend the analysis of Chapter 2 and develop a more general framework for modeling the buyer's process of gaining information for his choice among brands and its implications for sellers' sales-promotion strategies and market performance. I will examine the market for product information facing the buyer and derive the conditions which determine the buyer's strategy for gathering information to improve his choice of products. The analysis also considers his responsiveness to the various sources of product information available. The buyer's strategy for gathering information will be seen to guide the seller's choice of what portfolio of sales-promotion devices to employ. In determining the seller's sales-promotion strategy, the cost-efficiency of each sales-promotion device in providing information messages to potential buyers will interact wth the buyer's responsiveness to those messages and the policies of market rivals. Chapter 5 will then examine the link between the portfolio of sales-promotion devices chosen by the seller and his rate of profit. Sales-promotion devices will be seen to have differing implications for market power. In addition, I will be able to extend the sales-promotion-market power relation beyond that of previous work using my model of interbrand choice.

The theory presented in Chapters 2 to 5 leads to a large number of hypotheses about structure-performance relations in consumer-goods industries. In Chapters 6 and 7 I summarize some of the most important empirical implications of the theory and present the results of tests on a broad sample of consumer-goods industries. I find that important differences in industries' structure-performance relations are associated with differences in the buyers' process of interbrand choice and the power of the retail sector. I also find that differences in the strategies of an industry's member firms affect its profitability. By accounting for strategy differences, the power of the retailer and the variation among products in the buyer's choice behavior, I am able greatly to increase the proportion of interindustry variation in profit rates that can be explained.

In the final chapter, some general implications of the study for public policy towards manufacturing and retailing are raised. Some illustrative implications for business managers (and researchers on management) are sketched to suggest how the study can be applied to the problem of setting company strategy. Finally, I chart the course implied by the study for further research in industrial organization.

# 2

## *Manufacturer-Retailer Interaction and Product Differentiation in Consumer-Goods Industries*

The cross-industry variation in consumer buying characteristics and the coincident interaction between the manufacturing and retailing stages are important determinants of manufacturing marketing strategies and of economic performance in both manufacturing and retailing industries. If products were homogeneous and if the retail stage was atomistic, the outcome of the manufacturer-retailer interaction would be determined by the interaction of manufacturers with purely competitive buyers. In this world the retail stage would not affect the selling strategy of the manufacturer. In the presence of imperfections in both the manufacturing and retail stages, however, the outcome of their interaction depends on relative bargaining strengths (with the competitive solution identifying only the limiting cases). The retail stage can add in an important way to the differentiation of the product, because the retailer provides information about or influences directly some of each good's bundle of characteristics relevant to the consumer's choice between brands. Further, the retail stage can be characterized in terms of its structural elements in much the same way as the manufacturing stage, though the list of relevant structural traits for retailing is somewhat different. I will argue below that this structure is usually not atomistic in the relevant markets. The nonatomistic structure of retailing and other "imperfections" will provide the basis of the model.

My purposes here are two. The first is to provide a framework for introducing consumer buying characteristics explicitly into the cross industry analysis of consumer-goods manufacturing industries. The second is to introduce the retail stage directly into the analysis of these industries. I will develop a model of manufacturer-retailer interaction in consumer-goods industries and specify its empirical implementation. The model is in essence a bargaining model in that it predicts the outcome of the bargaining process which takes place between the manufacturing and retail stages in a world of "imperfections." The model is built on the foundation of interindustry variations in consumer buying behavior. In building the model the nature of the *process* of product differentiation can be illuminated. Product differentiation is a process because it is the outcome of firm selling behavior (constrained, of course, by intrinsic product characteristics). The manufacturer-retailer interaction will determine a mix of selling outlays, and it will be shown that the manufacturing and retail stages interact in an important way in determining product differentiation. Turning the analysis around, I will show that the characteristics of the retail outlets for a product signal the essential characteristics of buyer behavior for the product, and this can be used to advantage in empirical tests. The manufacturer-retailer interaction will also add to our understanding of entry barriers and will lead to the introduction of a concept which I will call the marginal costs of market share.

In building the manufacturer-retailer interaction model methodologically, it will be useful to segment the problem somewhat. I will focus primarily on explaining firms' conduct and performance in manufacturing industries.[1] In an earlier section I have suggested that the outcome of the manufacturer-retailer interaction is determined by: the "traditional" market structure of the manufacturing industry; the distribution of selling efforts between the manufacturing and retail stages; and the structure of the retail distribution system for the product. These determinants suggest a two-stage model building process. First, I will assume the retailer has no influence on the differentiation of the product and examine the impact of retailer structure on the manufacturer-retailer interaction. Then I will allow the retailer to influence differentiation. The two analyses are complementary.

### Retailer Structure and the Manufacturer-Retailer Interaction

I begin the analysis by setting aside the complications of retailer influence on product differentiation. It is perhaps not surprising that nearly all existing research has implicitly dealt with this case.[2] In its simplest

1. Explaining retailer performance is a different but related question.
2. See, for example, Scherer's comprehensive textbook (1970), chapter 9.

form, the manufacturer-retailer relationship involving a retailer unable to influence differentiation is closely analogous to the familiar model of the effects of *buyer concentration*. For a given manufacturing industry, the buyer-concentration model suggests that the larger and fewer the retail buyers of the manufacturing industry's product, the greater the retailers' bargaining power against the manufacturer. Thus the rate of return of the manufacturer will be reduced as the number of retail buyers decreases, other things being equal. Here the retailer's bargaining power is determined by his size relative to the total market for the manufacturer's product. Size leads to the recognition of mutual dependence between manufacturer and retailers (in contrast with the "competitive" case where any one retailer accounts for a negligible part of the manufacturer's sales) and opens the possibility that the retailer can bargain down the manufacturer's price subject to the limitations of the Robinson-Patman Act.[3] Technically, one can distinguish between simple oligopsony and the control by large retailers of significant numbers of customers. Both factors are of importance here. The retail stage can be thought of as achieving tacit cooperation by virtue of the fewness of firms which allows it to resist bluffing by manufacturers that they will refuse to sell. Symmetrically, the large retailer is able to inflict damage on the manufacturer by withholding access to his selling space.

Another (indirect) mechanism by which fewness of retail buyers may lower manufacturer's return is suggested by George Stigler's theory of oligopoly.[4] Stigler postulates that the willingness of the manufacturer to make secret price concessions to retailers depends negatively on the probability of detection by rival manufacturers (and subsequent retaliation). With numerous small buyers, the probability of detection is high: "When oligopolists sell to numerous small retailers, . . . they will adhere to the agreed upon price even though they are cutting prices to larger chain stores and industrial buyers."[5] Thus fewness at the retail stage tends to undermine the oligopolistic consensus at the manufacturing stage, while the presence of numerous retail buyers actually facilitates it. A related mechanism by which fewness at the retail stage undermines oligopolistic consensus in manufacturing, hypothesized by Almarin Phillips, is that a well organized adversary group increases the need for

---

3. The Robinson-Patman Act requires that all firms perceived as being in competition be treated equally. That is, the manufacturer cannot offer a better price to one retailer than another unless the differences can be justified in terms of cost variations.

4. Stigler (1964).

5. Stigler (1964), p. 47.

an interfirm organization.[6] The retail stage provides an obvious example of a potential adversary group, and fewness of retailers facilitates their "organized" stance against manufacturers. In all these models, fewness of retail firms provides the basis for their power.

An important necessary condition for the buyer-concentration hypothesis is *the elevation of price above marginal cost in the manufacturing stage*. As Morris Adelman has pointed out, the ability of buyers to extract price concessions from the manufacturer depends on the manufacturing industry structure, for if the manufacturing stage were perfectly competitive there could by definition be no concessions.[7] This is true in most, though not all, circumstances. Where the recontracting or "transaction" costs to the manufacturer of finding a replacement retail outlet are substantial, even atomistic manufacturers can be exploited.[8]

Returning to the examination of the buyer-concentration hypothesis and its variants, Adelman's caveat about the structure of manufacturing well taken, observation suggests that the applicability of simple buyer concentration may be limited in consumer goods.[9] Cases where the total number of retail buyers for a consumer good are small are few and far between.[10] If the number of retail buyers is small, then chain store development must be extensive. But multiple-outlet retail firms operate, in general, in different (and incompletely overlapping) sets of geographic areas, each constituting a market. This combined with the facts that the decision making level is the firm but that the relevant market's scope may be less than the firm's raises some interesting theoretical issues that cannot be explored here. However, it does appear that the ability of firms with incompletely overlapping markets to cooperate in lowering the manufacturer's price is limited except in the rare cases where the number of retail buyers for a product approaches the number of manufacturers in an oligopolistic market. Incompletely overlapping markets among competitors raises the complexity of the agreement relative to the usual oligopoly case.

Thus, using the traditional concept of buyer concentration, it has been easy to omit buyer concentration from the cross-industry analysis of consumer goods even when it was recognized that the manufacturer sold to a retail stage rather than directly to the consumer. Those studies that

6. A. Phillips (1962).
7. Adelman (1959), pp. 207–220.
8. I am indebted to R. E. Caves for this point.
9. Though not in producer goods, where fewness of buyers is more common.
10. Scherer (1970), chapter 9. The occurrence of large retailers is more common.

have emphasized effects of buyer concentrations have focused on the exceptional cases where the buyers are very large. Adelman's study dealt with A&P, and virtually all of Galbraith's examples of countervailing power involved very large retailers (Sears, A&P, and so on).[11] Nevertheless, existing evidence does lead to an initial hypothesis about the manufacturer-retailer interaction. As the total number of retail buyers for a product decreases, and retailers become large relative to the market, the rate of return in the manufacturing industry decreases, other things being equal. Our presentation of the theory suggests that the relationship is a strongly nonlinear one, where decreases make little difference until the number of firms gets relatively small or the shares of a few firms get very large.

Perhaps the most direct manifestation of this proposed relation would follow from the development of chain stores. To the extent that chain stores' penetration of a given class of retail outlet reduces the number of buyers of a product, our model suggests that manufacturers' profit rates will be reduced. Within a given industry, as chain store penetration increases over time our hypothesis predicts that manufacturing return will decrease, ceteris paribus. Ward's study of retailing in the United Kingdom concluded that the rise of chains there during the 1960s has reduced manufacturer margins, consistent with this view.[12]

The analysis of buyer concentration in retailing can be advanced a good deal by use of an observation made above about the structure of retailing. Retailers never sell a consumer good in a national market. Because the consumer must travel to the retail establishment [13] it must be in reasonable proximity to him. Hence the relevant market for consumer goods may be as large as a city or small region, but certainly no larger and in many cases much smaller. For some goods where convenience is important to the consumer, the relevant retail market may encompass that group of consumers within a five-minute drive of the retail establishment. In contrast with typically low national concentration ratios for a given retail outlet class, the concentration of retail establishments in the relevant retail market is often high. Two to five retail establishments commonly make up such a market.

The limited geographic extent of the market and the magnitude of demand within this market area impose a strong constraint on the maxi-

11. Adelman (1959) and Galbraith (1956). In addition, a recent Ph.D. dissertation by Hunt illustrates the great power of Sears in the appliance industry.

12. Ward (1973), pp. 135, 236.

13. The cases of door-to-door selling and mail order are interesting but not important.

mum number of retailers. The equivalent constraint on a national manufacturing industry is much weaker, so that the number of sellers in a retail market is typically smaller than that in even a "tight oligopoly" in manufacturing.[14] (One direct implication of this is that retail competition is positively related to population density.) Furthermore, other structural conditions favor coordination more in the typical retail market than in manufacturing. Locational proximity and substantial similarity of product lines promote the structural symmetry of competing retailers. Local demand trends, important input costs and other key structural market conditions are likely more similar than among manufacturers. Retail firms can quickly and accurately detect strategy changes by competitors, and the possibilities for secret changes are minimal. Unlike research and development or national marketing programs, retail strategic moves can usually be readily and quickly copied. A straightforward application of oligopoly theory suggests, then, that mutual dependence recognized among retail competitors in a given retail market will be higher than in an equally concentrated manufacturing industry because detection and retaliation lags are low.

Thus retailer concentration in the relevant market will typically be high, although it will vary markedly across classes of retail outlets, and recognition of mutual dependence is likely to be strong. It follows that competition may lack vigor and the chances for tacit agreement will be high as a result of the factors noted above. Unlike manufacturing, this result does not depend critically on barriers to entry due to capital costs or product differentiation attained by advertising. It does depend on barriers due to economies of scale, the cutting blade being the small size of the relevant market. The proportion of the market that the viable new entrant must claim will necessarily be high even if the size of the minimally efficient entrant is quite small in absolute terms. The risks of entry will be correspondingly higher than in manufacturing for this reason, and because perception of the new entrant by existing firms is assured and the likelihood of their reaction is increased. Thus although entry barriers due to capital requirements may seem trivial when compared to manufacturing, entry barriers can nevertheless be significant. In addition to scale economies other entry barriers may be important in retailing. In many types of goods the store's name, or product differentiation of the store as a whole, is important. In addition, location is often a critical source

14. The concept of "chain-linking," or overlapping market areas as introduced by Chamberlain (1962) pp., 103–104, militates somewhat against this point. Even accepting that competitive reactions spread without damping through a chain linking mechanism, however, the number of retailers in a given retail outlet class in most areas is very low.

of absolute cost or other advantages. Specialized service facilities subject to scale economies are sometimes required, and special requirements such as licensing of the store (liquor) or its personnel (pharmacists, opticians) in some cases block entry.

Although structural factors have been emphasized, any other factor that promotes cooperation among retailers or provides a means of preventing erosion of the retailer's position through entry is sufficient. Bowman cites liquor retailers and drug stores as examples of retail channels cooperative even on a national level.[15] Both of these channels are characterized by the use of the mechanism of strong dealer organizations or trade associations, perhaps flowing from the licensing requirement for liquor retailers and pharmacist licensing in drug stores.

What is the effect of retail structure on the sellers to that retail market? Retail sellers are few, so that opportunities for tacit collusion in bargaining with manufacturers place retailers in a market in a position of power with respect to the manufacturers.[16] The retailer bloc can threaten jointly to refuse to carry the product of a manufacturer. In the less extreme case where agreement among retailers is tacit, the fact that the manufacturer requires retail channels sets the retailers in a situation of partial monopsony. Since most retailers carry multiple products (and multiple brands of these), the manufacturers' threat of withholding products is asymmetrical to the retailers' threat to sell competing brands. The Robinson-Patman Act requires the manufacturer to sell to each competing retailer at the same price, subject to bona fide quantity discounts. The Act thus circumscribes the ability of chains or large retailers to bargain down the manufacturer's price because a concession given to chains must be given to all competing retailers. However, the Act generally does not apply to noncompeting groups of retailers. Hence, a tightly concentrated retailer group may win a concession from a manufacturer that is not necessarily awarded to all other retail market areas.

If only a few of the retail markets supplied by a typical manufacturer had these characteristics, the effect of their market organization on the manufacturer would be small. However, if many or all relevant retail markets served by the manufacturer had such a structure, then the manufacturer might be forced to make substantial concessions. Thus a second hypothesis about the manufacturer-retailer interaction is suggested. If a large number of the retail markets through which the manufacturer dis-

15. Bowman (1952), p. 258.

16. Retailer collusion vis-à-vis manufacturers does not imply excess returns at the retail stage. These returns may be competed away through excess capacity in retailing or through other means. But entry barriers into retailing may be substantial so that excess returns in retailing may be present.

tributes are tight oligopsonies or otherwise cooperative, then the rate of return of the manufacturing industry will be lower, other things being equal.

An interesting argument consistent with this hypothesis is given by Phillips.[17] He conceptualizes the oligopolistic manufacturing industry as an interfirm organization partially based on interests shared among the member firms. The better organized and more efficient are the other groups in conflict with this interfirm organization, the greater the tendency toward rivalry within the organization. Phillips asserts that the groups to and from which sales and purchases are made are probably the most important adversaries. Thus retailer structure can affect manufacturer performance through the subtle impact of well organized retail markets on rivalry within the manufacturing industry, as well as through bargaining power. This bargaining power of retailers need not yield them high rates of return because it is based on the *induced* effect of the retailers on rivalry among manufacturers. An example illustrating this analysis can be found in Bowman's study of retail liquor dealers based on a 1936 antitrust case.[18] Although his focus is on resale price maintenance, he illustrates how a well-organized group of liquor retailers can exert bargaining power over the manufacturer and extract concessions. Bowman's bilateral-monopoly model to explain the occurrence of resale price maintenance[19] is based on essentially the same analysis as our retailer-oligopsony hypothesis.

Although recognizing that retail markets are local has advanced our understanding, there remain further major structural features of retail markets that influence their relation to the manufacturing stage. Our discussion so far, and the bulk of economic literature, has assumed implicitly that a given product passes through homogeneous channels. A moment's reflection convinces one that this is not necessarily correct. Many products are sold through multiple types of outlets. Although development of a taxonomy of retail outlets will be postponed until a later section, it is clear that many products are sold by various types of retailers offering different product mixes and providing varying amounts of service with the sale. An example is motor oil, sold with service through gas stations and car-repair outlets, with sales assistance through automotive supply stores, and self-service in discount houses. Another example is cigarettes, sold through a wide variety of retail channels.

Different types of outlets with different product mixes and service offerings have different cost structures and are subject to different com-

17. Phillips (1962).
18. Bowman (1952), pp. 259–260.
19. Resale price maintenance will be discussed in Chapter 3.

petitive relationships. Thus even if the relevant retail market for a product is concentrated, the fact that multiple types of retailers sell that same product weakens the ability of the retailers to cooperate and enhances the power of the manufacturer. Our third hypothesis is, then, that the rate of return of the manufacturer will be higher where multiple types of outlets sell the product, other things being equal. It must be emphasized that we still exclude any power of the retailer to affect product differentiation and that we are comparing situations where the total number of retailers in the market is held constant.[20] This point will come up again when our focus is expanded to product differentiation and we will develop a counter-hypothesis under certain circumstances. In the present context, the importance of the hypothesis is primarily insofar as it interacts with retailer concentration (cooperation) in the relevant retail market.

A fourth hypothesis about the structural interaction between manufacturing and retailing depends on another key dimension of retail enterprises. The mean absolute size of the individual retailing firm under one management varies significantly from one retail-outlet class to another. In addition, the size distribution of firms varies quite markedly. From the manufacturer's viewpoint, what is the effect of dealing with a series of relatively small jewelry stores rather than a series of relatively large department stores?

It has been suggested by Palamountain [21] that the small retailer often lacks business training and has difficulty securing credit; in short, he faces the classic problems of small business to an especially great degree. While this may be an exaggeration, it does seem that a small retail outlet (in terms of total sales per outlet of all products stocked) will be in a weaker position than a larger retailer in its ability to secure favorable terms, credit, delivery, and so on, from the manufacturer even if retail market concentration stays the same. The larger individual retailer or the chain is likely to have greater specialization of management by function and thereby enhanced experience and bargaining skill. The larger retailer may indeed be able to attract higher quality management. Whereas differences in size among manufacturing firms may hold only minor implications for the quality of management, I would argue that the difference in management, for example, between a small local grocery store and a food chain or large department store is staggering. In addition to managerial advantages, the large retail outlet is more likely to

20. The presence of multiple retail outlet types (unequal product mixes, and so on) raises interesting questions of measuring the relevant number of competitors in the retail market. I will treat these in Chapter 6.

21. Palamountain (1955), pp. 10–13.

have an established credit rating and a larger sales throughput of a given product to justify more frequent deliveries by the manufacturer. The large retailer (who also stocks many products) may possess buying advantages on inputs not specific to the individual products it sells. Finally, large absolute size, if it implies financial reserves and access to credit, may give the retailer the ability to make and sustain credible threats toward the manufacturer.

The potentially greater bargaining ability, bargaining power, and the access to alternative credit lines of absolutely large retailers suggest the following hypothesis. As the absolute firm size of the retail outlets selling a manufacturing industry's product increases, the rate of return of the manufacturing industry will decease, other things being equal.[22] Since firms in many retail outlet classes vary greatly in size, this implies that both the average firm size and the skewness of the distribution toward large firms will be important. It is clear that the absolute size effect provides an additional mechanism for the impact of chain stores on manufacturing. To the extent that chains increase the size of the retail unit under one management in a given retail outlet class, I would predict the position of any manufacturer selling to that class to weaken, even if buyer concentration for the manufacturer's output stays unchanged.

A final structural manufacturer-retailer interaction follows from the related observation that most retailers stock the products of multiple industries. The effect of this is straightforward but conceptually separate from absolute size per se. Stocking multiple products reduces the impact of threats by a manufacturer of one product, by reducing the dependence of the outlet on that one product or product class. In a multiple product outlet, the manufacturer of a given product competes with the manufacturers of all other products sold through the outlet for shelf space, sales attention, and so on. The multiple product retailer will rationally optimize the total amount of selling space and equate on the margin the profit contribution of each additional brand of each product stocked. The potential *loss* to the retailer of the withdrawal of a given manufacturer's brand will depend not only on the response of the manufacturer's immediate competitors but also the willingness of all other sellers to the retail channel to compensate the retailer or increase their representation in the outlet. The retailer's alternatives in this regard will probably increase as more different products are sold. As the retailers selling an industry's product gain increasing proportions of their sales

22. It may be more costly to service large retailers who demand better service. Conversely, large size may imply offsetting economies in the distribution function. I concentrate here on bargaining power.

from other products, then the bargaining power (and return) of the manufacturer should decrease, other things being equal.

Let us review the hypotheses that the analysis has suggested about the effects of retailer structure on manufacturing industry performance. The arguments suggest that retailer power vis-à-vis the manufacturer will increase (and manufacturing industry return will decrease, all other things equal): 1. as the total number of retail buyers for the manufacturing industry's product decreases; 2. as the relevant retail markets through which the product is sold become more concentrated or recognition of mutual dependence increases; 3. as the number of different retail outlet types through which a product is sold decreases; 4. as the absolute size of the retail unit under one management increases; and 5. as the retail outlet class sells increasing proportions of other products. In other words, as the structure of retailing becomes more "imperfect" along these dimensions, retailer bargaining power increases and manufacturer return decreases.

### The Retailer's Influence on Product Differentiation and the Manufacturer-Retailer Interaction

Assuming that the retail stage has no impact on product differentiation, I have been able to develop a set of hypotheses about the way the structure of the retail outlets through which a product is sold interacts with its manufacturing industry. The model concentrated on the bargaining relationship between manufacturers and retailers, identifying the retailers' bargaining power with their ability to cooperate as a result of fewness, similarity of cost structures and competitive objectives, and their ability to extract concessions and sustain threats due to large absolute size and selling multiple products. By adding the retailer's ability to influence product differentiation to the framework, one can extend the interaction model greatly. Product differentiation will be shown to create the potential for additional power on the side of the retailer. The significance of this source of power, in my view, exceeds that afforded by the "cooperative" and structural bargaining effects stressed above.

The nature of the retail channels for a product will provide the key to measuring the essential characteristics of demand for the product. Those characteristics will in turn have implications for the manufacturers' choice of strategies for product differentiation, and for the height of barriers to entry into manufacturing. Access to retail distribution will be identified as a major component of overall barriers to entry into consumer goods industries.

Product Differentiation in Consumer Goods Industries

The focus of the model is on the consumer's process of choice among brands as the critical aspect of demand affecting industry performance.[23] Product differentiation is measured by the degree of cross price inelasticity of final consumer demand for a given product relative to competing brands.[24] Product differentiation is usually looked upon as resulting from a combination of physical characteristics of the product and selling efforts by the manufacturer, notably advertising. This view misses important elements of the problem, however. Product differentiation is a result of consumer choice, and choice in turn depends on the attributes of products and the investment the consumer makes in information about them. Products have multiple attributes of value to the consumer (brand image, reliability, styling, availability of servicing, and so on), on which he may base his purchase decisions.[25] The consumer seeks information about the various product attributes from numerous sources. Although some information sources (advertising) may have negative costs associated with them, in general the optimizing consumer acts on less than full information about product attributes.

If information were costless for the consumer and no uncertainty existed, he would consider all product attributes in his purchase decision and would employ the full range of sources of information available about all the attributes. When gathering information is costly, however, consumer buying behavior will depend on the balance between his perceived incremental benefits and costs of gaining product information. Gaining information about some attributes (reliability) is more costly than gaining information about others (brand image). This tradeoff will, in general, vary across products, with the result that the attributes on which choice is based will vary. I will model information equilibrium more fully in Chapter 5 below. For the purposes of the interaction model,

23. Conventional demand theory focuses on the problem of choice between different goods (not brands). Although the question it attempts to answer is interesting for many applications, it is of little usefulness in rationalizing industry performance. The manufacturer-retailer model is a starting point for a fuller theory of interbrand choice which will be developed in Chapter 5.

24. So-called "intrinsic" product differentiation ("differentiability") is of interest and is treated in Chapter 5. In terms of the structure-performance link, however, it is the product differentiation in the eyes of the ultimate consumer (as well as the impact of the retailer in developing it) which counts. For the differentiation–differentiability distinction see Caves (1962), p. 48.

25. The concept of attributes is due to Lancaster (1966). I differ from Lancaster in putting emphasis on the product characteristics perceived by the consumer rather than any intrinsic product attributes and stressing imperfect information as a major determinant of the choice problem.

however, I concentrate on the influence that the retailer exerts on this process of acquiring information and rely on the weakest model of buyer information equilibrium.

The retailer's contribution to product differentiation is the influence he exerts on the purchase decision of the consumer. This influence is applied in two major (and interacting) ways. First, the retailer controls or embodies some of the attributes the consumer may desire in the product. The store's reputation and image may reflect on the quality and image of the product. The physical amenity of the store as well as the quantity and quality of attendant services provided by the retailer (credit, billing, delivery, warranty, repair) comprise attributes of the product in the eyes of the consumer in much the same way as are price, packaging, or advertising image. The identity of the store may indeed be as important for some purchase decisions as the identity of the specific products found in the store.

The second way in which the retailer can influence the sale of the product is through the provision of information. The salesperson in the store can have a major influence on the brand of product the consumer buys. The influence is wielded through the selling presentation and personal recommendation or advice solicited by the consumer, and fortified by the perceived expertise of the salesperson with respect to the product. The retailer conveys information about the product's reliability, features, and method of use that may be difficult to obtain from other sources. In addition, the independence of the retailer from the manufacturer makes the information more credible to the buyer than would be similar information from the manufacturer himself.

The retailer's two influences on purchase clearly interact. On the one hand, the store's reputation, image, and other characteristics can be viewed as providing indirect information to the consumer about the product, in much the same way as the salesperson does directly. On the other hand, the perceived competence of the salesperson as an information source depends in part on the store's reputation and the nature and quality of the attendant services it provides.

The importance of the retailer's selling efforts and his control of product attributes depends on the consumer's process of choice. The consumer is willing to expend varying amounts of effort (cost) in buying different products and considers varying sets of attributes. The retailer will be more or less influential in the purchase decision, depending on the importance of product attributes controlled by the retailer, the perceived benefits of the range of product information disseminated by the retailer relative to the availability and cost of other sources of information, and how large an investment in information the consumer will make. If the amount of effort the consumer is willing to expend on selection is relatively large, he will shop several retail outlets in order to compare brands and solicit product information from the retailer, and the retailing sector will be influential in product differentiation.

The size of the rents attainable due to product differentiation depends on the amount of differentiation achieved at the manufacturing and retail stages together, and therefore so does the aggregated rate of return of the two stages. As the retailer's influence on product differentiation increases, the bargaining power of the retail stage vis-à-vis the manufacturer increases, other things being equal.[26] Since each retailer can withhold his selling efforts for a particular brand and in fact influence consumers to purchase another brand, the retailing sector for a product is in a position to bargain away rents from the manufacturing stage. Where the retailer is influential in differentiation, manufacturers will bid down their prices to retailers, increasing retailer margin, or expend resources in persuading retailers to promote their products (direct selling, advertising allowances, and so on). Thus the relative power of the retailing and manufacturing stages determines the distribution of rents between stages. However, the retailers' selling efforts enhance product differentiation and hence the total rents available. Therefore, the level of the rents to the manufacturing and retail stages depends simultaneously on the structure of the manufacturing stage, the structure of the retail stage, and the interaction between them. (The retailer structure hypotheses developed above apply directly, with no offsetting influence on the total rents available.)

Manufacturers' and retailers' joint influence on the consumer depends on the extent to which alternative sources of credible information are available or on what demand theory usually calls imperfections. If consumers had complete and costless information, the information supplied by the seller could have no influence in the purchase decision and no rents would accrue; sellers could give information, but it would not affect choice. Accordingly, retail channels would all be very similar, reflecting the similarity in consumers' need for information. Information is costly, however, and the manufacturer and retailer are jointly in a unique position to supply information more cheaply than alternative sources. Based on the characteristics of the product and its use, consumers' buying characteristics vary and with them the influence of the retailer. But the demand for information from the retailer will feed through to in-

---

26. Retailer power also depends on retailer structural traits. These two sources of power will be shown to interact below.

fluence the nature of the information and services that the retailer provides. Variations in the characteristics of retail channels, then, reflect variations in consumer buying characteristics.[27]

Recognizing that buying characteristics vary from product to product is only the first step. What is needed is a way of identifying and measuring the economically relevant differences. Our discussion above suggests a way: *the characteristics of the retail channels for a product will signal the relevant characteristics of consumer demand for that product.* Although the economically significant differences in buyer (and retailer) characteristics might be quite numerous, I suggest a principal dichotomy. I define two types of retail outlets:

*Convenience outlets:* Retail outlets where little or no sales assistance (information transfer) in the form of salesperson interaction is provided with the sale and the locational density of outlets is high.

*Nonconvenience outlets:* Retail outlets where sales assistance (information transfer) is provided with the sale, and outlets are selectively rather than densely located.

Examples of convenience outlets are supermarkets, gasoline stations, and liquor stores. Examples of nonconvenience outlets are furniture stores, appliance stores, and automobile dealerships.

These two prototype retail outlets are an abstraction from the numerous types of retail outlets which occur in practice, that can be arrayed on the taxonomy shown in Figure 2–1. As we move up the hierarchy of outlets in our taxonomy, the retailer's contribution to the product differentiation increases. This reflects the increasing specialization of the retailer's product line (and salespeople) and the decreasing locational density of outlets. Although this taxonomy will be useful later, I propose that the convenience-nonconvenience outlet distinction captures the major differences in buyer (retailer) characteristics. Therefore this distinction will provide the primary basis for the model and subsequent tests.

The prototypical product and consumer buying characteristics corresponding to these two types of retail outlet cannot be described formally without a full model. However, a classification scheme for products long used in the field of marketing can be used as an approximation that

---

27. Observed characteristics of retailing reflect buying characteristics as well as, in general, the production functions for the distributive activity. However, observation suggests that production function constraints are minor relative to the variations in retailer traits reflecting buying characteristics identified below. The effect of the retail production function on retailer structure will be examined below in the context of chain store development and exclusive outlets.

Outlet characteristics                                      Class of retail outlet

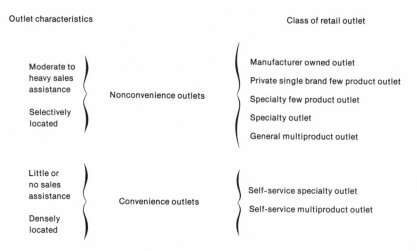

Fig. 2.1.   A Taxonomy of Retail Outlet Classes

captures the essential elements of the problem. In this classification, products are sorted into two groups defined as follows:[28]

*Convenience goods:* Goods with relatively low unit price, purchased repeatedly, for which the consumer desires an easily accessible outlet. Probable gains from making price and quality comparisons small relative to consumer's appraisal of search costs.

*Shopping goods:* Goods for which the consumer compares prices, quality, and style in several stores; the purchase can be delayed; the purchase is relatively infrequent (small appliance, clothing). Probable gains from making price and quality comparisons large relative to the consumer's appraisal of search costs.

The distinction between convenience and shopping goods can be seen, following the earlier discussion, to be a device to capture a fundamental distinction in consumer buying habits. The severe shortcoming of the convenience *good* and shopping *good* terminology, however, is the ambiguity in classifying individual products into the two categories. There is no clear way to decide just what constitutes low unit price, infrequent purchase, and so on, and these characteristics do not necessarily correspond to buying behavior.

28. Holton (1958) pp. 53–56. The earliest known use of a similar system is due to M. T. Copeland (1923). The "specialty goods" category has been dropped because it added no new information and was poorly defined in the literature.

Making use of the characteristics of the retail stage as a proxy for buying behavior, however, this problem can be avoided and the usefulness of such a classification system is increased. If a product is sold through retail outlets characterized by little or no sales assistance and locational density (convenience outlets) then we can safely assume that the product is one where consumer buying habits correspond to those ascribed to convenience goods. Similarly, if a product is sold through retail outlets that provide sales assistance and are located selectively rather than intensively (nonconvenience outlets), consumer buying characteristics for these products correspond to those of shopping goods. The characteristics of retailers are a more reliable and direct indicator of consumer buying characteristics than any single attribute of the product, such as unit price or purchase frequency or durability.[29] Furthermore, the simple dichotomy between convenience and nonconvenience outlet captures a critical distinction among products in the bundle of buying characteristics without the need for a complete theory.[30]

*Products sold through convenience outlets.* The convenience outlet provides little or no information with sale and is located close to the

29. It should be pointed out that non-convenience outlets may sell some of their products on a convenience basis, though the opposite is rarely the case. For example, a non-convenience hardware outlet may have little influence on the sale of lightbulbs though it has a great influence on paint sales.

Bucklin (1963) proposed a system of classification of retailers based on the buyer's patronage motives toward the retailer. His system bears some relation to mine, but is based on different criteria and is applid in different ways.

The convenience outlet–nonconvenience outlet system differs from the durable-nondurable distinction. The latter refers to goods and not to the way they are sold. Durables by and large fall within the nonconvenience classification but nondurables fall into both the convenience and nonconvenience groups. The durable-nondurable system also suffers from many of the same problems as the convenience goods classification, namely the problem of what exactly is a durable. A study by Greer (1971) divided products into three groups based on "product characteristics generally agreed to be relevant to optimal advertising expenditures." His system also failed to capture buyer characteristics and led to major differences in classification from the system suggested here.

30. It is clear that consumer buying characteristics, and hence retailer characteristics, depend on a set of intrinsic product characteristics, as partially mirrored in the convenience outlet-nonconvenience outlet system described above. Following on this, the observed level of advertising is an outcome based on these intrinsic product characteristics, other elements of market structure and firm conduct patterns. A complete theory would link intrinsic product characteristics (the true element of market structure) with consumer buying characteristics and retailer characteristics: my model thus can be seen as an intermediate stage. Chapter 5 will present a fuller theory.

buyer. For products sold through convenience outlets (convenience goods) low unit price and frequent purchase of the product reduce the desire of the consumer to expend effort on search. As signaled by the characteristics of the outlet, the consumer demands a nearby retail out- let, is unwilling to shop around, and desires no sales help. Thus the consumer considers the purchase relatively unimportant.[31] Since the purchase is not perceived to be important, the consumer is willing to rely on less costly information in making his purchase. For convenience goods, relatively costly information sources such as sales assistance by the retailer and direct shopping and comparison are not utilized by the buyer.

In view of these buying characteristics, the manufacturer's prime strategy for differentiating his product is to develop a strong brand image through advertising. If the manufacturer can develop a brand image, the retailer has very little power because: the retailer is little able to influence the buying decision of the consumer in the store; a strong manufacturer's brand image creates consumer demand for the product, which assures profits to the retailer from stocking the product and at the same time denies him the credible bargaining counter of refusing to deal in the manufacturer's goods.

In the model encompassing both the manufacturing and retail stages, it is clear that entry barriers extend beyond the traditional barriers of advertising, capital requirements, and production economies of scale. Gaining access to distribution is as important to the manufacturer, if not more so, as overcoming barriers to entry into production. A manu- facturer selling through convenience outlets must gain access to numer- ous retail outlets to achieve scale economies associated with dense coverage of a given geographical area, since the consumer is unwilling to travel large distances to purchase the product. Hence the manufacturer's sales force (or distribution system if wholesalers or jobbers are used) is required to deal with numerous outlets, many of which are typically small. Where the manufacturer has established a brand image, the per- suasion necessary to convince retailers to stock the product is minimal and the purely logistic aspects become paramount.[32] Furthermore, the

31. Ward (1973), in a different context, shows that convenience is the dominant buyer motive in determining his choice of outlet in confectionary, tobacco and drugs—all examples of convenience goods.

32. A throw-off of this discussion is clearly a suggestion about the efficacy or need for multiple products by the manufacturer for the various categories of products. Given the large number of convenience outlets, manufacturers of con- venience goods are likely to attain significant selling economies (as well as the obvious distribution economies) through development of multiple products sold

manufacturer need not convince the retailer to promote the sale of the product, since the influence the retailer has over the consumer is limited. Hence the manufacturer need not promote his product (once it is stocked) with retailers by means of manufacturer's salesmen or intermediaries such as wholesalers.[33]

Where due to product characteristics the manufacturer selling through convenience outlets is unable to develop a brand image through advertising, however, the convenience retailer becomes very powerful, and the manufacturer's ability to achieve product differentiation in the eyes of the consumer is severely limited. Entry into retail channels becomes extremely difficult because many outlets must stock the product for an efficient density of market coverage. Although manufacturers' salesmen (or paid substitutes such as wholesalers or distributers) may aid the undifferentiated manufacturer in gaining entry into retail outlets, their efforts will yield the manufacturer little or no product differentiation because the retailer can do little to influence the consumer's buying decision.

It is evident that a static notion of entry barriers no longer suffices when gaining access to distribution is considered. For convenience items in the initial stages of new product introduction, lack of a brand image makes barriers to distribution high; the distribution system will require enticement in the form of large margins, advertising allowances, and so on. As product differentiation is achieved over time through advertising and promotion, however, the willingness of retailers to stock the product will increase.

To capture this notion I introduce the concept of marginal cost of market share. The producer contemplating a long-run competitive move compares the present value of the extra profits he expects with costs (one-shot or continuing) of the most efficient way to attain the small increase in share. These costs include marginal barriers to entry different from, though related to, Bain's structural barriers to the attainment of a viable initial share for the new firm. The costly elevation of market share entails some method of increasing penetration of the distribution system—increased sales through existing outlets, more retail outlets selling the product, or both. The model suggests that the costs of increasing distribution will vary markedly across consumer goods indus-

---

through the same outlet class. Such diversification is indeed very common in convenience goods, witness Proctor and Gamble, American Home Products, Standard Brands, etc. Also see Chapter 4.

33. The retailer can to some extent influence the sale of the product through shelf positioning and inventory on hand. Some role for manufacturer selling remains, but much less than in the nonconvenience case discussed below.

tries. For products sold through convenience outlets, the discussion suggests that gaining access to distribution actually becomes easier as the product's brand image matures. The manufacturer, if he can convince an increasing proportion of consumers to purchase his product through advertising, will find that the distribution problem largely takes care of itself. Further, advertising space, the prime selling tool, is always available and can be tapped in increasing amounts. This will contrast sharply with nonconvenience goods.

Food products provide a good example of the concepts set forth in this entire section and also serve to introduce some other points. Food (except high-priced specialty food) is unambiguously a convenience item. Retail food outlets are primarily self-service outlets, conveniently located and, in the case of the larger retail food stores and chains, promote the store name and image through advertising. Food stores carry a wide variety of nationally branded products. Alongside these, and in some cases competing with them, the food store stocks undifferentiated (unadvertised) merchandise.

An indication of the power of the food store vis-à-vis the manufacturers of undifferentiated and differentiated food products is that the food chains have provided the impetus for the growth of private label brands in many lines.[34] For its differentiation, the private label product relies exclusively on the name and image of the retail store. The revealed preference of food chains for private label products, and their replacement of little advertised manufacturers' brands in many product areas, suggests a recognition of the chains' power vis-à-vis the manufacturer where a strong manufacturer's brand is not present and a desire to capitalize the value of the scarce resource they control—display space in well located outlets with a good image. The power to control access into distribution is utilized by the retailer to appropriate the bulk of the power and profits. (The profits may be low if competition among retailers is high.) The manufacturer of an unadvertised convenience item is forced by his lack of bargaining power to accept the inferior status of producing for private label rather than for his own brand (with private label the manufacturer himself has no differentiation at all). The large sales of chains may also entice manufacturers of branded goods to allocate marginal production capacity to producing for private label.

Adelman's study of A&P provides some evidence relevant to the

---

34. Private label products carry the name of the store as the brand, or other brand names associated with the store.

argument.[35] He found that relatively atomistic manufacturing industries supplying produce and other types of groceries offered no price concessions to A&P. As I have argued earlier, there was no incentive for them to do so. Adelman also found that strongly differentiated products seldom made concessions. A&P was most successful in obtaining concessions from those manufacturers who produced moderately differentiated products. Although Adelman was thinking largely in terms of traditional buyer concentration and offered no comprehensive explanation for this observation, his evidence is quite consistent with the model of the retailer's role in product differentiation. Makers of strongly differentiated products enjoy very high bargaining power vis-à-vis the retailer (even the chain), whence my theory would predict that few concessions would be made. The retailer's position would be superior, however, with moderately differentiated products.

What hypotheses has the discussion of products sold through convenience outlets generated about manufacturers' product differentiation strategies and performance? Because other forms of product differentiation activity by manufacturers offer little potential, direct advertising to the consumer is the dominant form of selling effort by the convenience goods manufacturer. As well as leading to product differentiation in the eyes of the consumer, advertising determines the manufacturer's power vis-à-vis the retailer and his ease of access to distribution. Where retailer power is high, the manufacturer's rate of return will be bargained down, ceteris paribus. Alternate means of product differentiation available to the manufacturer are likely to be ineffective. As a corollary, advertising is a relatively good measure of product differentiation for products sold through convenience outlets.

I can briefly extend this argument to encompass physical product characteristics and the content of advertising messages. The consumer of products sold through convenience outlets is swayed by relatively nonobjective factors and advertising appeals, since he is unlikely to shop and expend information gathering outlays. This suggests that physical product characteristics may be less important to the buyer's choice for these products; the payoff to superior product characteristics is limited and can be overcome through advertising claims. The same argument suggests that the content of advertising messages will be relatively less factual for convenience goods. Where the manufacturer can shift the basis of choice away from price or relatively objective product features, it is in his interest to do so. Price and objective product

35. Adelman (1959).

features are readily imitated, and competition along these dimensions erodes excess profits. I will have more to say about these issues in the discussion of nonconvenience goods.

*Products sold through nonconvenience outlets.* We now move to a consideration of products sold through nonconvenience outlets (nonconvenience goods). Nonconvenience outlets are those providing extensive in-store information through salespeople and those which are selectively located, requiring travel to shop and compare goods. The fundamental difference between convenience goods and nonconvenience goods is in the consumer's buying habits and hence the retailer's role in affecting the differentiation of the product. The purchase of a nonconvenience good is relatively large, postponable, and infrequent. The buyer views it as important and expends effort in comparing the various alternative goods available. The buyer's intentions and plans to purchase are more likely made in advance of purchase.[36] Although advertising and product differentiating activities of the manufacturer can induce the consumer to consider a particular brand or visit a store that carries it, the consumer's buying decision involves more. A critical adjunct to the information the consumer has from experience or media sources is physical demonstration and inspection of the product, the advice and counsel of the salesperson and the reputation and attendant services provided by the retail outlet.[37]

Physical product characteristics will take on more importance for products sold through nonconvenience outlets than for those sold through convenience outlets. Because the consumer shops around, solicits sales advice, and is willing to expend effort learning about competing brands, their physical characteristics will be noticed and are likely to be important. So should design and quality. Similarly, advertising messages are likely to be more informative, since they can be later verified or counteracted by the retailer.[38]

36. See Doyle (1968).

37. Because of these, the retailer rarely carries all the brands sold in the industry. The convenience retailer will carry a relatively greater proportion of brands. This is an example of retail structure adjusting to buyer behavior and manufacturer needs.

38. The deduction from store location and characteristics that consumers are willing to shop several stores for nonconvenience items and to spend more time and effort in the purchase decision is consistently supported by the various studies of shopping behavior which have been done in the marketing literature. Although a systematic study of shopping behavior across a broad sample of industries has apparently not been done, studies of individual or small groups of convenience and nonconvenience items have shown that nonconvenience buyers often shop several stores while convenience good buyers rarely shop (despite the greater

Products sold through retail outlets where sales assistance and other retailer services are provided are products where nonconvenience consumer buying characteristics are dominant.[39] As we move up our taxonomy of retail outlet classes (Figure 2–1), more and more sales assistance and attendant services, such as credit, billing, warranty, repair, are provided (the need for warranty and repair, of course, depend on the specific product). As the retail outlet becomes more specialized and carries fewer product categories, its power to influence the sale (contribution to product differentiation) will generally increase. Specialization of the outlet may signal more reliably good products to the buyer and leads to specialization in sales personnel, which increases their perceived competence. This retailer contribution also increases as more sales assistance is provided with the sale. These factors provide the basis for the construction of our taxonomy of retail outlets, and thus within the nonconvenience outlet category retailer contribution to differentiation increases as we move up the taxonomy. These retail characteristics mirror variations in consumer behavior within the nonconvenience group. Among convenience goods, consumer behavior along the dimensions discussed here is relatively more homogeneous.

The essential notion in the model for nonconvenience goods is the necessity of sales promotion by both the manufacturer and retailer. Even if the manufacturer advertises heavily, the policies of his retailers are critical to his success. A good brand image is not enough, and conventional measures of manufacturer's market power based on his own efforts to differentiate are inadequate.[40] This discussion suggests the following hypothesis. Among nonconvenience goods, as the retail outlet class through which the product is sold moves up the hierarchy of outlets in Figure 2–1, the bargaining power of the retailer increases and hence the retailer's share of returns.[41]

---

cost of shopping selectively located outlets); spend more time in the store and travel further to the store than convenience buyers; and plan the purchase days or weeks in advance of the shopping trip. See, for example, Voorhees (1955), May (1965), and Isaacson (1966).

39. Some products which are clearly convenience items, such as cigarettes, are sold through nonconvenience outlets. However, empirically the percentage of the sales of such products through nonconvenience outlets is small. See Chapter 6.

40. Conventional measures emphasize manufacturer advertising to sales ratios.

41. Ward (1973) presents some interesting data in another context which supports my model. He finds that distributive margins within a given industry are higher for the low advertised brands, consistent with my bargaining power hypothesis (p. 171). After computing expected retailer margins based on the inventory cost the retailer must bear, Ward finds margins to be higher than expected in radio and electrical goods and furniture (nonconvenience goods) and lower than ex-

B. Peter Pashigian's study (1961) of automobile distribution provides a good example of my characterization of nonconvenience outlets and consumer buying behavior in these outlets. Pashigian argues that automobile dealers can affect the consumer's selection of a brand. His data show that many automobile buyers shop among dealers, that most buyers travel more than four miles to the dealer they purchase from, and that dealers seem to be differentiated and buyers are loyal to particular dealers.[42] Consumers do not always buy from the nearest dealer, and dealers with reputations for good prices and service draw proportionally greater numbers of buyers than dealers without such reputations.[43] Finally, Pashigian's data illustrate that manufacturers have not been able to bargain away all the above-normal profits of automobile retailers even though the manufacturers control not only selling price to the retailer but also influence entry into automobile retailing.[44] This suggests the existence of retailer bargaining power.

There are other important aspects of the nature of retailing for nonconvenience goods. As we move up the hierarchy of outlets, selective rather than intensive retail coverage of the market becomes more and more important. The consumer is increasingly willing to travel to seek out product alternatives, and hence the manufacturer needs to have a few well chosen outlets rather than a large number of outlets. The reputation and image of the outlet becomes increasingly important in the dissemination of information. These characteristics have several effects. The manufacturer's sales force is oriented less towards the purely logistic function of distribution and more toward selling the retail outlets on the manufacturer's product. The nonconvenience retailer is in a position of power, and hence he must be convinced that it is in his interests not only to stock but to promote a product.[45] The sales-

---

pected in grocery and tobacco (convenience) goods (p. 173). While other explanations are proposed, a significant factor ignored by Ward is the retailer power hypothesis.

42. Pashigian (1961), pp. 38, 45–46, 51, 191.

43. Pashigian (1961), pp. 189–191.

44. Pashigian (1961), p. 16. I will discuss franchised or exclusive distribution (which occurs in automobile retailing) as a manifestation of retailer power in the next chapter.

45. It is appropriate to review here the assumption to ignore the wholesale stage, or more generally, the stages of distribution between the manufacturer and the retailer. In each stage of the argument, the emphasis of the selling function which the manufacturer must carry out to achieve retail distribution has been identified. Clearly these functions can either be carried out by the manufacturer or some intermediate stage. The more the intermediate stage is asked to do, the more it must be compensated. The functions to be performed remain, however, and it is these functions that are crucial to my analysis. Whether the manufacturer performs

person's time in explaining and demonstrating various brands is a major input in the nonconvenience retailer's decision to stock or promote a product. The retailers will allocate their time to those products where it is most cost effective. Among nonconvenience goods, the nonadvertising (and promotion) portion of manufacturer selling expense (primarily selling the retailer) is likely to be significant. The manufacturer's (or intermediary's) salesman must not only be concerned with getting the product into the outlet but also with training and motivation of the retailer's salespeople once it is there. The salesperson is so influential in the sale that in some cases manufacturers actually offer commissions to salespeople directly based on sales of their brand.[46] Thus advertising is a doubly poor measure of market power in nonconvenience goods. As a measure of product differentiation, it fails to account for the important contribution to product differentiation made by the retailer. As a measure of bargaining power vis-à-vis the retailer it omits an important variable: manufacturers' efforts to persuade the retailer.

In nonconvenience goods I have argued that the logistic aspect of distribution performed by the manufacturer's sales force (or intermediates) is less important than in convenience goods because there are fewer outlets to service. Also, functions such as stocking shelves and performing inventories, sometimes performed by salespersons selling to convenience outlets, are shifted to the retailer. Hence, the size of the manufacturer's total selling efforts towards the retailer (salesmen, intermediaries, and so on), which includes what I have termed the logistic aspect of distribution, cannot be unambiguously predicted to vary either way as we move up our taxonomy and as we move from convenience to nonconvenience goods. Manufacturer sales force expense (including the cost of intermediates) is not a clearly relevant structural variable for these reasons.

The nature of distribution for nonconvenience goods has further effects on manufacturers' selling strategies. The manufacturer of a product who lacks a strong advertised brand has better chance to succeed than the maker of a weakly differentiated convenience good. The manufacturer with a little advertised nonconvenience good with poor brand identification need not penetrate every outlet to be successful. Furthermore, advertising and promotion by the retailer are to a degree substitutes. The retailer can through his sales efforts compensate in large measure for a lower level of manufacturer advertising. This substi-

---

the functions or compensates an intermediate stage to perform them is not central to the analysis. [I will discuss intermediate stages more fully in Chapter 3.]

46. This occurs, for example, in hifi component retailing.

tutability raises the opportunity of alternative selling strategies within the same industry, which we will explore in Chapter 4. As evidence of the substitution possibilities and of retailer power in nonconvenience goods in general, witness the great success of Sears and Montgomery Ward in selling private brands of appliances, hardware items, and so on. Hence a manufacturer of a nonconvenience good can, though possessing little market power as measured by his rate of advertising outlay, be quite successful. To be sure a strategy that emphasizes persuading the retailer to promote the product will require compensation making it cost effective for the retailer to allocate his promotional inputs to that product. In addition, since the retailer is in a position of great power over nonconvenience manufacturers, most of the profits may flow to the retailer unless the manufacturing industry is concentrated. On balance, however, comparing two industries otherwise identical in market structure, one a convenience good and the other a nonconvenience good, with equal and low conventional measures of product differentiation (advertising), the model suggests that manufacturer rate of return in the nonconvenience good will be higher. Conversely, making the same comparison except for matching two industries with high conventional measures of product differentiation, my hypothesis is that the manufacturer rate of return in the nonconvenience good will be lower.

Barriers to gaining access to distribution are present in nonconvenience goods. The initial barriers to gaining access to distribution in nonconvenience outlets are lower than in the convenience outlet case, since intensive coverage of retail outlets is not required. However, mere access to nonconvenience outlets is not sufficient because of the power of the retailer to influence the consumer. The retailer must be induced through remuneration and persuasion by the manufacturer to cooperate in selling the product. The average return of selling efforts toward retail channels is equal in importance from the manufacturer's point of view to that from direct advertising to the consumer.

As the product matures, the manufacturer's requirement to remunerate and persuade retailers does not phase out, as it did in the convenience outlet case as the brand image developed. Thus whereas initial barriers to gaining access to distribution may be lower with nonconvenience outlets, the marginal costs of increasing distribution persist over time and probably escalate as the manufacturer's share increases. Higher market share means that more and more of the retailers selling the product must be convinced to aggressively sell the product vis-à-vis other brands, thereby increasing the market share of the product in their outlet. A key sales device in nonconvenience goods, namely retailer push, is not automatically there for the asking. Increasing retailer push may involve increasing cost per "unit of push." This relation between market share goods and costs of distribution is the reverse of the convenience outlet case and may provide a strong temptation for gaining exclusive control of retail outlets as the nonconvenience manufacturer increases market share.

The hierarchy of retail outlet classes (Figure 2–1) is based largely on the amount of sales assistance provided and number of products carried, reflecting a judgment that these are the dominant features. However, the retailer provides services that affect his ability to contribute to differentiation: credit, billing, delivery, warranty, repair. To the extent that these functions are performed by the retailer, they add to his ability to influence product differentiation and his relative power, with repair service obviously adding more than, say, credit. Conversely, the performance of these services (notably repair) by the manufacturer should subtract from retail power.

For products sold through convenience outlets, I have argued that advertising/sales is a relatively good measure of manufacturers' market power vis-à-vis the retail sector and of product differentiation. The effort of the convenience good manufacturer to persuade the retailer is likely to be only marginally effective. With nonconvenience goods, however, the manufacturer's persuasion of the retailer can make a difference. Studies of market structure-performance relations typically regress industry rate of return on measures of market power, using advertising as the sole proxy for product differentiation. The model implies that including solely advertising/sales biases measured structure-performance relationships. Those industries which expend relatively large amounts on persuading retailers will show up as "too profitable" based on their advertising/sales ratios. This will introduce a systematic error to the relationship between advertising/sales and profits. Whether that relationship will shift one way or the other will depend, of course, on the distribution of manufacturer's retailer oriented selling expenditures.[47] The presence of a logistics cost component will remain a problem, however, in any attempt to introduce into our equations a variable measuring the efforts of the manufacturer in persuading retailers.

*Summary of the basic model.* To summarize, my theory suggests that the characteristics of the retail outlets for a product reflect the nature of buyer choice for that product. For convenience goods, the retailer is not important in product differentiation, and advertising is the primary selling tool of the manufacturer. For nonconvenience goods, the retailer

47. The omitted variable bias depends on the relationship between the omitted and included variables. See Rao & Miller (1971).

is quite important in selling and advertising alone is a weaker measure of product differentiation. It is apparent that different structural measures of product differentiation should be used for the two groups.

The model of manufacturer-retailer interaction asserts that the power of the retailer vis-à-vis the manufacturer increases as we move up our hierarchy of retail outlets. Holding retailer structure (buyer concentration, and so on) and other elements of the manufacturers' market structure constant, the model suggests the hypothesis illustrated in Figure 2–2. For convenience goods the relationship between advertising/sales and profits is steeper because advertising aimed at the consumer is more effective in influencing him and has a powerful and direct influence on the bargaining strength of the manufacturer vis-à-vis the retailer. The manufacturer's other selling efforts are subsidiary. Because of the power position of the manufacturer, the relationship between advertising/sales and profits lies generally above that for products sold through nonconvenience outlets. For little-differentiated goods sold

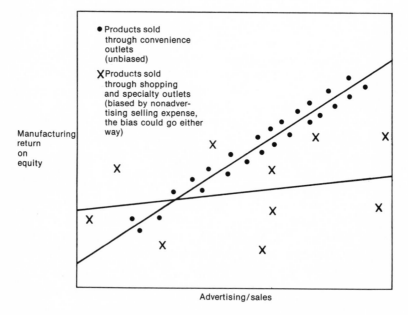

Fig. 2.2.  The Advertising-Profits Relation in Convenience and
          Nonconvenience Goods

through convenience outlets, however, the relationship dips below the one for goods sold through nonconvenience outlets.

For products sold through nonconvenience outlets, the advertising-profits relation is less steep because of the importance of the retailer in selling. The relationship is biased unless manufacturer selling efforts toward the retailer are included or controlled for. The direction of the bias can go in either direction depending on the sign of the advertising-manufacturer selling relationship.[48] Within the nonconvenience group, as the retail outlet through which the product is sold moves up our taxonomy, retail power increases.

The theory suggests that barriers to gaining access to distribution are a major component of overall entry barriers in consumer goods and that barriers to gaining distribution vary across outlet classes. The importance of advertising in convenience goods is reinforced by its impact on gaining access to distribution; in nonconvenience goods manufacturer sales efforts toward the retailer become essential.

The manufacturer-retailer interaction model highlights the potential shift in the distribution problem facing the manufacturer as the firm grows. Costs of increasing distribution were seen to vary between convenience and nonconvenience goods. In convenience goods, enlarging market share is primarily a problem of convincing more and more consumers to purchase the product through advertising. The problem of increasing distribution is largely solved through this advertising. In nonconvenience goods, however, the manufacturer must convince retailers to stock and more aggressively sell the product in addition to advertising directly to the consumer.

It follows that the successful large firms in nonconvenience industries would be less profitable relative to their industry than those in convenience industries.[49] The marginal cost of increasing distribution appears to be less in convenience goods. Contrary to the effect often noted with advertising, the activities incident to enlarging market share in nonconvenience goods would appear to offer less clear economies of scale. To increase retailers' sales-promotion efforts would seem to require increases in manufacturer expenditure which are proportional to sales or accelerating.

Another difference that the model suggests between large firms in the two sectors is that market shares in nonconvenience goods would be

48. Since there is no clear direction of this relation, the omitted variable will introduce noise into the model.

49. This assumes that other economies of large scale do not vary systematically across the two groups (such as production economies and capital market imperfections).

more stable. Manufacturers' relations with retailers would appear to be more lasting, harder to duplicate and less easily offset than would consumer advertising campaigns.[50] However, relative instability of market shares in convenience goods does not imply low rates of return if the convenience goods are differentiated. In nonconvenience goods, those industries with relatively unstable market shares would probably be less profitable because instability would signal costly and destabilizing competition for retailers' favors. Such competition, unlike advertising competition, would yield no offsetting support to profits by raising the level of product differentiation.

Multiple Outlet Classes and Types

In building a manufacturer-retailer model with products differentiated we encounter a sticky problem: how to deal with products that are sold through more than one type of retail channel. This question has already been discussed in the context of retail market structure in the first part of this chapter. There, multiplicity was identified with diverse types of retail outlets, with types distinguished by the general nature of products sold (for example, food vs. liquor), the breadth of product line, or quantity of sales assistance and services offered. Given the over-all concentration of retail outlets, multiple types reduced the chances for effective collusion among retailers.

The discussion of product differentiation suggests that the break-down of retailing by outlet types is not the only relevant one, although it is clearly the broadest. The taxonomy in Figure 2–1 separated retailers into groups based on the degree of product specialization and the amount of assistance provided. To distinguish these, I will term them retail outlet *classes*. Retail classes reflect differences in retailer power, whereas different types of retailers may have equal power but differ in the general nature of products stocked (for example, hardware versus sporting goods). In terms of the ease in achieving cooperation this distinction is relevant though probably not important, since in either case the patterns of competition and the likely objective and subjective characteristics vary across different outlets. This variance may be somewhat greater when specialization and sales assistance vary than when only the product mix varies.

It is evident from the discussion of retailer's role in differentiation that the hypotheses regarding the effects of multiple retailer types can be extended in two major directions. First, the model introduced the concept

---

50. If product quality is more important in nonconvenience goods, year to year changes in quality through research and development would work against this.

of barriers to gaining access to distribution. Multiple outlet classes or types obviously affect the problem of access into distribution. Second, multiple outlet classes complicate the influence of product differentiation on the balance of power between manufacturer and retailer because different outlet classes have varying degrees of retailer power.

I will first treat barriers to gaining access to distribution. As the number of outlet types through which a product is sold increases, gaining access to distribution becomes easier. This flows from the assumption that each retail outlet type occurs roughly in the optimal density for servicing its customers. That is, convenience outlets such as food, drug, and liquor stores are densely located whereas the nonconvenience outlet types are considerably less densely located. Taking convenience goods as an example, each convenience outlet type has sufficient locational density to satisfy the convenience criteria, the ability to sell through more than one outlet type clearly reduces the problem of gaining adequate distribution. As a component of overall barriers to entry into manufacturing decreases, manufacturer rate of return potential would decrease using the usual structure-performance model.

This effect goes counter to the earlier hypothesis about the effects of multiple retailer types, which predicted the opposite sign. There, however, I was assuming an equal total number of retail outlets. In practice, multiple outlet types selling the product will increase the number of outlets and thereby result in an offsetting tendency to enhance manufacturer power through the buyer concentration hypothesis. The net effect is an empirical question.

The effect of multiple types may be asymmetrical as between convenience and nonconvenience goods. In convenience goods, intensive locational density requirements make distribution barriers important. Among types of convenience outlets the density of outlets is roughly constant. Therefore the number of different outlet types selling a convenience product is a sufficient measure of the multiple outlet effect. Among nonconvenience goods, however, the variation in the number and density of outlets of each type is large (compare clothing stores and department stores). Hence not only the number of outlet types is important but the number of individual retail firms represented by that outlet type is important. Obviously the sale of luggage through luggage specialty stores as well as department stores will not affect barriers to gaining access to distribution significantly if luggage specialty stores are rare. While the number of outlets would be most important to distribution barriers, the effect of multiple outlet types in reducing retailer cooperation and hence bargaining power would depend most strongly on the relative sales shares of the retail outlet types.

There is another effect of multiple type selling that is of interest. The analysis has assumed that gaining access to one type of convenience or nonconvenience outlet would yield efficient market coverage to the manufacturer. However, in the group of convenience goods sometimes known as impulse goods, repeated exposure to the product (seeing it on a retailer's shelf) may increase primary demand; thus selling through multiple outlet types may provide a direct benefit to the manufacturer in these cases, offsetting at least partially the potential decrease in return due to the reduced entry barriers. Examples of products where such effects might occur would be candy, chewing gum, soft drinks, periodicals, and perhaps cigarettes. In fact, if multiple outlet type selling increases demand significantly for impulse goods, net barriers to gaining access to distribution will actually be increased. Establishing and maintaining distribution channels is likely to involve fixed costs and be subject to economies as the number of separate channels increases. The potential entrant faces the classic scale economies dilemma of accepting inferior sales effectiveness due to lack of multiple channels or bearing the fixed costs.

*Selling by multiple outlet classes: discount houses.* Empirically, the sale of products through multiple outlet classes is rare.[51] Few products sold through convenience outlets are also sold through nonconvenience outlets and vice versa. This is quite plausible intuitively, in view of the major difference in the retailing function of the two groups. The major exceptions to this general rule are the so-called discount houses, which sell primarily on low price and high volume. The last decade has seen the emergence of discount stores both in convenience outlet categories such as drugstores and nonconvenience categories, primarily department stores. In convenience goods the discount house raises few issues for the model, because the retailer's contribution to product differentiation is already low. In fact, the model suggests that discount selling is to be expected in convenience goods because the retailer has relatively few dimensions on which to compete besides price. In convenience goods, discount selling would seem to have little effect on the manufacturer (except insofar as discount selling implied large chains or large absolute size). Among retailers, the discounter is likely to be a destabilizing force leading to lower retailer rates of return. Competing convenience retailers would have limited opportunities for offsetting discounters' price advantages with other strategies to raise buyers' utility and hence the discounter may weaken margins in the entire market. Historically this may explain why supermarkets and drug chains which were discount ori-

51. See Chapter 7.

ented, at least during their period of growth, came to dominate their respective forms of retailing.

Among nonconvenience goods, discount selling affects the model's predictions more fundamentally. Discount houses typically sell nonconvenience products with a minimum of sales assistance and at reduced prices, apparently contradicting the hypothesis that the retailer is important in selling nonconvenience goods. The range of goods carried by discount houses is quite broad—from clothing and automotive supplies to appliances.

Let us, however, analyze the discount house selling function more fully. It is important to point out initially that the difference is a matter of degree and not fundamental selling strategy. Discount stores are selectively located, and all employ salespersons. The difference between a discount store and a conventional outlet involves less emphasis on store amenities and perhaps a somewhat reduced degree of sales assistance. Given our characterization of consumer buying characteristics for nonconvenience goods, it would appear that consumers purchasing these goods in discount houses fall into two groups. One group has shopped around and received sales assistance elsewhere and patronizes the discount outlet because the lower price available there is worth more to them than the greater services of conventional outlets are (nicer buying atmosphere, credit, delivery, and so on). The second group are those consumers who are persuaded to purchase based on manufacturer advertising alone and require no sales assistance. The size of this latter group (never zero) probably decreases as the normal, dominant outlet selling the product moves up our taxonomy (Figure 2–1). The significance of the former group of consumers would also increase as the normal outlet grows less specialized. The more specialized outlet, influential in differentiation, can offer the buyer benefits to offset the lower price of the discounter. The extent of true discount sales of nonconvenience goods appears likely to stabilize at a level determined by the size of the pool of very price conscious consumers.[52]

The effect of discount houses on competition among retailers in the nonconvenience outlets will be noticeable but not nearly so severe as in the convenience case. Discount houses are not likely to affect retailer power in nonconvenience goods beyond the effects of multiple outlet types already noted. It is interesting that nonconvenience discount stores have evolved toward conventional department stores in recent years, while convenience discount stores remain a stable and important influence. This is consistent with our model.

---

52. The term true discount house is used because there is an observed tendency for discount houses to become more like department stores over time.

*Simultaneity: The determinants of multiple type selling.*    Before concluding our discussion of the effects of multiple retail types selling a product, it may be useful to consider the manufacturer's reasons for utilizing multiple types of outlets. The underlying consumer buying characteristics probably constrain products to distribution through either convenience or nonconvenience outlets, for the reasons given above. Why, though, are some convenience products sold through multiple outlet types, for example, supermarkets, drug stores, and health and beauty aid stores?

One reason is the possibility that impulse purchase products benefit from maximum possible exposure. More broadly, depending on the manufacturer's cost of servicing more outlets (the marginal cost may be zero) the manufacturer can weigh the incremental sales of more outlets against the cost. A manufacturer's success in differentiating a product through direct promotion to the consumer might tend to encourage selling by multiple outlet types.[53] A strong brand image may imply large retail sales and a well known brand would heighten the willingness of the consumer to buy a product in an outlet other than the traditional one. Such a chain of causation would tend to reinforce the positive effects of multiple outlet types on rate of return stressed above—it would provide a direct indication of the manufacturer's market power. Multiple outlets would imply lower retail bargaining power and higher profits for manufacturers.

### Interaction of the Structure of Retailing and the Retailer's Ability to Influence Differentiation

Retailer power has been separated into two categories based on its source. Retailer structure is comprised of the number and size distribution, variety, and absolute size of retail outlets and the breadth of their product lines. The structure of retailing influences competitive behavior in the retail market and retailers' ability to coordinate behavior. Power also accrues to the retail stage based on its contribution to the differentiation of the product.

It was asserted above that the major basis for retailer power lies in product differentiation. The sector's ability to exercise this bargaining power, however, depends in part on retailer structure. For retailers to extract higher margins and other concessions from the manufacturing stage, competition among them must be moderated. For retailer competition to nullify retail bargaining power vis-à-vis the manufacturer, however, it would have to take on a special form. Competing retailers would have to bid up the manufacturer's wholesale prices for the right to stock

53. I am indebted to R. E. Caves for this point. Also, see Holton (1962), p. 303.

the product. This scenario seems unlikely; a more plausible one would be a Chamberlinean retail industry which ate up excess returns resulting from bargaining strength vis-à-vis the manufacturer in the form of over-capacity.[54] Exercise of retailer power vis-à-vis manufacturers is not at all inconsistent with normal retailer rates of return.

It was argued above that small retail market size and other character-istics of retailing tend to lead to a high degree of mutual dependence recognized among retailers. Rivalry among retailers may thus be both reduced and shifted away from areas where all retailers stand to lose, namely, in dealings with the manufacturing stage. Retailer recognition of mutual dependence in dealing with the manufacturing stage is not in-consistent with strong competition in selling prices and service.

The conclusion is that an oligopolistic retail structure is not a prere-quisite for the realization of retailer's bargaining power vis-à-vis the manufacturer. It seems clear, however, that retail structures conducive to mutual recognition among retailers can enhance the retailers' ability to extract concessions. Thus retailer power due to product differentiation interacts positively with power due to oligopolistic structure. In con-venience goods, retailer power based on differentiation is low, so that it rests on retailer structure if it exists at all. In nonconvenience goods, however, the effect of retailer structure is twofold. In addition to its direct effect on bargaining, retailer structure influences the realization of bargaining power based on differentiation. A small number of strongly interdependent retailers will make more effective use of this bargaining power based on differentiation. In view of this, retailer structure is likely to be a very important variable explaining variations in rate of return in nonconvenience good industries.

Just as was true in the general case above, though, the realization of bargaining power based on differentiation is not completely determined by structure in nonconvenience goods. This power is based on the re-tailer's individual efforts to sell the particular manufacturer's product, and not on the mere presence of the retailer in the market. In the face of retailers with multiple products and multiple brands, there remains an incentive for the manufacturer to stimulate retailer sales effort even if many retailers are in the market, and the individual retailer can resist the pressures of individual manufacturers on his margins.

### The Characteristics of Retailing and Technical Progress

Although our focus has been on the effect of manufacturer-retailer interaction on allocative efficiency, some theoretical implications of dif-

54. Caves (1970).

ferences in retailer (and consumer buying) characteristics can be derived for the process of innovation. Buyer characteristics appear to be neutral with regard to the attainment of technical efficiency or process innovation. They can, however, have important implications for product innovation.

The level of product innovation across industries is dependent upon two factors: the potential for product innovation (technological opportunity) and incentive. I will concentrate on incentives. The incentive of the manufacturer to innovate depends on the responsiveness of consumers to innovations and the likely reactions of competitors. The model suggests that consumer response to meaningful product innovation and the benefits which accrue vis-à-vis rivals will be greater in nonconvenience goods. Tangible performance characteristics and features will carry weight in the purchase decision and are difficult to imitate or nullify without lags. Consumer search will likely uncover meaningful product differences. Furthermore, the retailer (a surrogate informed buyer) is in a position, through his influence on the consumer decision, to highlight meaningful changes in products and discount superficial differences.

In the case of convenience goods, the consumer engages in less information gathering in purchasing them and is unwilling to search and compare products. This posture dampens his responsiveness to product change, because brand perceptions change only with a lag. Effective advertising claims appear to be a more powerful influence on consumer choice than product innovation per se. Innovation can facilitate the design of advertising campaigns, but meaningful innovation is not a prerequisite for advertising success. Meaningful product changes can be neutralized by defensive advertising and hastily concocted "cosmetic" product changes.

These characteristics also have implications for the character of innovation in the two groups of industries. In nonconvenience goods, innovation will likely involve substantive changes in the product (though some may argue the social utility of some of these changes). In convenience goods, however, innovation may take the form of cosmetic product changes designed to form the basis for advertising campaigns. Indeed, a progression of such changes may have important implications for the effectiveness of advertising (see Chapter 5). In convenience goods, the innovating firm will not realize the benefits of product innovations unless it is accompanied by heavy advertising. This implies that large firms will be the major source of innovations, whether the innovations are real or cosmetic.[55] Large firms should be the major source of

---

55. In some cases significant product innovation may be a partial substitute for advertising as a means for small firms to achieve entry or increase market share

innovations, and the major beneficiaries of innovations made by smaller firms. An illustrative example of this is the disposable pen market. Both Bic with the stick pen and Gillette with the soft tip pen (Flair) used heavy advertising to dominate markets where the products were introduced earlier by small firms.[56]

In nonconvenience goods, however, scale economies in promotion do not constrain the effectiveness of the small or medium sized firm as an innovator. The retailer provides a mechanism for the promotion of innovations through direct contact with consumers. The consumer's propensity to engage in product search will further aid small or medium sized firms in gaining acceptance for an improved product. Therefore, product innovations, and research outlays, should be less concentrated in nonconvenience goods.[57]

To summarize, the manufacturer-retailer interaction affects product innovation in three ways. First, it suggests a greater incentive for product innovation in nonconvenience goods. Second, the research or innovative activity in convenience goods may be directed to socially undesirable cosmetic product change, while the tendency for this to occur in nonconvenience goods is relatively slight. Third, expenditures on product innovation will be more concentrated in convenience goods because of the requirement for large-scale sales promotion.

---

in convenience industries. In view of the importance of advertising in bringing innovations to the attention of the consumer in convenience goods, one would expect such cases to be infrequent.

56. *Bic Pen Corporation*, Boston: International Case Clearinghouse 4–374–305.

57. R. E. Caves suggested this point. Small firms are successful innovators, for example, in appliances (Maytag, Magic Chef).

# 3

## Extensions of the Manufacturer-Retailer Model

In Chapter 2 I presented a model of the interaction between the manufacturing and retail stages and developed its implications for product differentiation strategies in consumer goods industries, and for manufacturing industry performance. In this chapter, I extend the model in several directions. These can be divided into two major sections. In the first section, I will examine a number of implications of the model for selected aspects of the observed behavior of manufacturers and retailers and of the occurrence of retailing structures. First I will briefly examine some of the implications of the model for general manufacturer and retailer behavior. Next I will derive the implications of the model for the cross-industry variations in intermediate stages of distribution and the cross-industry incidence of chain retailers and private label goods, examining Galbraith's theory of contervailing power in the process. In the second part of the chapter, I will extend the model to analyze the continuum of contractual relations between manufacturer and retailer, including resale price maintenance, exclusive dealing and manufacturer ownership of outlets. The implications of the model for the incidence of these contractual relations and their characteristics will be developed. The analysis will then be applied to antitrust policy regarding these practices.

### Applications of the Model

#### The Manufacturer-Retailer Interaction and Retailer and Manufacturer Behavior

A straightforward implication of the manufacturer-retailer model is that the retailer can possess bargaining power and thus has the incentive and perhaps the ability to increase it. A retailer's bargaining power can be increased by promoting the store image and reputation (perhaps through store advertising), enhancing the credibility of the information he provides (and thereby its effect on the sale). It follows directly from the model that the retailer's efforts to build power will likely to be proportionally greater in nonconvenience goods. Because of the buyer's choice process, in convenience goods building retailer power will generally be restricted to publicizing competitive prices and emphasizing the quick services and convenience of the outlet. In nonconvenience goods, outlets may publicize salespersons' competence and the presence of attendant services; they can also invest in physical amenities in the store to convey an image of quality (and hence quality of information), and so on. Retailer's advertising is likely to be proportionally more important in nonconvenience goods, especially in cases where the retailer has a narrow product line. It should also be more oriented to image and transaction terms other than price.

Symmetrically, the manufacturer has the incentive to improve his power position vis-à-vis retailers. Besides the selling efforts directly to the consumer and persuasion of the retailer already mentioned, the manufacturer may move to develop exclusive arrangements with retailers. The manufacturer may also have the incentive to diversify into other products sold by his retail channels. This allows him to bargain with a larger block of the retailers' sales and correspondingly increases his bargaining leverage. Such a move may also allow the manufacturer to shift from wholesalers to his own distribution or to demand more specialized wholesalers. This can offset any bargaining power resident in the wholesale stage and improve the manufacturer's representation with retailers. This latter effect is more important in nonconvenience goods. Finally, the manufacturer may also be able to use the threat of withholding a successful product with a strong brand to induce the retailer to stock a new or less successfully branded product if he sells a number of products through the same retail channels.

The Manufacturer-Retailer Interaction and
Intermediate Stages of Distribution

Chapter 2 focused on the interrelation between the manufacturing and retail stage, yet intermediate stages of distribution occur in many industries (wholesalers, distributors, jobbers, and so on). I will use the term wholesalers to characterize all forms of intermediate distribution. Wholesalers make no contribution to the differentiation of the product to the consumer but rather serve as the manufacturer's representative to the retail stage, for which they receive remuneration. Wholesaler salespersons may take over the task of persuading retailers to stock and promote a product (and sometimes a limited amount of advertising on the manufacturer's behalf) or may do so in conjunction with manufacturer salespeople. Unlike retailers, therefore, wholesalers have little incentive to advertise themselves to consumers. Their presence merely shifts the locus of where the retailer persuasion function occurs.

Since wholesalers have little or no influence on differentiation, their power depends on their structural features. If wholesalers are few, and possibilities for manufacturers (or retailers) assuming the wholesaling function are limited, wholesalers may have some bargaining power vis-à-vis the manufacturer. This power is limited, of course, by the ease of entry into wholesaling. Entry into wholesaling will be impeded by scale economies in the wholesaling function, differentiation of wholesalers through retailer contacts, and capital requirements for inventory.

Our manufacturer-retailer model has implications for the cross-industry incidence of wholesalers relative to direct sales from manufacturers to retailers. Wholesalers are less likely to occur in nonconvenience goods where the manufacturer's persuasion of and interaction with the retailer is crucial, others things being equal. Where they do occur in nonconvenience goods, wholesalers are likely to have more specialized products lines and distribute few, if any, competitive brands. These implications flow directly from the importance of persuading the retailer to promote a particular brand in nonconvenience goods. The wholesaler is an independent entity whose profit maximizing strategy potentially diverges from the manufacturers to the extent that he carries other products and brands. In nonconvenience goods the manufacturer faces greater risks in having wholesalers loyalties divided among his brand and other brands and products. The potential efficiencies of broad-line wholesalers are thus sacrificed because of the importance of the wholesalers' function of representing the manufacturer in nonconvenience goods.

Overlaying these effects is the technology of the distribution function. The previous literature on the cross-industry penetration of wholesalers has focused on this to the exclusion of product differentiation.[1] The cost tradeoff between manufacturer distribution of his own line and wholesaler distribution of multiple products will vary across industries. Products sold in small quantities through widely spread retail outlets may be inefficient for the manufacturer to distribute himself or even for wholesalers to specialize in (due to scale economies). The key factor is the size of the individual order: the smaller it is, the more likely wholesalers will occur.[2] These factors may reinforce the tendency for whole-

---

1. See Ward (1973), part 2. The classic work is Jeffries (1950).
2. Ward (1973), p. 136.

salers to occur in convenience goods.[3] The important point for the analysis is that the optimal distribution arrangement for selling purposes will be balanced against the relative costs of alternative distributive strategies to determine the strategy chosen in any given industry. Insofar as individual firm product lines or output volumes vary within an industry the optimizing set of distributive arrangements may vary within industries as well.

### The Determinants of Retail Structure

For methodological, if not for other reasons, it is of interest to consider the problem of what determines the structure of the retail distribution system for the given product. Does the market structure of the manufacturing industry affect the concentration of retailers selling its product, the position of these retailers on our taxonomy, and so on? If so, then retailer structure is an endogenous variable in studies of manufacturer market power. Galbraith's *American Capitalism* suggests that manufacturing industries with high market power will beget powerful retailers.[4] To support this view Galbraith cites cases such as Sears, A&P, Woolworth's, and so on. Thus Galbraith views retailer and manufacturer structure to be causally related. Richard Holton in part supports this view.[5]

It is clear from Galbraith's examples that his notion of countervailing retailer power is solely in terms of buyer concentration. In view of my model this is a serious weakness. However, let us use Galbraith's hypothesis as an excuse to make an analysis of whether manufacturer structure is related to retailer (buyer) concentration, leaving aside for a moment any possible linkage between manufacturing industry structure and the position of the retail outlet on our taxonomy. Galbraith, in his exposition of the rise of countervailing power, is in essence speaking about the rise of large chains in certain retail outlet classes. Does the rise of chains occur in retail outlet classes which sell the products of powerful manufacturing industries?

In the first place, the chains Galbraith refers to are all characterized by their handling of a large variety of products which are sold by industries with the entire range of manufacturer market structures. Thus any one-to-one relation between manufacturing and retailer structure is evidently nonexistent. Second, it is instructive to inquire more generally

3. The presence of chain retailers reduces the potential for wholesalers by increasing the order per buyer. Ward (1973) finds that increasing chain store penetration in the United Kingdom has reduced wholesaler share (p. 232).

4. Galbraith (1956), pp. 108–134, esp. p. 113.

5. Holton (1962), p. 269.

why chains have occurred. Holton speaks to this point.[6] Reviewing the incidence of cases where chains are important, he argues that chain stores are likely to be important where: the volume of goods is so large and the assortment demanded at the retail outlet so standardized that much can be gained from reducing to a routine the  physical movement of goods through the wholesale and retail levels (distribution economies); personal service required at the retail level is limited; pricing can be easily centralized; entry is sufficiently difficult to prevent the constant entry of large numbers of entrepreneurs. Although the development of countervailing power may be one motive which might be added to this list, these other factors provide a convincing set of reasons for the development of chains even in the absence of countervailing power motives. Hence, Galbraith's stress on the countervailing power motive must rest on shaky footing, and his simple  buyer concentration model  is  correspondingly  of  limited value.[7]

My model suggests that the major element of retailer power results from the retailer's ability to influence product differentiation. We thus have a situation of countervailing power which, as in Galbraith's model, provides a significant check on the power of the manufacturing industry. Unlike Galbraith, however, I do not argue that manufacturer structure and retailer structure are directly dependent. Instead, there seems to be a partial though important dependence.

For convenience goods with a strong brand image, the manufacturer power vis-à-vis the retailer is very high, and manufacturer's problem of gaining access to retail outlets relatively modest. Chains indeed occur often in convenience goods, collinear with the countervailing power notion. However, in convenience goods the very characteristic which limits the power of the retailer provides the opportunity for successful development of multiple unit operations by the retailer. The keys to chain development are distribution economies and ease of replicating the critical requirements for success in the retail outlet type.  In convenience outlets personal service is minimal, and requirements for physical distribution are substantial due to the locational density of the outlets. Indeed, since personal selling is minimal the convenience retailer will tend to sell a large array of convenience goods, increasing the number of purchases

6. Holton (1962), pp. 276–281.

7. Hunter (1958) concludes, in reference to this point, that chains have developed mainly in order to exploit considerable economies of scale open to them through organizational and merchandising techniques. Galbraith (1959) replies: "I would not argue that the deployment of bargaining power is the only reward to size in marketing. The efficiencies of scale are symbiotic with the rewards of bargaining power" (p. 169).

the buyer can make in one shopping trip. The broad product line in convenience goods reinforces the advantages of chains. Lack of retailer influence in selling, then, is an important factor for facilitating chain development though hardly in the same way as implied by the countervailing power hypothesis. The influence of the retailer on the differentiation of the product flows from consumer-buying behavior reflecting intrinsic product traits.

In the case of convenience outlet chains the occurrence of chains does not necessarily affect the power balance, a view again not consistent with Galbraith's. The occurrence of chains may not affect in an important way the retailer's power vis-à-vis manufacturers of highly differentiated products—witness Adelman's observations about A&P's inability to extract concessions from such manufacturers. Chains, I would argue, have a greater effect on industries selling moderate to low differentiated products.

For nonconvenience goods, retailer power to influence differentiation is much higher. Large chains are correspondingly more rare, again collinear with the countervailing power view. The rarity of chains may be explained, however, by the difficulty of gaining economies of repetition of nonconvenience outlets because of the high personal selling component of the selling task. Further, the strategy of increasing the number of products sold in the nonconvenience outlet to provide the chain store with greater economies in distribution is constrained by the cost such lessening of specialization may have on the influence of the nonconvenience retailer on the buyer's purchase decision on any given product. Broad product lines will generally be rarer in nonconvenience goods. Where chains do develop, the model would predict that they are extraordinarily powerful by combining power in product differentiation with large sales volume. The basis of the countervailing power is far different from simply size and fewness, however.

I have, therefore, argued for a link between manufacturer structure and retail structure of a very different sort from Galbraith's. Retail structure is most of all determined by product characteristics as they affect consumer buying behavior rather than by manufacturer structure. These same consumer buying characteristics influence the structure of the manufacturing industry. The historical growth of chains did not seem to be motivated by the political motives stressed by Galbraith but rather by the potential offered by convenience goods for mass selling and distribution economies. The link between retailer structure and manufacturer structure is thus a more fundamental one, stemming from intrinsic product characteristics. This relation is sketched below; its further exploration must await a future work.

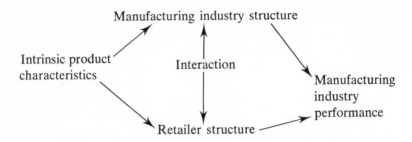

### The Manufacturer-Retailer Interaction
### and the Incidence of Private Label

In Chapter 2 I identified private label goods as a manifestation of re-tailer power. Closely related to the discussion of the incidence of chain retailers is the question of predicting the pattern of occurrence of private label goods across consumer goods industries, and its relationship to chain stores.

In convenience goods where the retailer is unimportant in product differentiation, the presence of retail chains is a prerequisite for private label. Since the retailer contributes little to product differentiation, the appeal of private label goods to the consumer is contingent on offering a lower price. Unless the retailer is in a position to purchase large quan-tities of unbranded goods, the possibilities that he will be able profitably to offer these goods for sale at a price sufficiently lower than that of the manufacturer's branded products to attract sales is reduced. Thus the incidence of private label in convenience goods should follow the extent of chain penetration, other things being equal. It is not surprising in view of this that private label goods are common in food items and health and beauty aids, because of the strong position of food chains, drug chains, and discount health and beauty chains. In wines, liquors, and beer private label goods are much less common. This is consistent with my view, since liquor store chains are rare. Private labels of some liquor products (but not wine and beer) can be found in the few high-volume liquor chains that have developed. The cost of processing liquor is very low relative to its selling cost.[8] Thus despite the typically low sales volume of liquor retailers, some liquor products offer tempting targets for private label. The selling cost/production cost relation is much less favorable in wine and beer. An interesting case is soft drinks. Here, supermarkets are relatively important in sales and private label soft drinks have begun to appear in some supermarket chains.

One would expect private labeling first in those product areas where

8. *Heublein, Inc.* Harvard Business School case, Intercollegiate Case Clearing House, 9-373-103.

the logistics cost savings of chains are large (for example, in bulky products) and where manufacturer selling costs per unit are high, so that the chain can offer price advantages over the branded good. In addition, private label would be promoted by the absence of high setup costs or other substantial economies in long production runs. Each private label product must at very least have been given a different package or label and may involve a different product formulation. The more costly the production changeover to produce the private label good, the greater the selling cost and logistics savings that must be present to justify private label, or the greater the retail store volume must be before private label is a viable strategy.

In nonconvenience goods where the retailer's contribution to product differentiation is relatively large, private label merchandise need not be priced lower than manufacturer branded merchandise. Indeed, the image and reputation of the store may be more important to the consumer than the manufacturer's brand. The presence of retail chains enhances the possibilities for private label in a given manufacturing industry; it is not, however, a prerequisite. Retail chains such as Sears, Montgomery Wards, and so on, offer a wide variety of private label nonconvenience goods. The importance of retailer selling makes these private label goods relatively more successful in competing with branded goods than is the case with private label convenience items. There are also numerous cases where private label nonconvenience goods occur in the absence of retail chains. Common examples are furniture, clothing, and some sporting goods. In these cases, the manufacturer is sometimes known, but the essential part of the selling job is the sales effort and reputation of the retailer. Since a cost advantage over manufacturer branded goods is not necessary for the success of private label nonconvenience goods, large retailer volume is not necessary and thus neither is the presence of chains. It follows that the need for retailer volume to justify private label decreases as the outlet moves up the hierarchy of outlets in our taxonomy, reflecting increasing retailer contribution to differentiation.

## Contractual Relations between Manufacturers and Retailers

The model of the interaction between manufacturers and retailers flows from the ability of the retailer to influence product differentiation, and market power resulting from the structure of retail markets. One observes in practice a series of contractual relations between manufacturers and retailers. These can be roughly arrayed on a spectrum, ranging from exclusive dealing arrangements and resale price maintenance to franchising and manufacturer ownership of retail outlets. This section derives the implications of my model for the incidence of the various forms of contractual relations and the effect of contractual relations on the bargaining relation between manufacturer and retailer. In the process, the lessons of the analysis for antitrust policy toward vertical relations are explored.

Direct Manufacturer Involvement in Retailing

I proceed first to consider that portion of the taxonomy of retail outlets that I chose to ignore earlier, namely those retail outlets where the manufacturer is directly involved in retailing either through manufacturer ownership of retail outlets (formal integration) or granting of exclusive territorial rights in essentially single product outlets. The phrase *direct outlets* will cover both categories above. The first category is straightforward and includes such well-known outlets as Singer, Sherwin-Williams, and so on. The second category refers to those outlets which carry no other brands of the product and where the outlet is identified by name with the product. This includes such outlets as automobile dealerships, gasoline stations, and farm equipment dealerships where the outlet is identified explicitly with the brand, and the product line is relatively narrow. These outlets may or may not be franchised. The essential characteristic of direct outlets is the total identification with one brand of a single product category. The more general case of exclusive dealing, where the retailer need not specialize in one product or brand, will be discussed in the next section.

There are two questions to be answered about direct retailing. First, how and why do manufacturers adopt direct outlets? Second, what is the significance of direct outlets to our model? The second question will be treated first.

*Direct outlets and the manufacturer-retailer bargain.* Once a manufacturer has developed direct outlets it is clear that the manufacturer exercises a strong degree of control over the outlet. In the case of manufacturer-owned outlets the control is complete and the retailer's bargaining power is correspondingly nil. In the case of outlets independently owned but identified solely with the manufacturer the situation is similar. The outlet has little choice about whether or not to push the products of the manufacturer. Anything the outlet withholds to hurt the manufacturer will reduce its profits as well, and thus it has little bargaining strength. What bargaining strength it does have is based on its ability to terminate its exclusive agreement with the manufacturer. This gives it significant power only if customers are loyal to the outlet per se and not the product it sells and if there is not a supply of able outlets to replace it.

The issue of recontracting or transaction costs was raised in Chapter 2 as significant to the manufacturer-retailer interaction. Here, the transaction cost to the privately owned direct outlet of changing to another manufacturer is very high if not infinite. A comparable franchise from another manufacturer may not be available, and in any event much of the goodwill and reputation associated with the outlet will be lost if the outlet changes manufacturers. What is more, there exists a strong asymmetry in the bargaining relation. The manufacturer is much better able to get along without one particular dealer than vice versa.[9]

Tempering this power is the manufacturer's requirement to recruit willing and able candidates for taking on his brand name. The significance of this offsetting influence will vary depending on the investment and technical expertise required to establish an outlet of the required type. Also a factor is the time it would take a new outlet to establish itself, with the sales lost in the process a cost to the manufacturer of changing outlets. All this suggests that the manufacturer is well advised to take relatively good care of privately owned outlets. Since the outlet carries only a few products (perhaps none) not produced by the manufacturer, the manufacturer's policies will be largely responsible for the financial success of the outlet. The ability of the outlet to sell effectively, maintain adequate showroom and service facilities, and so forth, may be dependent on some degree of financial success. This observation tends to moderate the power of the manufacturer to a limited extent in such situations. Over time, the direct outlet must earn at least a near normal return.

Direct outlets represent a discontinuity in my hypotheses. Whatever the nature of the product and wherever the outlet is positioned on the taxonomy, the low level of retailer power in the direct outlet case suggests the hypothesis that the manufacturer's rate of return will be higher than in a similar industry having "normal" independent outlets.

*The incidence of direct outlets.* Moving to the first question, it is evident that the manufacturer-retailer model provides a clear hypothesis about the industries where manufacturer owned or nearly owned outlets will arise. In view of the increasing importance of the retailer in selling as we move up the hierarchy of retail outlets (Figure 2–1), I would predict that the likelihood of owned or nearly owned outlets would increase as the type of outlets used under private or non-direct circumstances moved up the hierarchy.[10] Examples such as autos, sewing machines, light aircraft, high-priced men's shoes, recreational vehicles, and pianos and organs seem quite consistent with this view. Where direct outlets occur,

9. For a discussion of these issues for farm equipment dealers see Dirlan and Kahn (1954), p. 178. See also White (1971), p. 151.

10. Holton (1962) makes a similar observation, pp. 268–269.

the substance of the manufacturer-retailer relation is unchanged whether the contractual agreement is termed a franchise or exclusive dealing agreement. The situation is one where the retailer is influential over the sale and consequently the manufacturer goes to direct distribution to better control this power.

Direct outlets, via franchising, sometimes though rarely appear in convenience goods, however. For example, gasoline stations and fast food outlets are heavily franchised. In these cases the motivation for direct outlets is quite different. The differentiation of the product is greatly enhanced by bundling a number of products together for sale. As noted by Donald Dixon (1962) on the basis of evidence from the United Kingdom, gasoline may be difficult to differentiate in the absence of direct outlets which allow the manufacturer to tie gasoline sales with service and tire, battery, and accessory sales. The buyer then selects the station, rather than the gasoline per se. In convenience good franchising situations there may be economies of scale in nationwide sales promotion coupled with the requirement for local production (hamburgers) and mobile customers who do not shop a particular outlet but many outlets. The ability of the manufacturer to differentiate may be related to his ability to control quality and service in multiple outlets and hence provide a motivation for franchising to gain such control. In convenience direct outlets, the power relation between manufacturer and retailer is, therefore, quite different—the ability of the outlet to influence the individual purchase is much lower than the nonconvenience case. Thus franchisers are less likely to extend their control of outlets by purchasing them in convenience goods than they are in nonconvenience goods.[11] Further reasons for the occurrence of direct outlets in convenience goods are found below.

Lawrence White's study of the auto industry considers the motivation behind direct outlets for automobile manufacturers.[12] White concluded that the "forcing" of dealers to sell large volumes was the primary reason for franchising automobile reltailers and limiting their number. Critical to the welfare implications of this argument and to White's judgment

11. This section relies on R. E. Caves and W. F. Murphy, "Franchising: Firms, Markets and Intangible Assets," *Southern Economic Journal* 42 (April 1976), a fuller discussion of franchising, including its occurrence in service sectors. This paper contains a discussion of the application of my convenience-nonconvenience dichotomy to franchising.

12. White (1971), pp. 136–170. See also Pashigian (1961). Pashigian ignores the influence of the auto retailer on differentiation in his analysis of why the direct outlets occur there. See p. 117.

about auto manufacturer's motives was the notion that economies of scale in automobile distribution are present. These economies of scale, however, were contingent on the dealer providing ample showroom space, service facilities, and inventory. In the absence of franchising, it seems clear that the same level of services may not be provided and hence the economies of scale in automobile distribution would be sharply curtailed. A more fundamental explanation for the motivation of auto producers for franchising in automobile distribution rests with my model. Because auto dealers are critical in product differentiation, which requires ample showroom facilities and a high level of dealer services, the manufacturer is motivated to franchise outlets and control entry. If only sales volume were desired and retailer product differentiation not important (and hence showrooms and repair facilities leading to scale economies), the manufacturer would not need to force but rather could let dealer competition drive down dealer prices and the extent of their repair facilities. Another complementary manufacturer motivation may be the ability to extract greater rents through bundling the sale of automobiles and parts to the dealer system instead of dealing with separate selling and repair outlets.

It is clear that other factors are important in determining whether direct outlets occur; the model by itself is primarily useful in checking the consistency of those examples that exist and making a judgment about the power relations between manufacturer and retailers in them. First, not every product can support an owned or nearly owned outlet. The ability of one or few products to cover the overhead of an appropriate outlet based on its reasonable expected sales volume is obviously critical. For example, it seems unlikely that a manufacturer owned pen store could survive without carrying many other products. Once many other products are stocked, however, the problems for the manufacturer compound and many of the benefits of owning outlets largely disappear. It would appear to be possible to make a judgment about the feasibility of owned outlets for a product, or at least their prior probability, based on the sales per typical outlet and the nature of the services required to be provided with sale. (Of course the latter can be influenced by the manufacturer and are not strictly given.)

Second, in the case of owned outlets substantial financial resources are required of the manufacturer. The possession of such resources may imply an already concentrated and powerful manufacturing industry.

Third, where the manufacturing stage is highly capital intensive, the proclivity to integrate forward and backward may be enhanced. High capital intensity implies high fixed costs and benefits in ensuring steady sources of supply and distribution. Policies in supply and distribution may also be manipulated to best utilize the large capital investment where direct distribution occurs.[13] This factor may be important in explaining direct outlets in gasoline distribution and automobiles, as suggested by Dixon and White respectively.[14]

Fourth, where private individuals retain ownership of the retailing stage, their willingness to give up what power they might have to sign exclusive or franchising contracts is suggestive of a number of possible preconditions: large inventory and other ·financing is required; the manufacturer is already strong and has a strong brand image. A great deal of casual empirical evidence supports these hypotheses. Manufacturer financing for inventory and facilities is a central feature of many direct contract relations (for example, light aircraft, farm equipment and recreational vehicles).[15] Also, direct outlets often develop as an industry matures rather than in its introductory phases. Those manufacturers with successful brands are able to recruit direct retailers, while less differentiated brands must rely on conventional outlets. In early phases of the industry's development, no manufacturer usually has the brand identification nor the resources to aid retailers in financing.[16]

Fifth, the manufacturer's willingness to integrate forward will be tempered by the reluctance to get involved in the problems of retailing, and perhaps by the low return which might be available in retailing.[17] Although the second is a somewhat empirical question, the importance of these factors seems subordinate to the other considerations mentioned.

It seems clear that where the economies of covering overhead are conducive, all manufacturers, especially in nonconvenience goods, would prefer to control outlets. Those cases where such control has occurred may be symptomatic of existing market power, and the presence of direct outlets merely enhances this power through elevating barriers to entry and removing any bargaining strength from the retail side.[18] A model for assessing the probability of direct outlets for a given product might be diagrammed below:

13. I am indebted to J. L. Bower for this point.

14. See Dixon (1962), p. 43, and esp. p. 46; White (1972), pp. 139–140.

15. *Note on the Light Aircraft Industry,* HBS Intercollegiate Case Clearing House 9–370–036.

16. *Note on the Recreational Vehicle Industry,* HBS Intercollegiate Case Clearing House 9–375–092.

17. Preston (1965) makes these points in somewhat different context (p. 512).

18. Entry barriers increase because of foreclosure of retail outlets. Since direct outlets are unavailable to potential entrants, the potential entrant must enter both manufacturing and retailing or face a disadvantage.

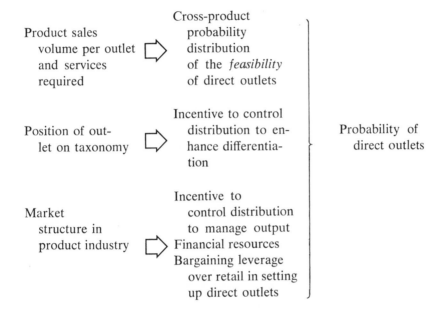

The Manufacturer-Retailer Model and Vertical Agreements

Direct outlets are a special case of the more general question of manufacturer contractual relations with the retail stage. We can broaden our look at such vertical relations by considering the practices of exclusive dealing and resale price maintenance. There is extensive literature on both these practices, yet it can perhaps be characterized by only weak theoretical underpinnings. Following along the lines begun in the last section, my model can serve as a basis for rationalizing these practices and offering policy guidance for their regulation.

*Exclusive dealing.* I will begin by describing the mechanics of exclusive dealing, because the literature on it suffers from misleading terminology. Exclusive dealing involves an agreement between the manufacturer and retailer for the retailer to sell only the particular brand of that manufacturer (which I will term *exclusive selling*). *Customer restrictions* are restrictions the manufacturer places on the classes of customers whom the retailer may serve. Typically such agreements prohibit sales to certain very large customers, institutions and federal, state, and local governments. Exclusive selling agreements and customer restrictions may or may not be combined with the delineation of an *exclusive territory,* that is, the manufacturer agrees to make his product available to no other retailers within a given area. An exclusive territory may also be granted even though the retailer sells other brands of the same product.

Thus, there are three elements to exclusive dealing, at least one of which is present in any given situation: exclusive selling (only brand $X$); customer restrictions; exclusive geographic territory. In most cases all three aspects are present, and I will begin the analysis with this case.

Exclusive selling involves a concession on the part of the retailer, who gives up his freedom to choose his product line and may sacrifice potential sales that would result from stocking other brands. Similarly, the retailer sacrifices potentially lucrative sales by accepting customer restrictions. Granting an exclusive territory, on the other hand, involves a concession on the part of the manufacturer. When he gives a retailer sole rights to handle his product in the area, he becomes dependent on the performance of that retailer and forgoes the advantage of rival promotional efforts by competing retailers. He may also sacrifice market coverage, reducing his ability to reach all the potential buyers in a given area.[19]

Our manufacturer-retailer bargaining model suggests that exclusive dealing in all its possible forms will tend to increase as the outlet through which the product is sold moves up the taxonomy.[20] Along this scale, the retailer becomes more and more important in selling, and the manufacturer finds it increasingly important to enlist the undivided loyalty of the retailer. Thus he is more likely to accede to the retailer's desire for an exclusive territory, perhaps even without demanding an exclusive selling arrangement in exchange. The manufacturer thereby sacrifices flexibility and perhaps coverage of the market. Exclusive territorial arrangements, then, signal the presence of retailer power.

The primary economic consequences of exclusive dealing are the reduction in intrabrand competition and the enhancement of manufacturers' market power through greater product differentiation.[21] Let us compare the significance of these consequences in convenience and nonconvenience goods. Because the consumer shops for goods sold through nonconvenience outlets, the effect of exclusive dealing on intrabrand competition seems least severe with such goods, provided the exclusive dealing agreement includes an exclusive territory provision.[22] An exclusive selling arrangement in the absence of an exclusive territory provision

19. Preston's model of territorial restrictions and market coverage is not directly applicable to consumer goods retailers because of its assumptions. However, turning around the model's requirement that the retailer contact the consumer, it is complementary to mine.

20. Scherer (1970) recognizes this distinction in passing in his discussion of exclusive dealing (p. 509n).

21. For a discussion of these consequences, see Comanor (1968).

22. Watkins (1940) briefly and incompletely discusses this latter point (p. 216). Watkins also notes that the retailer can be important in selling (p. 210).

is a unilateral exercise of manufacturer market power. Its purpose can only be to enhance the manufacturer's market power through improving his product differentiation and by foreclosing access to distribution. Thus exclusive selling agreements or customer restrictions without a companion exclusive territory agreement are per se undesirable.

In such cases the significance of the resulting increase in entry barriers is affected, however, by the nature of nonconvenience good distribution. Since only selective distribution is required for nonconvenience goods— more selective as we move up the taxonomy—foreclosure of outlets may not be as restrictive as in convenience goods. Some authors have argued (and the current antitrust standard is) that exclusive dealing should be illegal if a substantial number of outlets are foreclosed.[23] In view of the distribution process for nonconvenience goods, this criterion may be useful only in extreme cases where the manufacturer forecloses outlets in excess of what would be required for adequate market coverage. If the maximum allowed number of outlets controlled were set low enough to preclude unreasonable foreclosure in convenience goods, the consumer's propensity to shop for nonconvenience goods would surely make foreclosure ineffectual there. However, parallel action by dominant sellers of a nonconvenience good could effectively transfer the market structure of the manufacturing stage to the retail stage with undesirable results (for example, farm equipment). The antitrust standard for nonconvenience goods should therefore focus on parallel action, not proportional foreclosure by individual sellers.

The argument has often been made that exclusive dealing undesirably prevents intrabrand competition among retailers. This is perhaps confusing. By insulating the retailer somewhat from intrabrand competition, exclusive dealing makes it possible for the manufacturer to assure the retailer a high margin for which the retailer is expected to promote the product aggressively. If intrabrand competition were allowed to go unchecked, the retailer's margin would soon be at least partially competed away. A manufacturer wishing to grant the retailer a higher margin would be required by the Robinson-Patman Act to offer it to all competing retailers. This added margin would be vulnerable to undercutting, because each competing retailer might be willing to sacrifice some of this margin in an attempt to expand his market share. Unless the retail sales price is controlled, the ability of manufacturers to give incentives to the retailers to promote their products is greatly enhanced by the option of exclusive territories.[24] But what of the effect on interbrand competition?

23. See Watkins (1940), p. 210.

24. This point has been raised by Comanor (1968), pp. 1426–1427. It depends to a degree on the market structure of the particular retail channel used by the

Because consumers will shop for nonconvenience goods, we presume little if any negative effect on interbrand competition unless parallel action by leading firms forecloses a large portion of the retail outlets for the product.[25] The retailer whose profits are derived from a particular product is likely to promote it aggressively, countenance price reductions (unless the price is maintained) and provide the maximum of attendant services. Were each retailer to carry a parallel assortment of brands, greater recognition of mutual dependence among retailers would amplify the reduced incentive for promotional effort as a source of soft and ineffective retail competition. Possessing exclusive rights to the product, conversely, makes the fruits of such competitive efforts at least partially appropriable to the retailer.

Countervailing the potential benefits is perhaps a lessening competitive pressure on the manufacturer. If each retailer carries several brands, each manufacturer is induced to court each retailer to promote his particular product. In the process the manufacturer's price is likely to be bargained down. Thus exclusive dealing narrows the options of the retailer and hence his bargaining power. As a partial offsetting factor, the retailer with an exclusive arrangement can terminate his agreement or simply refuse to cooperate unless the manufacturer cooperates. Unlike the case of owned or nearly owned outlets, the exclusive retailer may have other products, so that the transaction costs of terminating the agreement are not nearly so large. A special sales effort by the retailer who sells products other than the exclusive product will come only at the price of favorable treatment by the manufacturer. On balance, however, more effective rivalry among retailers when exclusive dealing is in use may be at the expense of less effective competition among manufacturers. Furthermore, foreclosure of a large proportion of retail outlets via exclusive dealing elevates entry barriers into manufacturing and compounds the stifling of competition there.

The proposition that exclusive dealing allows greater product differentiation is in clear agreement with our manufacturer-retailer model. William Comanor appears to assume that the effects of this are appropriable by the manufacturer and work against the consumer.[26] However, exclusive dealing reflects retailer power and the enhanced product differentiation is retailer based. Thus there may be no net harm to the con-

---

manufacturer. It assumes that the retailer structure is competitive, which may not always be the case.

25. Or unless the exclusive arrangement improves the ability of the retailer to sell, in which case buyers presumably are better off.

26. Comanor (1968), pp. 1425–1426.

sumer. To the extent that the enhanced product differentiation allows a higher rate of return, I would agree that this is undesirable.

Goods sold through convenience outlets represent quite another situation with respect to exclusive dealing. The protection afforded the consumer by his propensity to shop is no longer present. Although the consumer can and does switch stores, which is an important competitive check among retailers, the consumer is quite unlikely to make a competitive search for a single item. More important, the retailer is not important in influencing the sale, so that the manufacturer has no motive to promote interbrand competition among retailers. Thus with convenience-outlet products, exclusive dealing is presumptively bad. The only likely purpose of exclusive dealing is to raise entry barriers and enhance the manufacturer's market power. For example, it may restrain price cutting in such products as gasoline.[27]

Joel Dirlan and Alfred Kahn, like Lee Preston, argue that exclusive dealing, requirements contracts and tying should be considered together analytically. Preston would also include customer restrictions. I object to this view. Exclusive dealing in many cases represents a bargained outcome of the mutually dependent relationship of manufacturer and retailer. Requirements contracts and tying arrangements in nearly all cases represent a unilateral exercise of market power by the manufacturer. True, the logical distinctions among these arrangements are fine ones. Exclusive dealing and requirements contracts both reduce to a common form (If any $A$, then all $A$), and a tying arrangement (If any $A$, then all $B$) is built into an exclusive dealing contract that covers multiple products carrying the same brand name but enjoying different degrees of effective differentiation. The difference lies in the auxiliary terms of the exclusive dealing arrangement analyzed above, which reflect a mutual accommodation between manufacturer and retailer. In contrast, requirements contracts and tying arrangements in their pure forms represent all-or-nothing offers and price discrimination imposed by a seller with monopoly power. Antitrust policy should—and largely does—make this distinction. The substantiality test for economic harm from exclusive dealing set forth in the *Standard Oil* case differs from the one applied to tying arrangements in *International Salt* [28], and requirements contracts must serve the reasonable interests of both parties.[29] Rather than lump exclusive dealing with tying and requirements contracts, I chose to con-

27. Dirlan and Kahn (1954), p. 200; Preston (1965), pp. 507–509.

28. *Standard Oil of California et al. vs. U.S.*, 337 U.S. 293 (1949). *International Salt Co. v. United States,* 332 U.S. 392 (1947).

29. *United States v. American Can Co.*, 87 F. Supp. 18 (N. D. Cal. 1949). *Tampa Electric Co. v. Nashville Coal Co.*, 365 U.S. 320 (1969).

sider it in tandem with resale price maintenance for reasons that should become clear below.[30]

*Resale price maintenance.* Resale price maintenance (RPM) refers to the practice of a manufacturer of a branded product setting the price at which the product can be sold at retail. There is extensive literature on the alternative hypotheses for the existence of RPM as well as its legal and legislative history. Joseph Palamountain develops the political aspects of RPM that are important in understanding its legislative history.[31] From an economic point of view, Ward Bowman's bilateral-monopoly model offers the most convincing theoretical structure for explaining the incidence of the practice, and I develop its relation to the analysis of manufacturer-retailer interaction.[32] Obviously, as Bowman points out, RPM can only occur for branded goods where the product is physically distinguishable from rival products. The rate of return earned by the manufacturer of the branded good is based on the manufacturer's price to the retailer (wholesale price). Thus only the retailer can gain from RPM unless: the maintained retail price allows the manufacturer to obtain a higher wholesale price; or the maintained retail price favorably affects the sale of the product. Let us concentrate first on the second point because many of the arguments found in the literature are premised on this relation.

The classic justification by manufacturers for RPM turns on a professed desire to prevent loss leader sales by retailers on the assumption that aggressive cutting of the prices of advertised products will somehow tarnish the image or perceived quality of these products. This assumption of an upward sloping demand curve is itself unconvincing. If the manufacturer simply allowed the market to function, the retail price of the product would be bid down by such aggressive price cutting. The result would leave undamaged the manufacturer's price and lower the retail price, which the manufacturer would presumably welcome as leading to increased sales. There may be adverse effects on product image during the adjustment period, though these would seem relatively minor in an industry where most branded products would presumably be similarly affected. It will be necessary, then, to go beyond the loss leader hypothesis.

---

30. Customer restrictions by themselves involve a unilateral restriction on the retailer's behavior and a curb on intrabrand competition. In practice they often appear as part of a bargained settlement that involves exclusive dealing and territorial protection, so their competitive significance cannot be determined independent of the overall effects of these agreements.

31. Palamountain (1955).

32. Bowman (1952).

Bowman proposes that RPM occurs in cases where there is mutual dependence: both the manufacturer and the retailer possess partial monopoly power. The manufacturer must possess some monopoly power in order to induce low-cost and efficient retailers of the product to sell at the higher maintained price, sheltering higher cost retailers. Unless the manufacturer's brand is strongly differentiated, low-cost retailers could sell a competing product not subject to RPM and reap the benefits of their competitive advantage. A strong brand image limits this option by causing buyers to expect the retailer to stock the particular brand in question. Another condition for RPM is that the retailer must possess some monopoly power in the retail market which the manufacturer needs and cannot obtain without RPM; otherwise the manufacturer could sell his product through some alternative channel without the requirement for a higher than necessary retail price. Bowman adds that RPM is introduced by the manufacturer "because there is no other feasible way of remunerating them [the retailers] for the services they perform to the product."[33]

In spelling out the nature of the retailer's market power, Bowman uses the example of ethical retail opticians and optometrists. He asserts that these retailers "had a substantial degree of 'monopoly power' in recommending products."[34] Bowman's other example involves book retailers. His general point is that retailers have power that can be exercised for the benefit of the producer, and the guaranteed retail markup is a payment for the exercise of this power.

Using my model I can sharpen the specification of Bowman's ideas, with which I basically agree, and then extend them. RPM is likely to occur where the retailer can add significantly to the promotion of a product, or where the retailer's contribution to product differentiation is relatively high. As the analysis suggests, the retailer's contribution to product differentiation is the primary (although not the only) source of his market power. It is significant that Bowman's chief example, optical goods, involved a highly specialized outlet high on our taxonomy. The retailer's importance in differentiating the product gives the manufacturer an incentive to accept a retail price higher than necessary in the same way it promotes exclusive territorial agreements.

Bowman's model, however, is incomplete. He asserts that RPM is the only feasible way of remunerating these important outlets. Why cannot the manufacturer simply lower his own selling price to compensate the retailer, without elevating the retail price? The answer lies in the market structure of the relevant type of retail outlet. Cutting the manufacturer's

33. Bowman (1952), p. 212 *in reprint.*
34. Bowman (1952).

price is ineffective where the retail sector is relatively competitive so that the effect on retailers' margins of any price cuts by the manufacturer would be competed away. Resale price maintenance provides a second-best solution (under current conditions where RPM agreements are not legally enforceable). It is easier for the retailers to agree on resale price maintenance than for them to agree not to cut prices when the manufacturer reduces his selling price. With the manufacturer using the various methods available to enforce his retail price, retailers are protected from price competition with each other. The maintained price provides a focal point for agreement that is not present otherwise.[35]

RPM is likely to occur, then, where: a strong brand exists (manufacturer market power); retailer contribution to product differentiation is significant (or retailer power is otherwise high); the structure of the relevant retail outlet class is competitive.

We would expect RPM to be much less prevalent among convenience goods, especially those sold primarily by single outlet types. The incentive for the manufacturer to compensate the retailer is lacking. When multiple outlet types sell the product, however, I have shown how the manufacturer's presence in these yields him an advantage in some cases. The different cost structures of diverse outlet types may lead to the tendency for the least-cost outlet to prevail (which is possible following the logic that each convenience outlet provides intensive distribution). RPM may be employed to preserve multiple outlet types. The maintained price provides an umbrella which allows the higher cost outlets to enjoy a comfortable margin on sales of the product. The benefits to the manufacturer of multiple outlet types justify the higher retail price. RPM may serve, for example, to protect conventional outlets against discounters. Once again, RPM provides the focal point for an agreement among different outlet types that would otherwise have trouble reaching an accord. Because the power of the manufacturer is very high for branded convenience goods, the problems of enforcing the maintained price are reduced: the threat of brand removal is probably sufficient. The Robinson-Patman Act severely hampers the ability of the manufacturer to charge different prices to different outlet types, a more direct approach the manufacturers might take to preserve multiple outlets.

The use of RPM to sustain multiple outlet types is especially important in convenience goods. Here no important differences in retail service exist to sustain price differential among outlets. The conventional outlet has little or no defense against the price cutter. Though recognizing the symptoms—little retail price competition—rather than the full sig-

---

35. Suggested retail prices with little effort at enforcement are an intermediate case.

nificance of RPM in convenience retailing, Basil Yamey has suggested the further (and interesting) point that RPM may actually retard the development of retail chains with their concomitant bargaining power.[36]

This analysis suggests that among convenience goods, highly differentiated food items that are sold primarily through a single type of outlet will not be price maintained, while health and beauty aids, chewing gum, and cigarettes will. This result is consistent with observation.[37] Of course, high differentiation attained by the manufacturer's direct persuasion of the consumer is a prerequisite.

Bowman's example of liquor, which is a convenience item sold exclusively through one outlet type in the majority of states, illustrates a final unusual case (it is ironic that one of Bowman's examples is an exceptional case in our model). Where structural factors allow convenience outlets to develop the capacity for agreement or cooperation, their power vis-à-vis the manufacturer increases and resale price maintenance seems more likely to occur. Bowman and others have discussed how licensing requirements and strong trade associations lead to a somewhat unusual degree of unity of interest among liquor retailers.[38] Also, direct state involvement in the industry in many cases facilitates price maintenance.[39] Hollander notes that dealers' organized efforts have at times forced manufacturers to adopt RPM in drugs, cosmetics, and liquor.[40] These are all convenience goods, a condition constant with my theory.

I have serious reservations about Bowman's characterization of RPM as a monopoly problem at the retail level. The monopoly at the retail level is a special one based not on the structure of the retail market (in fact, my argument suggests that monopoly in this sense is not likely to be present) but on the retailer's ability to influence the purchase of the product. Bowman's analysis is misleading because it does not make this distinction. My interpretation of Bowman's analysis shows it to be based, implicitly, on the notions of retailer power developed in Chapter 2.

Dirlan's and Kahn's discussion of exclusive dealing in gasoline sales triggers a final addition to my framework.[41] They report the existence of

36. Yamey (1966), p. 10.

37. See, for example, Yamey (1966), p. 12n. Retail price maintenance, Yamey observes, has rarely been strong in the grocery trades.

38. Through licensing requirements, liquor chains are very rare despite the seeming benefits of chains in this retail channel because of ease in repeatability and distribution economies. Lack of chains greatly heightens the likelihood of cooperative behavior among retail firms. Chains have been a major destabilizing influence in other retail channels. See Palamountain (1955).

39. S. C. Hollander, p. 76, in Yamey (1966).

40. S. C. Hollander, p. 81, in Yamey (1966).

41. Dirlan and Kahn (1956), p. 182.

a form of RPM in gasoline sales, where the supplier suggests the proper price to the dealer. The explanation for this case, one contrary to the conditions set forth above, is suggested by the fact that gasoline retailers are primarily dependent upon one product. In this situation, price cutting and price warring will directly affect the manufacturer. Price cutting that weakens the dealer's ability to sustain operations threatens to reduce the long run sales of the manufacturer, and the manufacturer is likely to be required to step in to support the dealer. RPM in this case offers an obviously superior solution. Since the manufacturer's power is very high in convenience goods, especially single brand outlets, there is little difficulty in enforcement.[42]

42. In view of my arguments the normative question with regard to resale price maintenance is clear—it is unjustifiable. For arguments about the welfare implications of the consumer justification of resale price maintenance, see Yamey, pp. 3–22, in Yamey (1966).

There are other plausible effects of resale price maintenance such as its elimination of a source of instability, which tends to enhance the possibilities for pricing agreements. Yamey, p. 12, in Yamey (1966). These, however, appear to be a possible offshoot of resale price maintenance rather than a cause. For causation I suggest that the basic model is dominant.

# 4

## Firm Strategy, Oligopolistic Rivalry, and Industry Performance

The manufacturer-retailer model explains variations in strategies for differentiating the product from one consumer-good industry to another, thereby filling a gap in previous analyses. But the model can contribute to the development of a further implication of great importance for the theory of industrial organization. Within an industry, firms' behavior and marketing policies vary significantly. This chapter will lay the conceptual groundwork for analyzing the significance for market performance of these variations of firms' behavior within an industry. Defining the concept of strategy to capture the important elements of firms' conduct, a model will be presented of the relation between an industry's performance and variations in the strategies of its member firms. Finally, the retail stage will be introduced explicitly into the analysis and the theory extended.[1]

### The Firm and Its Strategy

Early students of business focused squarely on the firm as the relevant unit of economic analysis for industrial organization. The idiosyncrasies

1. Since this study was completed further work on the significance of strategy differences within industries has been done. This chapter (and the empirical tests which follow) focuses on differences in marketing strategy, linking these to the characteristics of the retail stage. More recent work has extended the model to any dimension of firm conduct. See M. E. Porter, "The Structure within Industries and Market Performance," unpublished manuscript; and R. E. Caves and M. E. Porter (1975b).

of the large firm, its peculiar management, policies, and so on, were felt to dominate any influence of the industry (whatever that meant) in which the firm operated. The Bain-Mason tradition shifted the focus in the direction of the industry.[2] The industry replaced the firm as the locus of analysis, but more fundamentally, the structuralist [3] viewpoint subordinated the firm's conduct as an influence on its performance. This view posited that the structure of the industry determined the behavior of the firm to a major degree. Thus all firms in an industry were treated as identical organisms (except for some recognition of the effect of different market shares). Their methods of marketing, production, and finance were identically determined by the constraints of industry structure save for a random component, asserted to be unimportant. What determined industry structure was left open.

The recent and continuing debate over the importance of conduct can be seen to represent a renewed appreciation of the significance of the firm's behavior. Those urging the relevance of conduct declare that the firm does indeed have scope to exceed (or influence) the bounds of industry structure through its pricing behavior, marketing policies, and so on. I will have more to say about the notion of firm conduct later; suffice it to say here that it represents the revival of an old viewpoint.

While economics dwelt in the realm of the industry, business schools were maintaining the focus of interest squarely on the firm. Business schools have emphasized the functional skills the manager of the firm needs to be effective: marketing, production policy, organization structure, finance, and the like.[4] Rather than learning the lessons of the industry for firm behavior, the emphasis is on "beating" the industry by outperforming competitors through excellence in the functional areas. As the methodology of business instruction progressed, some graduate schools of business (notably Harvard) developed the concept of corporate strategy.[5]

Corporate strategy is defined, in the simplest terms, as a set of goals for the firm and a set of functional strategies for achieving those goals. It follows that every firm, explicitly or implicitly, will have a strategy and this strategy is a way of describing the important aspects of firm

2. See Bain, "The Comparative Stability of Market Structure" (1972). Basic sources are listed therein.

3. Scherer (1970), p. 2.

4. The functions of business, using common terminology, are marketing, finance, control, accounting, and so on. I will maintain this usage below.

5. See Learned et al. (1969). Here and later in this chapter, areas familiar to students of the literature on business management but perhaps unfamiliar to economists will be discussed. In view of this, an effort has been made to err in the direction of a full explanation.

behavior. The literature on strategy has added a normative dimension as well—a loose set of characteristics of a good strategy. I will focus initially on strategy as a descriptive concept.

The strategy of the firm is the vector of the firm's choices with respect to its major decision variables. The elements of firm strategy can be characterized as follows:

Product-market strategy
    pricing policy
    type of product
    channels of distribution
    means of differentiation
    diversification or acquisition
Production strategy
    plant location and organization
    degree of vertical integration
    capital labor ratio
R&D strategy
    amount and nature of R&D performed
Financial strategy
    forms of financing
    financial leverage
Organizational strategy
    organization structure
    rewards and incentive systems

I could add to this list of the elements of strategy, but this would not change the essential features of the concept. A firm's strategy contains a large number of components or substrategies.

The strategy of the firm is its search for a comparative advantage in its industry. The firm not only sets its price and quality but simultaneously determines a large number of other parameters of its competitive posture within its industry. A critical feature of this vector of decision variables is that they are interrelated. For example, a firm competing with low price and ample customer service may locate plants near customers, integrate vertically to minimize production cost, and allocate its research dollars to cost-saving process innovation. Its organizational structure and incentive systems may emphasize minimizing costs. A differentiated producer, in contrast, may set a higher price and spend resources on advertising and product R&D. Interrelation in strategic elements implies that cross-firm or cross-industry variations in one decision variable, such as the use of advertising, are likely to be associated with variations in other decision variables. It follows from this interrelation that an important normative test for a firm's strategy is internal consistency. It is clear, for example, that the competitive position of the firm is enhanced by ensuring that its pricing strategy is supported by the emphasis placed on quality and cost in its production process.[6] Thus the firm's effort to maximize profit intensifies the interdependence among its substrategies.

If the elements of the firm's strategy comprise a mutually determined (and consistent) set, we cannot logically treat individual strategic elements as if they were determined independently and could therefore be adjusted independently in interactions with rival firms. Bain's view treats the determination of the industry's pattern of market conduct as a two-stage process. Individual firms form their preferences about the key decision variables (such as price, advertising, outlays and research and development outlays), and then their preferences are reconciled in the market to determine an independent market equilibrium for each decision variable. For this model to hold, it is necessary but not sufficient for firms to set their key decision variables independently. If firms hold preferences over the set of decision variables rather than over individual variables, however, general equilibrium requires the simultaneous equilibration of the *sets* of values adopted by each firm. Reconciliation in the market, under these circumstances, involves trades among the set of decision variables. Firms may be willing to adjust decision variable $A$ (for example, price) in conjunction with a compensating adjustment in variable $B$ (for example, research outlays). This interdependence is most evident in the various dimensions of marketing where there is a great deal of substitutability.

Much research in industrial organization has focused on the market determinants of individual decision variables such as prices, product quality, advertising, and research and development. Unless the values of other decision variables are held constant or are determined by variables included in the model, this procedure is incorrect, and models employing it can exhibit misleading results and low levels of explanatory power.

6. The proposition that strategic elements are internally related needs qualification. First, although firms apparently seek internal consistency in their strategies, they differ in their skill at achieving it. That internal consistency is desirable is both logical and in concert with established doctrine in the study of corporate strategy. See Learned et al. (1969). Second, external factors may constrain certain strategic elements. If the firm is a division of a diversified parent, the policies of the diversified firm may constrain behavior of the subject division. For example, it may have special financial arrangements, peculiar control systems and incentive systems, and so on. There are many reasons why the diversified firm, presumably maximizing on the sum of its parts, would not act in the same way as a single firm. (See Hunt, 1972). Finally, where firms have monopoly power, they may trade risk reduction or managerial utility maximization for the profit maximizing interrelation of strategy elements.

And the procedure contributes to the suspicion with which researchers in business administration view economists' models.

Armed with the concept of strategy, one can get to the heart of the controversy over whether the firm or the industry is the appropriate unit of analysis. Let us define a *strategic alternative* as an internally consistent set of values of the firm's key decision variables. The firm can choose its strategy from a large number of strategic alternatives. The business school approach asserts that the firm has discretion over this choice. Its strategic choice is influenced, but not bound, by the structure of its industry because the firm can influence the structure of its industry through its behavior. Furthermore, in any given industry different strategic alternatives may maximize the objectives of different firms depending on each firm's initial position and the strategic choices of its competitors.[7] Implicit in this view is that optimal strategies may change over time.

The structuralists' deterministic models of markets imply, conversely, that the structure of an industry defines the strategy of the firm; the latitude for choice of a strategy by the firm is very limited if not absent. The firm reacts to its industry's structure in its marketing, production, and financial decisions. The industry structure facing all firms in it is constant, and hence all firm strategies should be similar. Also, the firm's strategy will remain constant so long as the structure of its industry remains essentially unaffected by outside forces. Thus by studying the structure of the industry we can learn most of what is important about the firm's behavior and hence market performance, subject always to random noise. There are, then, two major areas of disagreement between the structuralist and business school (firm dominant) positions; whether an industry's structure determines the strategies, and whether all firms within an industry choose strategies that are similar in economically important ways. Let us first examine the former; the latter question is more fundamental, since economically important differences in firm strategies within an industry necessarily imply that the industry's common structure does not define all the firm's strategies.

Whether or not an industry's structure defines the strategies of its firms is essentially the conduct versus structure debate in industrial organization. We describe the characteristics of the conduct of an industry, not of its individual members; all firms in an industry take part in a common pattern, and conduct is the amalgam of all their strategies. Those who view conduct as important argue that this common pattern is not fully determined by the industry's structure, and that the firm's decisions about pricing, advertising, R&D, and other strategic elements

---

7. Some of the dynamics of this process are explored in Caves and Porter (1976).

affect market performance as does the industry's structure. Bain, representing the structuralist view, responds to the conduct hypothesis that although the form of conduct can indeed differ among industries in ways that reflect the firm's discretion, the substance (or effect on performance) of these differences in conduct is largely if not totally determined by each industry's structure; therefore conduct is irrelevant.[8] Even though firms think they have a choice, they really do not.

The real controversy is apparently based on two factors. First, over what time horizon is the interaction of conduct and structure observed? Second, are there fundamental elements of industry structure that do not change? It has been recognized that advertising (conduct) indeed affects the level of product differentiation (structure) and that R&D spending (conduct) can affect absolute-cost barriers to entry, minimum efficient plant scale and product differentiation (all structure). Hence, conduct clearly affects structure over the long run. However, it might be argued that the true structural traits of an industry are more fundamental and unchanging characteristics such as the intrinsic differentiability of the product determined by the nature of its buyers, the technological opportunity for R&D, and so on. But then conduct does not affect this new concept of structure.

However, empirical evidence on the determinants of R&D spending point to important other factors besides technological opportunity.[9] Little empirical evidence supports the proposition that the level and character of advertising and the degree of product differentiation ultimately achieved are closely constrained by the intrinsic (or structural) differentiation of the product, though the relevant underlying product traits are elusive to measure.[10] In fact, the amount of product differentiation ultimately achieved seems more related to the nature of the buyer and his buying behavior than to the nature of the product. Even commodities such as household bleach and aspirin have been strongly differentiated to the consumer (but not to the industrial or commercial user).

My position on the analytical significance of conduct is that conduct is important insofar as it affects structure. Much conduct involves alternative ways of reaching the same structural result and is thereby unimportant for industry performance. For example, firms might use varying combinations of the elements of marketing strategy (packaging, cents-off deals, advertising, and so on) to achieve essentially the same level of product differentiation. Economically significant conduct wields its effect

8. Structuralists concede that firm-specific differences in conduct may arise out of differing managerial attitudes.

9. Scherer (1970) chapter 15.

10. See Caves (1962), pp. 48–50.

over time, gradually modifying dimensions of structure other than the number of sellers. "Snapshots" of the structural characteristics are still important because the current values of the characteristics determine current market performance. However, a rapidly changing structural trait can blur the snapshot and distort the estimated relation. Those testing structure-performance relations have perhaps been fortunate in their use of advertising (conduct) as a measure of product differentiation (structure). This practice happily captures some mixture of the level and rate of change of product differentiation. But my view is that there is some set of fundamental traits of an industry which are unchanging and which place some bounds in the strategies firms may choose over the life of the industry. Within these bounds there are broad ranges of possible strategies, and these change over time as innovations in selling and producing the product occur.

The extreme, firm dominant view is misleading too, however. The current performance of an industry is strongly influenced by its number of sellers, barriers to entry, growth, and so forth. While the firm can influence this industry structure through its strategy, this influence is incomplete, gradual, and depends in part on the behavior of competitors. For example, a firm could focus R&D efforts on increasing the minimum efficient plant scale or integrate vertically to increase absolute cost barriers to entry. But such changes would involve risk and long lead times, and imitation by competitors would nullify any short term benefits.[11] The ability to alter technology or enhance product differentiation may be sharply constrained, and the firm's ability to influence some important elements of industry structure such as the number of competitors and overall market growth may be absent. Thus in understanding firm and industry performance, both current industry structure and firm strategy are important. Treating one or the other as dominant is seriously misleading.

### Differences in Firm Strategy within Industries

I have identified the important elements of conduct, or the amalgam of firm strategies, as those that affect industry structure. Can such meaningful differences in strategies prevail within an industry? Industrial organization economists implicitly answer no when they assign a single level of product differentiation and a single condition of entry to an industry. A major thesis of this study is that such a procedure is incorrect. It will be argued below that an industry's members can adopt strategies that not only differ but differ in economically meaningful ways. Hence the notion of a unique industry structure is in many cases inappropriate.

11. See Caves and Porter (1976).

Common observation suggests that the firms in an industry often differ from one another in their degree of vertical integration or diversification, the extent to which they advertise and brand their product, whether or not they use captive or exclusive distribution channels, whether they are full-line or narrow-line sellers, whether they operate in the national market or only regionally, whether they are multinational in operation, and so forth. That is, strategies differ among firms in an industry. An industry thus may consist of groups of firms, each group composed of firms that have similar strategies. We define such groups as *strategic groups*. A typical pattern in consumer-good industries is the presence of a small group of producers of a full line of nationally branded goods and larger group of producers of unadvertised goods, regionally branded goods and producers for private labels. Producer-good industries often contain extensively integrated makers of full lines or systems, using controlled distribution networks, and a larger group of firms specializing in parts of the line or components, often utilizing independent sales agents. Because of their structural similarity, strategic group members are likely to respond in the same way to disturbances from inside or outside the group, recognizing their interdependence closely and anticipating their reactions to one another's moves quite accurately.

Not only may firms' strategies for competing in a given industry differ, but where firms are diversified the relationship between the business units competing in an industry and the other components of their parent firms may differ. For example, two divisions of diversified firms may compete in a given industry, but one is related vertically to other divisions in the corporate parent while the other is not. Strategic groups can thus be defined by important differences in the extra-market relationships a business unit possesses which affect the way it competes in its particular industry. I will concentrate here on intra-market strategy differences, but the analysis can be readily extended to extra-market strategy differences.[12]

The presence of strategic groups affects industry profitability in two ways. First, the standard sources of entry barriers vary among groups. For example, vertical integration and full-line production may heighten economies of scale in production, distribution and selling. Absolute-cost barriers will be higher into full-line and vertically integrated production because of the greater capital outlays required for entry into these strategic groups. Entry barriers, then, become group specific and impede

12. For recent work pursuing this idea see Newman (1974). Hunt (1972) first introduced the concept of strategic groups in a more limited model. I will explore it below.

not only the entry of new firms but the mobility of established firms from group to group.[13] Similarly the number of resident firms varies across strategic groups. If the resident number of firms and barriers to entry vary across groups, conventional industrial-organization theory would predict that performance varies across groups. I will term this the *indirect* effect of strategy variations on performance. Within an industry firm strategy differences lead to strategic groups with different "structures" and hence different profitability among groups. Strategy, through its power to influence groups, then, affects the aggregate structural traits of the industry and its profitability. The second way strategic groups affect industry profitability is that the presence of a structure of groups within an industry affects oligopolistic rivalry in the industry. Certain group structures enhance oligopolistic rivalry and hence lower predicted profitability for the entire industry. I will term this the *direct* effect of strategy variations on performance.

My concept of strategic groups within an industry inevitably raises the question of industry boundaries. I stress that the following discussion does not reduce to a redefinition of the homogeneous set of sellers as a group instead of an industry, for two reasons. First, although I suppose that oligopolistic interdependence is recognized more fully within groups than between them, I also suppose that it is recognized more fully by firms in the same industry than by firms in different industries. The industry becomes segmented but does not disappear. Second, groups may be distinguished from one another because their products are imperfect substitutes, but that is not necessary. Groups can be differentiated by factors that affect the conditions of sale of a good but not the good itself (such as the width of the product line of which it is a part or the manufacturer's policy toward the retail stage), or by factors (such as vertical integration) that differentiate the product not at all in the eyes of the customer.

It follows from this general statement of the model that many differences in firm strategy will feed through to industry performance through these two effects. The primary concern in this study is with consumer-goods industries and the process of determining marketing strategy in these industries. Indeed, marketing influences product differentiation, which has proved to be an especially important dimension of strategy in consumer goods.[14] Thus although the model is general across all industries and encompasses the full range of strategy variations, I will defend

13. This idea is developed in Caves and Porter (1976).
14. Bain (1956).

and apply it here in the context of marketing strategy variations in consumer goods.[15]

Variations in Marketing Strategy within Industries

Conventional demand theory implies that consumer's demand for an industry's output can be looked upon as relatively homogeneous. The manufacturer of each individual brand thus uses the same basic formula for sales promotion (a marketing mix of price, advertising, packaging, and so on), although some products achieve greater success in applying the formula than others. Phrases such as price-conscious consumers and quality-conscious consumers sometimes appear but to little apparent consequence.

The literature on marketing has long recognized, however, that aggregate demand facing an industry is fractured into market segments with differing characteristics. A modified form of Lancaster's demand analysis provides a useful way of making this notion operational.[16] Each brand in an industry can be looked upon as possessing a set of discrete attributes that yield utility to the consumer. These attributes include cost, numerous dimensions of product quality, packaging, service supplied with the product, and many more. Each brand has its own vector of attributes. Consumers have different preference rankings over the attribute space; for example, some consumers place more weight on cost while others weight service or quality over cost. Over the attribute space, consumers with a similar preference rankings constitute market segments.

For example, one might characterize market segments for hair shampoos (a convenience good) as follows. Some consumers will buy the cheapest shampoo irrespective of its other traits and not be swayed by advertising. They place a very heavy weight on price in their attribute rankings. The bulk of consumer most likely will buy one of the nationally advertised brands, desiring a high quality product and being persuaded by advertising that they are getting one (at a higher price, of course). Price here is weighted less heavily while quality is weighted more heavily in the buyer's attribute ranking. A few eccentrics will probably hold out for specialty shampoos made from exotic substances at very high prices. Within each category there are further variations in the dominant attribute. For example, some quality-sensitive consumers heavily weight mildness, others aroma, and so forth (quality is not unidimensional).[17] In addition, other attributes such as packaging, service, and

15. See Porter, "The Structure within Industries and Market Performance," for a complementary view encompassing other elements of firm strategy.
16. Lancaster (1966).
17. This observation was suggested by R. D. Buzzell.

the like, may be important determinants of variation in consumer tastes within market segments. Thus one could potentially subdivide industry demand to the point where there was a market segment to correspond to each consumer—scales of preference may be continuous. However, as I will explain below, relatively broad groups of attributes may capture the essential characteristics of the demand space for our purposes.

The clear implication of segmented industry demand is to induce differences in marketing strategies within industries. I assume that technology and cost conditions do not preclude product variety. Nonconvexities in the supply of goods preclude infinitely many brands with infinitesimally small gradations between them. But differences in preferences lead to profitable opportunities for increasing product variety in the market to reflect important dimensions of preference change, to the point justified by the cost of variety. To continue the shampoo example, a firm may plan its marketing strategy to attack the large middle-market segment. Or, it may address the price-sensitive segment, thereby avoiding the necessity for advertising but probably with the expectation of a lower profit-maximizing price and perhaps more difficulty in gaining access to distribution channels. Opportunities for market segmentation increase wth the number of product attributes, and so the analysis suggests many if not infinite opportunities for marketing strategies to differ among firms, constrained only by the cost/variety tradeoff. But are these differences in marketing strategies economically significant?

The earlier discussion suggests at least one criterion for weighing their significance, namely their effect on structure. If differences in firms' marketing strategies leave their products similarly differentiated, and marketing strategy differences do not imply differences in other strategy elements which affect structure (for example, relations with the retail sector, production strategy, and scale economies), one would predict little effect on allocative performance. (Product variety is itself a dimension of market performance which I do not emphasize here.) If, however, different strategies result in significantly different levels of product differentiation or other structural traits, profitability would be affected (via the indirect effect).[18] And the variation in marketing strategies within an industry may itself prove to be an important structural trait of the market (via the direct effect).

To illustrate, I will draw on general observation of the large proportion of consumer goods industries whose firms can be crudely divided into two strategic groups based on their marketing strategies. One group consists of firms that produce highly differentiated, nationally advertised

18. Product differentiation, as defined throughout this study, is the degree of price inelasticity of demand.

products. These products follow the differentiated marketing strategy (I will call them the D group). The other group consists of producers for private label and others that produce essentially unadvertised products. These producers follow a marketing strategy which I will characterize as undifferentiated at the manufacturer level (the U group). Industries displaying this dichotomy include canned soup and other foods, household paper products, soft drinks, tires, and so on.

Clearly, a single degree of product differentiation is not appropriate for characterizing such consumer-goods industries. Nor are barriers to entry the same for both groups. Barriers to entry into the D group are obviously higher than barriers into the U group because D sellers need to engage in costly product-differentiation expenditures, which raise absolute-cost barriers to entry into the D group. Thus barriers to entry take on a rather different character when intraindustry strategic differences are allowed. They become, in part, specific to the strategic group.

In this industry two segments are present with significantly different structural characteristics rather than a single industry-wide set. The usual analysis of industrial organization predicts that these two subgroups will display significantly different levels of profitability (the indirect effect). The D-group firms seem likely to enjoy higher rates of return. The number of a group's members will be related to its set of entry barriers. If, as has been suggested, scale economies in advertising exist, D-group firms will be fewer and their average size larger.

As I argued earlier, the presence of strategic groups within industries does not invalidate the industry as an appropriate entity for analysis because the two groups interact to some extent. Products in the D group may command a price premium, but the existence of U-group products constrains its size. Conversely, the existence of D-group products of higher perceived quality also constrains the elevation of the price of U products. This interaction between the D and U groups would not, however, eliminate the basic differences in performance between the two groups. The presence of the two groups may also affect the possibilities for oligopolistic consensus. For present purposes, one need only establish differences in performance across the groups.

If a single set of structural characteristics is ascribed to a consumer-good industry and measured by product differentiation and other variables from the attributes of the leading firms, then the presence of a U group which is variable in size distorts structure-performance relationships.[19] The industry's rate of return in this case would be a mixture of two classes of rates of return. If the size of the U group and the product-differentiation differences between the D and U groups are the same in

19. For a study using this approach see Mann (1966).

each industry, this practice does not pose too great a problem for testing structure-performance relations.[20] Although the absolute rate of return is affected, relative rates of return across industries are not. If the size of the *U* group and extent of *D*-group product differentiation varies greatly from industry to industry, however, differences in industrys' rates of return will reflect not only the influence of traditional structural differences but also the *D-U* dichotomy.

The *D-U* dichotomy of marketing strategies can be generalized. A continuum of marketing strategies is normally available to an industry's firms, with the *D* and *U* strategies representing polar extremes. For any given level of differentiation there exist alternate combinations of the components of marketing strategy to achieve this level of product differentiation. Alternative combinations of the components of marketing strategy may either reflect different approaches to the same market segment or approaches to different market segments. As these marketing strategies cluster into groups which differ from each other in the degree of ultimate product differentiation achieved or other structural variables, the model suggests a difference in profitability between these groups.[21] The cross-group variation in marketing strategy will also enhance the rivalry between firms in the industry. The cross-group variation in entry barriers due to product differentiation may be enhanced by linkages between marketing strategy and other strategic elements.

I have thus far concentrated on marketing strategy, guided by judgment from previous research that product differentiation exerts a dominant influence on performance in consumer-goods industries. Earlier I argued that the elements of a firm strategy were interrelated. This suggests that variations in marketing strategy will be associated with variations in other elements of strategy. Marketing strategy reflects the foci of competition. Market segment choice establishes whether price (low-cost production), quick delivery, offering a full line, or brand advertising is important to the firm. The firm competing on price (*U*-group) may, for example, vertically integrate its production process if this reduces unit cost, structure its incentive system and organizational arrangements to support and reward efficient production, and concentrate on imitative R&D rather than on basic research. A firm emphasizing brand image (*D*-group), on the other hand, may concentrate organizational efforts and incentives on marketing, hire an advertising agency and allocate a

20. Distortion also will not occur if the size of the *U* group is correlated with some other independent structural trait.

21. As I will show below, the presence of the retail stage can lead to important alternative mechanisms for achieving a given level of product differentiation. These alternative mechanisms will have important performance implications as well.

large budget to it, emphasize new-product R&D, and buy more components of its product rather than produce them internally in order to minimize the complexity of production. Firms with similar marketing strategies—a strategic group using my earlier terminology—would tend to resemble one another in the other strategic dimensions as well.

The relationship of marketing strategy to other elements of strategy raises an important theoretical issue. The theory of the firm traditionally portrays cost minimization as the unambiguous problem of minimizing the cost of a given level of output. Failure to minimize costs is ascribed to insufficient managerial diligence, reflecting so-called managerial slack. The discussion suggests two important problems with this simple view. First, through strategy differences, firms in the same industry may produce importantly different outputs, so that the costs of their outputs cannot be compared. Second, minimizing unit production cost and maximizing profit do not necessarily coincide. Cost minimization, contrary to the idealized assumptions of the competitive model, is a costly activity. The profit-maximizing allocation of the firm's resources may involve more or less effort in minimizing unit production cost depending on its overall strategy. Since product differentiation potentially leads to above normal rate of return and complicates buyer comparison of rival products, firm resources spent on marketing could yield a greater return than resources (on engineering, vertical integration, and so on) expended minimizing cost. Thus in the presence of product differentiation, cost minimization takes on a greatly different character. If the firm is unconstrained in the amount of managerial and financial resources it can bring to bear, the firm will minimize costs to the extent that it will expend resources in cost minimizing up to their marginal product.[22] However, other firms will provide no competitive check on the level of production costs. In view of this, any attempt at measuring $X$-efficiency is suspect.

Marketing and other elements of strategy are always causally linked, but the direction and strength of causal relations can vary. Whether the firm lets its marketing strategy determine the other elements of strategy, or whether it sets production strategy and then adjusts marketing and other elements to match will depend on the company's individual situation. In some cases, notably oil and perhaps automobiles, characteristics of the production process and other nonmarketing factors may strongly influence the choice of marketing strategy. Causality, however, is not important to the influence of differences in marketing strategy on performance. The interrelation between strategic elements does allow us to

22. If the firm is constrained in its managerial or financial resources, it will not minimize production costs in any sense.

take variations in marketing strategy as a proxy for variations in a broader set of strategy elements.

To the extent that differences in marketing strategies are associated with parallel differences in production and other strategic elements, the previously noted variance in barriers to entry across strategic groups defined by marketing strategy may be affected. For example, a marketing strategy of selling a full product line probably requires producing a full line. This requirement may greatly enhance entry barriers into that strategic group due to scale economies or large capital requirements for plant.[23] A marketing strategy emphasizing price and quick delivery may similarly increase requirements for production capacity because it demands more vertical integration, reserve capacity, or decentralization of plants.[24]

### Strategic Asymmetry and Oligopolistic Rivalry

In the previous section I explored the indirect effect of strategic groups on market performance via differences in entry barriers, using marketing strategy as the group-defining trait. A study of the major home appliance industry by Michael Hunt has suggested a second important effect of strategy variations on performance—their direct effect on market rivalry.[25] Hunt argues that the use of asymmetrical strategies reduces the ability of oligopolists to achieve tacit cooperation in setting prices, advertising rates, R&D expenditures, and the like. The essence of Hunt's argument is that different strategic groups of firms exhibiting different levels of product differentiation, different organizational structures, and so on, will find it difficult to agree upon common courses of action (appropriate behavior). These differences in strategy lead to destabilizing differences in preferred prices, pace of new product introduction, and in other elements of firms' conduct. Expected profit rates will therefore decline for the industry as a whole.

### An Expanded Model

Hunt's model of the effect of intraindustry strategy differences on market rivalry and performance can be extended. Following the main

23. The pure product differentiation barriers would be the additional advertising expenditure necessary to offset the selling advantages of the full-line producer.

24. The fact that business strategy is broader than marketing strategy raises one problem in associating marketing strategy differences with performance. Other strategic elements could conceivably vary to offset the effects of marketing strategy differences in leading to differences in group entry barriers. I have no reason to suspect this occurs.

25. See Hunt (1972), pp. 12–23. Hunt's model considers solely what I have termed the direct effect and is sketched below.

thrust of this study, I will develop the argument in the context of consumer-goods industries. However, the model will pertain generally to all industries.

In the presence of strategy variations within industries, an industry contains a set of strategic groups which I will term its *group structure.* Group structure affects rivalry by making mutual dependence asymmetrically recognized within the industry. If all firms had the same strategy and differed only in scale of operations their mutual dependence would be recognized to degrees related solely to scale and to random factors. Strategic differences among firms causes mutual dependence to be recognized more fully within a strategic group than between groups.

Firms within a strategic group through their common strategy will tend to be objectively and subjectively quite similar. While the number of firms in the group and other standard determinants of oligopolistic rivalry have an influence, the common strategies of group members means that their cost structures, price preferences, relationships with distribution channels, and so on, will be similar. Their opportunities for interaction via common customers, suppliers, and channels of distribution will facilitate both their ability to predict each other's responses and their ability to detect cheating or competitive moves. Firms in different strategic groups, however, will in general have different cost structures, price preferences, selling strategies, and the like. Their ability to anticipate each other's reactions will be diminished. Their interaction through common relationships will be less, reducing the two-way flow of information about each other and the ability to rapidly detect cheating. If group differences rest on differences in the way businesses competing in the industry relate to their corporate siblings in a diversified firm, businesses may adopt different goals in the particular industry under study flowing from the maximization of the overall corporate position. These arguments suggest that the ability to achieve coordination will be greater within groups than across strategic groups. The presence of a group structure will imply more vigorous rivalry among firms than would be the case in a homogeneous industry. The competitive pressure of outside groups may also upset the consensus within a given group.[26]

These arguments support the destabilizing effects of a group structure on rivalry. At this general level, however, important questions are unanswered. Are all strategic groups equally influential on rivalry? What is the effect of changes in the makeup of the group structure on rivalry? To consider these questions, let us return to our $D/U$ dichotomy and consider the destabilizing effects of the strategic asymmetry inherent

26. This is consistent within Almarin Phillips' idea that the presence of powerful outsiders may upset the ability of a group to coordinate (Phillips, 1960).

in that industry structure. Hunt's thesis implies that the existence of $D$ and $U$ groups would lead to lower industry profits due to intergroup competition. If the collective sales of firms in the $U$ group are small, however, the effect of asymmetry on the ability to reach agreement in the industry is probably negligible. Following the simple leader/follower case in oligopoly theory, the $U$ group is likely to take the conduct of the $D$ group as given, while the $D$ group is likely to act independently of the $U$ group's conduct. Thus the potential for strategic asymmetry to affect performance depends on the relative sizes of the strategic groups. Further, the potential for intergroup rivalry is likely to increase as the number of groups increase. Other things being equal, then, we would expect rivalry to increase as the number of strategic groups become more numerous and more similar in size. Thus the conclusions of oligopoly theory regarding the influence of the number and size distribution of firms translate to the number and size distribution of strategic groups.

The effect of strategic asymmetry on rivalry will also depend on the nature of the strategic differences between firms. The nature of strategy differences is important in two major ways. First, varying strategy differences imply different degrees of objective and subjective variance among groups. The more dimensions of difference between group strategies, the more difficult the coordination problem. Groups differing only in their use of advertising are likely to face fewer difficulties in coordinating than those following different strategies with respect to breadth of product line, new product innovation, use of salesforce and advertising. If we look upon groups with different stategies as selling different bundles of attributes, as the bundles of attributes become increasingly dissimilar coming to terms on any given bundle becomes more difficult. Nonproduct dissimilarities also enhance the difficulty of coming to terms. Thus the effect of strategy differences rivalry increases as the *distance* between strategies increases.

Second, the effect of strategic differences on rivalry depends on the degree of *market interdependence* between groups. The presence of market segments within industries means that market interdependence is not homogeneous among firms in an industry. If one group sells primarily to price conscious buyers ($U$-group), then conduct changes in the group may have little effect on sellers in quality sensitive groups. However, if strategic groups use different approaches to selling to the same customer segment, then the intergroup impact of conduct changes will be more important. I will discuss this more fully in the context of the manufacturer-retailer interaction below.

Mutual dependence recognition among firms then, takes on a rather different character within a group. Within groups strategic similarity is high, facilitating coordination and leading to similar predicted responses to competitive challenges from outside the group,[27] and market interdependence is very high, since by definition there is the same target customer segment or segments. Across groups, strategic distance (affecting the ease of coordination and policing the agreement) varies as does market interdependence (affecting mutual dependence recognized). The net effect on rivalry depends on the balance between these two forces:

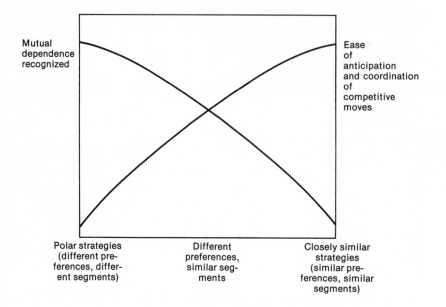

Relationship of group strategies

Fig. 4.1.   The Relationship of Group Strategies and Intraindustry Rivalry

The relationship is probably nonlinear, with the most volatile situation likely to occur where target segments are similar yet approaches to reaching the segment dissimilar.

It is interesting to relate the group model to the theory of oligopoly as it has developed. Oligopoly theory has long pointed to the destabilizing effects on rivalry of objective and subjective differences among

27. An illustrative example is the metal container industry. American Can and Continental Can follow strikingly similar strategies, have reacted almost identically to external stimuli such as innovations in packaging materials and slowing growth. Crown Cork and National Can have reacted very differently and have provided the major competitive stimulus in the industry. Other examples are watches, farm equipment and mobile homes.

firms.[28] In this sense the group model is nothing new. However, the group model supplies an important ingredient missing from oligopoly theory: a persuasive rationale for persistent objective and subjective interfirm differences and the groundwork for predicting their incidence. While it is easy to accept the traditional view of interfirm objective and subjective differences, it was difficult to see why these would not occur randomly across industries and randomly over time. The group model, as it will be developed, shows clearly why strategy differences are likely to be present and persistent. Further, the model predicts significant variations in strategy asymmetry across industries.

### Strategic Variations within Industries and Performance

I can now restate a full model of the effect of strategic variation on consumer goods industry performance, building on preceding sections. Strategic variation affects performance through two mechanisms. The first is in the indirect effect. Differences in the strategies of firms (which may or may not cluster into strategic groups) resulting in different economic structures (barriers to entry, number of group occupants) lead to different levels of potential profitability between groups. A high-barrier group ($D$-group) will have a higher potential rate of return than a lower-barrier group ($U$-group). Thus there are *structural* differences between firms within an industry, and therefore variations in rates of return among the firms in an industry will not be random. The second effect is the direct effect. Differences in firm strategy within an industry weaken the ability of firms to coordinate their actions. The presence of different groups enhances cross-group rivalry and depresses rates of return below the potential group returns determined by the indirect effect.

Returning to the $D/U$ example, the indirect effect establishes a difference in potential rates of return between the $D$ and $U$ groups. The extent to which this potential difference is realized, and consequently the mean level of profits in the industry, depends upon the strength of rivalry between the two strategic groups. The strength of rivalry depends on the relative size of the $D$ and $U$ groups, and the level of product differentiation (and hence market segmentation) that the $D$-group firms are able to achieve, as well as any other differences in preferences between the $D$ and $U$ firms that follow from their differing strategies. As strategic asymmetries reflected in the group structure increase, leading to a stronger direct effect, intergroup rivalry will increase and the industry's aggregate profit rate will decline. Thus there are two mechan-

---

28. For a classic statement, see Fellner (1949).

isms for increasing rivalry among firms: increasing strategic asymmetry among a given number of firms and increases in the number of firms.

The group model is clearly relevant to the distribution of rates of return within an industry. Strategic groups, through the indirect effect, lead to the potential for persistent intraindustry differences of rates of return. The direct effect will tend to narrow the differences in return between strategic groups. The greater the intergroup rivalry, the more bunched rates of return will be. Pure adjusted variance of firm rates of return around the industry mean may thus be an extraordinarily poor measure of risk in an industry.[29] Risk in an industry may be appropriately proxied by the strength of the direct effect or the strength of intergroup rivalry—in this case the closeness of firm rates of return to each other (hence to the industry mean) could represent very high risk.

The group model suggests a reorientation in the appropriate way of looking at an industry. It implies that a critical unit for analysis is the strategic group. The effect of the traditional industry is in defining, structurally, the possibilities for group structures and in setting the boundaries within which intergroup rivalry occurs (the direct effect). The industry defines the set of interdependent strategic groups. The structure of the strategic group is mirrored by the structure of the firms in it. In view of the group model, then, the structure of the firm (its advertising/sales, plant scale, breadth of product line, and so on) is much more important than is commonly held in determining the firm's profitability. With the concept of strategic groups, then, we have come an additional degree back to the business school position that the firm is the dominant unit of analysis rather than the industry. While I argued before that the joint conduct of all firms in an industry can influence its structure, the model suggests that firm conduct in an industry is not homogeneous along economically important dimensions. Perhaps the reason why the industry oriented and firm oriented approaches have both yielded useful results is because they are both right.

### The Retailer and the Incidence of Intraindustry Strategic Variation across Industries

The model of manufacturer-retailer interaction developed in Chapter 2 can be used to specify further the effect of strategic variation on consumer-good industries' performance, particularly variations in

---

29. See Fisher and Hall (1969), who use such a measure. See also a comment by Caves and Yamey (1971). My argument supports Caves and Yamey's argument that the level of risk is not purely exogenous; the firm can influence the level of risk.

marketing strategy embodying policy toward distribution channels. By integrating the retailer into the analysis, I will be able to sharpen the definition of marketing strategy. In the process, I will consider the important question of how the possible range of strategies in an industry varies across industries. The answer to this question will prove to be important for empirical testing.

Chapter 2 identified two primary sources of retailer power, structural traits giving rise to fewness and oligopsony in the relevant markets, and the retailer's contribution to product differentiation. Both sources of retailer power contribute significantly to the potential for variations among marketing strategies within industries. The influence on strategy variation of the retailer's contribution to product differentiation is most important and will be considered first.

The manufacturer-retailer model establishes a taxonomy of retail outlet classes (see Figure 2–1). The higher the position in the taxonomy of the outlet class selling a product, the greater is the contribution that the retail stage makes to product differentiation. The convenience retailer's contribution to product differentiation is small. As we move up into the categories of nonconvenience outlets, however, the retailer's contribution can become quite large. This is illustrated in Figure 4–2. The figure shows proportional contribution to product differentiation,

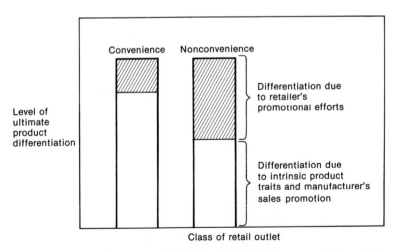

Fig. 4.2.    Manufacturer and Retailer Contributions to Differentiation in Convenience and Nonconvenience Goods

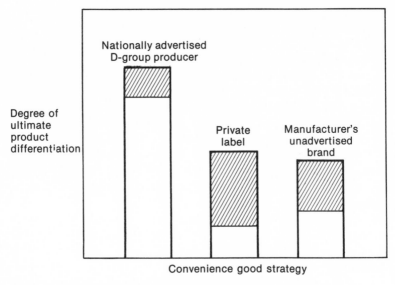

Fig. 4.3.   Marketing Strategy Options in Convenience Goods

with the shaded area representing the retailer's. The overall height of the block represents the ultimate product differentiation, or product differentiation as perceived by the final consumer.[30]

It is immediately clear that the possibilities for intraindustry strategic variation are substantially greater among nonconvenience goods than among convenience goods. For convenience goods, strategic variation among manufacturers is confined to something approaching the simple $D/U$ dichotomy introduced earlier, as shown in Figure 4–3. Variations in strategy are limited by the paucity of the retailer's role in differentiation (the relative power of the retailer may still be high, as against the maker of private-label merchandise or an unadvertised brand). The manufacturer's alternative to a strategy of heavy advertising is a moderate-to-undifferentiated product.

The case of nonconvenience goods differs greatly. Figure 4–4 shows a range of typical strategies. Push strategies encompass many options ranging from no contractual dealer arrangements to exclusive dealerships to direct outlets. To the extent that these alter the nature of the relationship between manufacturer and retailer, they contribute to strategic asymmetry. The nonconvenience manufacturer may also choose from a range of possible strategies offering similar levels of ultimate product differentiation or from a set of strategies involving less

30. Intermediate stages of distribution make no contribution to differentiation, though they may affect the bilateral power relations.

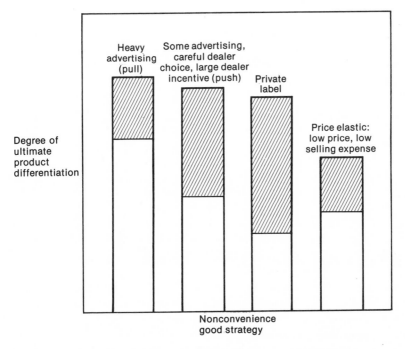

Fig. 4.4.  Marketing Strategy Options in Nonconvenience Goods

product differentiation and oriented to price competitiveness. An important feature of strategies open to nonconvenience manufacturers is that similar ultimate levels of product differentiation can result from very different approaches to sales promotion.

The possible variations among industries' marketing strategies may also be affected by the pure structure of the retail distribution network for a product, especially the presence of chains. As was explained in Chapters 2 and 3, their presence may make the private label strategy possible, especially in convenience goods. Sale of the product through many outlet types may also enhance the possibilities for strategy variation. The manufacturer may become a specialist selling through one outlet class, or he may use all outlet classes. Thus both the retailer's contribution to product differentiation and retailing structure greatly enhance the possibilities for intraindustry strategic variation.

It should be emphasized that the theory refers to the potential for strategic variation. Industries with high potentials should also display high degrees of strategic variation. But the pattern of strategic variation actually observed in an industry will be based not only on this potential but on historical, managerial, and other factors including a random component. And an industry's structure of strategic groups may evolve over time as the industry matures.[31]

The presence of a powerful retail stage modifies the strategy-profitability link presented above. In the presence of the retail stage the *indirect effect* of the strategic group structure on profitability depends on two factors. The ultimate level of product differentiation achieved determines the potential profit margin of the manufacturer and retail stages taken together for each strategic group, ceteris paribus. The distribution of the return between the manufacturer group and the retail stage depends on their relative power and their respective structures. Because the distribution of potential profits depends on the relative power of the retailer and manufacturer, group strategies that lead to the same level of ultimate product differentiation will offer, in general, different potential profits to firms in the respective strategic groups.[32] This is illustrated schematically in Figure 4–5 for the hypothetical strategy options diagrammed in Figure 4–4. The pull and push strategies yield similar potential total profits if the product differentiation ultimately attained is the same, but the manufacturer's share may be reduced when he pushes through the retail sector. The private label and price sensitive strategies yield similarly low levels of differentiation

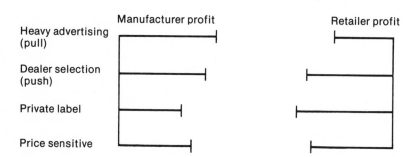

Fig. 4.5.   Composition of Total Profits under Alternative Marketing
            Strategies

31. For example, group structures involving vertical integration may be dependent on the industry's growth in total shipments.

32. Ward (1973) found that the distribution of margins within a given industry are higher for the low advertised brands, a finding consistent with my hypothesis.

at the factory gate. Yet the retailer garners a higher profit from private labels, and that may affect the manufacturer's profits. Different groups' strategies involving different levels of ultimate product differentiation may yield similar profit rates if the power of the retailer varies.

The direct effect of the strategic variation on performance is also affected by manufacturer-retailer interaction. In the expanded model the retailer is a major source of strategic variation among subgroups. Even though the same level of ultimate product differentiation may result from two subgroup strategies, differing reliance on the retailer's contribution means that the groups are following different strategies. (In the earlier model the major criterion for strategic variation was the level of product differentiation.) Strategies differing in their reliance on the retailer but attaining similar levels of ultimate product differentiation are very potent sources of destabilizing interaction. These strategies are targeted toward the same general groups of consumers; hence while there is substantial strategic distance between them, market interdependence is high and there is a large potential for destabilizing rivalry. That is, the strategic groups are strongly interdependent, yet their strategy asymmetries are likely to impede tacit competition. This pattern contrasts with strategy differences that reflect very different consumer targets (for example luxury-oriented consumers versus price-conscious consumers) and subsequently lower interdependence between strategic groups. Hence where retailer-based strategy variation is important, one expects more powerful direct effects of strategic asymmetry on market rivalry and on performance.

In nonconvenience goods, where the power of the retailer to influence differentiation is high, both the indirect and direct effects will be important. Because alternative strategies may be aimed at similar consumer classes (or market segments using the earlier terminology) the potential for destabilizing interaction between strongly interdependent strategic groups is enhanced. In convenience goods nearly all industries will have only $D$ and $U$ groups, with the relative sizes of the two groups differing. Cross-industry changes in the pattern of strategic variation are relatively small. The effect of this strategic variation on performance, through the indirect effect, will be easily measured, since the retailer has relatively lower power. In nonconvenience goods, however, strategic variation is difficult to measure because of the varying role of the retailer. The potential for the effect of strategic variation on performance is large and actual patterns of strategic variation in an industry may, consequently, vary markedly. Thus omission of measures of strategy variation will have more serious consequences in nonconvenience goods.

Hunt's descriptive work provides some support for our group model.[33] The interaction (my direct effect) of several of the strategic groups identified by Hunt was strong. Three of these were analogous to the push group (for example, Hobart, Tappan), the pull group (for example, General Electric) and private label group (for example, manufacturers selling through Sears and Montgomery Ward) respectively. All three groups achieved roughly the same amount of ultimate product differentiation, and the strong interaction Hunt observed between them is consistent with the model. Although the data available in Hunt's study are limited, it also appears that the rate of return distribution within the industry followed the prediction of the direct effect, namely, the manufacturer with high manufacturer differentiation tended to earn a higher rate of return.

33. Hunt's dissertation (1972) contains a good discussion of alternative strategies in white goods. It also chronicles the effect of the rise of large retail chains on the manufacturers.

# 5

## *Interbrand Choice, Information Equilibrium, and Market Power*

In Chapter 2 I argued that the buyer's process of choice among competing brands of a product (interbrand choice), rather than the choice among products, was the critical aspect of demand for understanding market performance. A simple model of interbrand choice proved sufficient to establish the influence of the retail stage in differentiating consumer goods. Among its implications was a difference in the impact of advertising among consumer goods industries.

This chapter extends the analysis in Chapter 2 and develops a more general framework for modeling the process of interbrand choice and its implications for industries' sales-promotion strategies and market performance. The buyer's demand for information and costs of obtaining it determine how the various information sources available to the buyer affect his choice. Information on some of these sources is provided directly or indirectly by the seller, who weighs the buyer's responsiveness against his own cost of supply to determine what portfolio of sales-promotion devices to employ. His profit maximizing portfolio is influenced by existing and potential competitors in the market for the product and the market for information.

The resulting equilibrium distribution of sellers' sales-promotion devices determines the sellers' market power due to product differentiation. The model of interbrand choice provides the link between sales promotion and the seller's market power. Different sales-promotion devices will be seen to have asymmetrical implications for market power, with advertising the premier device for erecting it. I will present an expanded theoretical link between advertising a market power from that of previous work and show that different advertising media have different market power implications.

This chapter concludes that we must consider three interrelated equilibria in understanding the effect on market performance of the buyer's uncertainty about choice: the buyer's information equilibrium, the seller's equilibrium portfolio of sales-promotion devices and equilibrium in the market for consumer information. Previous work focusing on a single information source (typically advertising) or a single partial equilibrium has led to conclusions that lack generality. Although my discussion is framed in terms of consumer goods, following the main thrust of this study, the model presented pertains generally to all buyers (and industries). I will briefly apply the model to producer goods in a later section.

The emphasis in my treatment will be on modeling the relevant equilibria rather than surveying the literature in these areas. The substantial literature (both in economics and marketing) on advertising and on consumer behavior provides fragments of the general framework and supporting evidence. I will note the important contributions to that framework below, leaving it to the reader to fit smaller ones in himself.

### Buyer Information Equilibrium

The buyer has numerous sources of information available to him about the array competing brands of a product, which we initially assume to be given: his own experience with the product; advice from friends and acquaintances; salesmen; reputation of the retail outlet offering the product; physical comparison of competing products; independent technical product information (*Consumer Reports,* government publications, and so on); media advertising (television, radio, magazines, newspapers, billboards). The buyer demands information about competing products to maximize his utility by choosing the brand that best meets his needs. Information is costly, however, and thus the buyer optimizes the amount and sources of information he obtains rather than maximizes them. The buyer never makes a perfectly informed choice but rather an optimally informed choice.

The buyer simultaneously determines his total outlay on information and the composition of the portfolio of information sources he consults, and thus the quantity of information consumed from each source. There are five major elements to this buyer information equilibrium: [1] the

1. Stigler's (1961) pioneering article first introduced formally the idea that the buyer makes an imperfectly informed choice and that he will search for informa-

desire of the buyer to make an informed choice; the product attributes about which information is desired; the set of product attributes about which each information source informs the buyer; the quality of each information source; the utility loss in obtaining each information source.[2]

The buyer's desire to make an informed choice is determined by the cost he perceives of making a bad decision. The cost of a poor decision is the buyer's *a priori* expected loss of utility resulting from that decision. This is related to the expected absolute difference in utility between good and bad purchases and the costs of changing the bad decision. The buyer will desire extensive information about products that are durable and require a large expenditure.[3] If utility increases with cost, equiproportional expected utility differences between a good and bad choice of a product will imply a larger absolute difference for costly products. In addition, for costly and durable products the buyer must live with a poor choice of such a good for an extended period, and its high cost precludes scrapping an inferior choice.[4] Products for which a poor choice substantially reduces utility for any reason will be chosen on a larger stock of information. For example, the buyer is likely to perceive that his standing with others is adversely affected by a poor brand choice among articles of clothing, other products worn on the person such as perfumes, and the broader class of products where styling is important. Products for which there are significant externalities in consumption are thus ones where the buyer will desire to make a well-informed choice.

The set of attributes on which the buyer places a utility value and on which the buyer would base a fully informed choice varies among products. The nature of the product defines this attribute set. For

---

tion until its marginal value equals its cost. Stigler's model treated price as the sole product attribute about which the buyer searched for information, and travel to stores as the method of securing information. My model extends that benefit-cost tradeoff to situations where there are many product attributes (differing among products), many sources of information about assorted subsets of these attributes, and expected utility maximization as the buyer's objective rather than Stigler's more narrow monetary objective.

2. The reader will recognize that some parameters of equilibrium taken here as given are determined in the overall cross-product information market. My model is to this extent a partial one.

3. The total expenditure affected by the decision is the appropriate datum and not the unit price.

4. The used or trade-in market for durable goods is partly offsetting here. However, the depreciation of durables is typically very high in the first year after purchase, with consequently high costs of early sale. Akerlof (1970) provides an interesting argument for the low price of used durables.

example, the buyer of a loaf of bread is probably uninterested in the style of the loaf, while the buyer of clothing is very interested in the style of a suit. The buyer of a washing machine is interested in its repair record, while the buyer of laundry detergent is not. The set of attributes which contribute something to utility may be very large. The buyer will not consider all product attributes to be equally important—they will contribute differently to his utility. For example, the color of a washing machine will carry less weight than its features, capacity, and so forth. Each buyer can be viewed as having a priority ranking of product attributes based on their contribution to his utility.

In general, indivisible bits of information pertain not to the product but to its individual attribute components. Information sources inform the buyer about the product's price, style, reliability, and so on, rather than about whether or not the product is good or bad overall. A different set of information bits will be secured for each of these attributes and in general each source of information informs the buyer about a different set of product attributes, and provides information of differing quality (to be defined below) about given product attributes. It follows that the buyer will expend a given total outlay of information in different ways for each product depending on the set of attributes he values. And since the set of attributes the buyer values varies across products, the value of individual information sources will vary. For any given product some information sources may not be used because they make no significant contribution to the expected quality of choice.

Not all information sources are perceived to be of equal quality by the buyer. The quality of information is the degree of confidence the buyer places in it, or the probability he perceives that it is accurate. The perceived quality of an information source depends on its perceived objectivity and on its perceived expertness. Objectivity is the degree to which the information is perceived expectationally to be independent of the seller. The expertness of the information source depends on the source's level of knowledge about the product and its flexibility in adapting information to the buyer's particular utility function. The source's ability to apply information to the particular buyer's utility function depends on the degree to which its message can vary with the needs of particular buyers (rather than remain a fixed message) and the technological limits on the source's content.[5] Product attributes are buyer-subjective to varying degrees—all buyers may measure repair record equally but each may have a different view about desirable styling.

5. For example, a salesman's presentation offers broader and more flexible content possibilities than a newspaper ad.

Differences in buyer-subjectivity of product attributes will manifest themselves in the perceived expertness of a given information source. Objectivity refers inversely to the likelihood that the information provided by the source is skewed toward the interests of the seller rather than the buyer. But objective sources may have little expertness and therefore their information is of low quality or usefulness to the buyer; thus both dimensions matter.

The buyer's own experience with a brand is perhaps the most objective information source. It may therefore be weighted very heavily in choice, and such weighting is the source of the high degrees of brand loyalty that are observed for many products. Physical comparison of competing products may similarly be treated as objective. Independent technical information and advice from friends and acquaintances are also objective sources of information, though less so because the utility function of the producers of the technical information and the utility functions of friends may influence the information presented to the buyer (though not necessarily in any seller's interests). The importance of advice from friends and acquaintances as an information source is well documented in the literature on marketing, which demonstrates that information flows freely among buyers, and that certain individuals (called "opinion leaders") take on a disproportionate influence as sources of advice to others.[6]

The retailer's image and advice from salesmen are sources of information of intermediate objectivity. While the retailer is an independent agent maximizing his own self-interest, except when he deals exclusively in one brand the retailer carries multiple brands and is independent of any one seller. Similarly, the retailer's reputation stems from the buyer's past experience with the retailer's entire product line and not solely the brand and product being investigated. The salesman's information may be questioned and its consistency tested by the buyer, who can thus in part verify its objectivity. On the low end of the spectrum of information sources ranked by objectivity is media advertising. The media advertising message is directly controlled by the seller and is presumably designed to represent his interests. Further, the buyer is unable to question or alter the content of this information source.

As objectivity varies by information source, so does each source's perceived expertness. While objectivity is specific to the information source, the perceived expertness of the source is a function of both the source and the particular product attribute about which the buyer is seeking information. A given information source may be perceived as more

6. See, for example, Engel et al. (1973), chapter 17.

expert about technical matters, for example, then about styling. Thus the quality of an information source varies by product attribute.

While the buyer may perceive his own prior experience (and physical product inspection) to be objective, the reliability ascribed to his own experience depends on the buyer's perception of his ability to judge the quality of a product from its use. This may vary among products; with regard to products with consumption externalities, technical complexities, or other difficult-to-measure qualities it may be difficult for the buyer to define and judge quality.[7] For such products media advertising (and other information sources) may be complementary with experience. The buyer may receive needed reinforcement that his purchase decision was correct through advertising. As the criteria for choice become less measurable, the need for such reinforcement may increase. The buyer's perception of his expertness will also vary across product attributes—he may perceive himself expert in style but not in technical characteristics, for example.

Independent technical information is objective and provided by knowledgable sources. Depending on the particular form of technical information consulted, however, it may or may not provide information about the attributes which make up the utility the particular buyer derives from consumption of the product. In addition, the buyer may or may not have the technical knowledge to understand the information presented by independent technical sources.

Friends and acquaintances may be perceived as more or less expert depending on the product being purchased and their experience correspondingly discounted. Limits on their knowledge about the product may be partially offset by their knowledge of the buyer's utility function, however. Where the utility the buyer derives from a product depends heavily on its perceived style and the reactions of other people to the buyer's ownership of it (externalities), friends and acquaintances may provide extremely important bellwethers. In general, friends and acquaintances will be perceived as more expert on matters of taste and style than about technical matters.

Reputation of the retail outlet is derived from the buyer's own

7. Nelson's (1970, 1973) argument that buyers obtain all the information about the products they desire for choice from either search (by which he seems to mean physical comparison) and experience through prior purchase not only ignores a number of important information sources but assumes that the buyer can fully judge the merits of competing brands by these two means. This assumption appears to be unacceptable when actual purchasing behavior (and the literature on marketing) is examined. Darby and Karni's (1973) credence goods idea, introduced in the context of the analysis of fraud, recognizes the consumer's difficulty in judging quality for many products.

experience and is therefore subject to the same limitations on the buyer's expertness noted earlier. A salesman's information, on the other hand, may come from a source very knowledgable about the product. Though the salesman presumably seeks to further his own interests, provision of assistance and advice by the salesman is an interactive process: he can respond to requests for information tailored to each buyer's preferences. The range of information the salesman can provide is extremely broad, from information and advice about style to technical product details. Information from salesmen is likely to be perceived either as equally expert across product attributes or, more likely, as very expert on technical matters and less so on more buyer-specific matters such as styling. In addition, the salesman can provide information at the level of detail and complexity most understandable by the buyer. It may be extremely difficult for the buyer to obtain the more technical information about products in a form understandable to him from any other source.[8]

Advertising comes from a source knowledgable about the product—the seller. But the content of advertising messages may or may not be that which the buyer would request and cannot be altered to fit the individual buyer's utility function, since the information provided by a given advertisement is the same to all buyers. However, the content of media advertising messages can and does vary across products and across media, from purely price and buying location information to technical product characteristics. The perceived expertness of advertising information is likely to be higher for style, taste and other non-technical product attributes. The nature of the information the buyer seeks in his choice will influence (but not determine) the content of media messages within the constraints placed by the technological limits on the content of each source. One important effect of advertising may be to tell the potential buyer what characteristics of the product to look for in subsequent search.[9] Thus the content of messages is determined jointly with the portfolio of sales-promotion devices adopted by the seller.

The final element in the buyer's information equilibrium is the loss in utility he experiences in obtaining information from the various sources. Utility is lost in information gathering in three ways. First, the

8. Other technical sources may be inaccessible to the buyer, and expert advice from friends on technical matters may not be available, especially as the product becomes more complex.

9. If it is assumed that the buyer does not have a well-formed ranking of product attributes, advertising may have the effect of influencing what product characteristics the buyer believes are important. The same may hold true for any form of product information.

buyer makes dollar outlays in acquiring information including direct media costs and the cost of transportation in search. Second, the cost of time in obtaining information reduces utility. Finally, the subjective displeasure of acquiring information from different sources can vary. The utility cost of time spent shopping may be different from the cost of an equivalent length of time spent reading technical publications or watching advertisements, depending on elements of the buyer's utility function unrelated to the product itself. As evidence of this, marketing studies have found that some people are "shoppers" and others are not, despite controls for the cost of time.[10]

The utility cost of obtaining information varies markedly among information sources. The cost to the buyer of his experience is zero. Experience is only costly to the buyer if he fails to use it. The cost of experimenting with a new brand is the loss in expected utility of not purchasing the best brand previously discovered.[11] Similarly to prior experience, knowledge of the reputation of the retail store is essentially costless, unless the buyer uses other costly information sources to gauge this reputation. Typically this knowledge is secured jointly with information gathering about other proucts.

The utility cost of media advertising may be low if not negative. While each medium is different, the time required to absorb the message is low and the message is bundled with the content of the media reducing the disutility of absorbing it. In the case of electronic media, the disutility of acquiring the advertising message is especially low, since reading the message is not required. The buyer's willingness to listen to or read low-cost information sources such as media advertising (and hence part of its cost) is influenced by the interest and perhaps entertainment value of its content. Thus it is not at all inconsistent with buyer optimization to see ads containing white tornados rather than dull recitals of technical product traits. It is generally difficult to consume the content of the advertising medium without being exposed to the advertising message. Finally, the advertisers subsidize the media and hence the value of the content may well offset the nominal price to the buyer of the media, resulting in the information being supplied at negative cost to the buyer.

All other sources of brand information have a cost. Advice from

10. For a review of studies illustrating the importance of factors other than resource outlays and cost of time (for example, personality traits, social class, and so on) in influencing shopping see Engel et al. (1973), pp. 381–383.

11. Not the actual lost utility as Nelson (1970) argues. The actual loss is a sunk cost which does not affect the buyer's *a priori* decision to engage in information gathering with respect to a particular purchase.

friends and acquaintances may involve costs of time and out-of-pocket costs of communication. These are likely to be relatively minor, though not necessarily so. Information gathering from friends and acquaintances may be pleasurable subjectively or may occur jointly with other utility raising activities of the buyer involving friends and acquaintances, reducing its cost. The cost of gathering information from independent technical sources involves the acquisition cost of obtaining the source as well as the costs of time and subjective disutility of absorbing the information. Unlike media advertising, independent technical information is not usually subsidized and hence its acquisition cost is not offset by other value. In addition, the cost of time in absorbing the information is typically greater than that required to read an advertising message. The infrequent use of technical information, despite its availability (in understandable form) for many products, is evidence of its time and subjective disutility cost vis-à-vis other information sources. Physical comparison of competing brands and securing salesmen's advice involve expenditures of time, resources for transportation and other purposes, and the potential high disutility of time spent in these activities.[12] These last three forms of information gathering are likely to be substantially the most costly than the other ones.

The inherent cost of obtaining complete information varies across products. A corollary to the cross-product variation in the set of attributes that enhance the buyer's utility is that different attribute bundles will require different information outlays. Gaining information about some product attributes, such as reliability, relative technical performance characteristics, and the like, is more costly than gaining information about others, such as price and image. Some attributes can be judged easily by prior observation of the product, some cannot be easily determined even after repeated use. Items which perform well-defined functions such as food may be inherently easier to gather information about than products like toothpaste or aspirin, where the function of the product is hard to test.[13] Products vary in complexity: automobiles, hi-fi equipment, and cameras are highly technical and sophisticated items, while furniture and sporting goods are less so. Products whose utility stems from perceived style and good taste (externalities) may be inherently very difficult to gather accurate information about. Buyers

---

12. Included in the costs of time is time spent in determining where to engage in physical comparison and solicitation of salesman assistance.

13. These are products with the so-called "hidden qualities" identified by some authors (Borden, 1974). Nelson (1970) and Darby and Karni (1973) build models around the variation in the inherent difficulty of gathering information about some products. As I have argued, there is but one element of information equilibrium.

who choose to make equivalent total outlays on information gathering will make a more-or-less informed choice across products as the inherent difficulty of gaining information about them varies.

The utility cost of information gathering may be allocated to researching a greater number of product attributes for fewer brands, or fewer attributes for more brands. For any given total outlay on information, the buyer's choice of the number of brands to research and product attributes to learn about will be determined by balancing the contribution to utility of the next attribute with the expected gain in overall utility (based on the initial set of attributes) from researching the additional brand. The margin between additional attributes and additional brands will vary, in general, as the total outlay on information varies, since the expected utility gain from an additional brand will decrease with the number of brands and the gain from an additional attribute varies with the number of attributes.

The tradeoff between the number of brands researched and the set of product attributes investigated may be resolved using a two stage process. Some information sources will be utilized to make an initial screen to determine the set of brands justifying careful investigation. Inexpensive and lower quality information sources such as advertising will rationally be used for this purpose—for example, Philip Nelson and others have argued that the fact that a brand is advertised is information that may lead the buyer to place it among those brands to investigate seriously. Other information sources, such as friends and acquaintances or technical publications like *Consumer Reports* may also serve the screening function. Once screening has occurred, additional information gathering will occur on the chosen brands. Following such a two-stage process, the buyer can economize on his use of the more costly information sources by directing his outlays on these toward the set of brands among which expected utility payout of making an informed choice is highest. In the two-stage process, the second-stage costly information gathering will receive the weight in the buyer's purchase decision, while the information gathered for screening will serve to influence choice only to the extent that it places the brand before the buyer with some probability that it will be chosen.

### The Properties of the Buyer's Information Equilibrium

The buyer making interbrand choice will continue to gather information to the point where the marginal net benefit is zero. The marginal net benefit equals the reduction in the expected utility lost from making a wrong choice minus the utility cost of the additional bit of

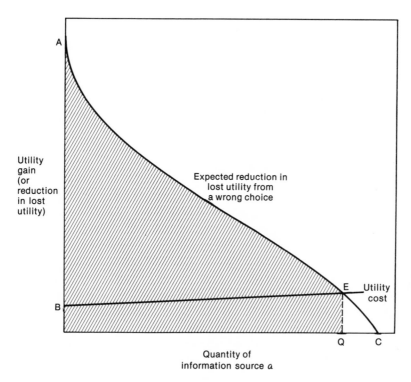

Fig. 5.1.  Buyer Information Equilibrium

information. This is illustrated in Figure 5–1. The quantities of information consumed from the various information sources are simultaneously adjusted so that each individually satisfies this marginal condition. Thus the buyer's information strategy consists of a total outlay on information in addition to a quantity of each individual source consumed. In general, the buyer will consume a portfolio of information sources.

Reduction in the utility cost of an information source will increase its net benefit and the quantity of it consumed if that is initially positive. Similarly, anything that improves a source's perceived quality enhances its expected contribution to making an informal choice and therefore increases the expected reduction in the utility lost from a poor choice from any given outlay on that source (shifts *AEC* in Figure 5–1 upward). Because attributes are bundled in products, information sources are not necessarily all substitutes. In addition, since attributes are bundled, increase in a supply of information about attribute $i$ could raise the demand for information about attribute $j$.

The weight the buyer places on any given information source in his purchase decision is determined by its total expected reduction in lost utility, or the area under the curve *(AEQ)* in Figure 5–1, relative to that of other information sources (and not necessarily the buyer's utility outlay on it). The various information sources consumed are accorded different weights in the buyer's purchase decision because they are of differing quality and provide information about different product attributes. The buyer wishes to make the utility maximizing choice subject to an information expenditure constraint. While the buyer may collect information from many sources, the highest quality sources which inform him about the product attributes which make the greatest contribution to his utility will be weighted heavily in the purchase decision and information sources which provide information about less important product attributes will have little influence, especially if they are of low quality. As the expenditure on information constraint becomes tighter, the buyer becomes increasingly willing to choose in ignorance of product attributes for which information gathering is costly (for example, technical characteristics) and settle for a less informed choice based on more easily researchable attributes. The equilibrium quantity of each information source consumed combines with the weight the buyer places on each source in choice to fully describe the interbrand choice process.

For costly durable goods (nonconvenience goods), for example, the buyer will base his choice on such attributes as technical characteristics, reliability, and ease of obtaining service and will likely expend time shopping several retail outlets, consulting independent technical sources, reading seller technical literature about the product, and actively seeking out information from friends and acquaintances. Such costly information sources provide especially high quality information about these attributes. While advertising may be consumed because of its low cost, its influence in the purchase decision will be small. For low priced, frequently purchased goods, the buyer will base his choice on more easily researched attributes such as packaging and image. He may base his choice on technical characteristics, but his information about these will be of greatly inferior quality. He may infer quality from his impressions based on advertising messages or even from his ability to remember the name and message of a brand at all. He is unlikely to consult salesmen, shop several retail outlets, or read technical literature about the product. Advertising is likely to carry an important weight in his purchase decision.

Individual Buyer Influences on the Information Equilibrium

We have been implicitly assuming that the buyer was the same for all products along relevant dimensions, and that within a given product class all buyers were equivalent. But this is clearly not so, and buyer differences will add to the variation in the information gathering strategy due to product differences. Cross-product differences in the group of buyers purchasing the product will supplement variation in the equilibrium portfolio of information sources due to differences in the nature of the product, and within-product variations in buyers will lead to market segments (see Chapter 4) for which the influence of given information sources varies.

Buyer differences affect the information equilibrium in four major ways. First, the utility cost of gaining information from the various sources varies across buyers. Second, the perceived benefits of making an informed choice vary across buyers. Third, for a given product the buyer's set of attributes which increase utility and their rankings vary. Finally, the buyer's exogenous level of technical expertise applicable to the brand choice may vary, which affects his cost of making an informed choice.

The cost of time, the disutility of time spent in information gathering, and required resource outlays on information gathering (such as costs of transportation) all vary across buyers, leading to variations in the utility cost of gaining information through some or all of the information sources. The cost of time varies with buyer's income, and hence higher income buyers should expend less on gathering information, other things being equal. The cost of outlays on transportation varies with the buyer's location and his available transportation means and their cost. The disutility of information gathering depends on the externalities the buyer gains from shopping trips and consulting information sources such as friends and publications. This is likely to vary by individual. The buyers education level may also affect the disutility of information gathering; one study by Mathewson (1972) found that the time buyers allocated to print media versus electronic media increased as buyers became more educated and earned higher wage rates.

The perceived benefits of making an informed choice will vary by buyer as well. The cost of making a poor choice is less important to buyers with higher incomes and buyers who purchase smaller quantities of the product per purchase or purchase relatively frequently. Similarly, for a given product, different buyers will rank different product attributes unequally. As described in Chapter 4, most markets can be partitioned into market segments. Some consumers weight price most heavily, others different aspects of product quality. Since different information sources provide information about differing bundles of attributes or differing quality of information about given attributes, the portfolio of information sources chosen and the weights placed on each source in choice will vary within markets as buyers' attribute rankings differ.[14]

The final major dimension along which buyers may differ is their exogenous level of technical expertise as it relates to the choice of a given product. Buyers differ in educational background, in experience with products having similar technological (though not market) characteristics to the one for which choice is being made, and buyers may differ in their skill in information gathering. For example, an engineer may engage in a different choice process for lawn mowers than a teacher because he need not gather information about some technical characteristics that the teacher might and because he is able to understand better or experience less disutility in consulting technical journals. These differences will translate themselves into differences in the information portfolio and weights for the two buyers.

## Information Equilibrium for Producer Goods Buyers

Most attention to buyer information gathering has been directed toward consumer buyers. However, the equilibrium described in the model applies generally to all categories of buyers. While the magnitudes vary, the same elements determine the responsiveness of producer goods buyers to information, although the buyer choice process is often more complex than for consumer goods.

Most previous research has portrayed the buyer of producer goods (commonly identified as the purchasing agent) as an informed, professional buyer, whose choices are based on technical product characteristics (for example, Preston (1965)). Indeed, the direct cost of search and the opportunity cost and disutility of time spent on information gathering per unit of product may be less for such buyers. More important, the perceived benefits of making an informed choice are likely to be great, justifying extensive information gathering. The benefits of an informed choice are measured by reductions in cost or improvements in the quality of the firms' purchased inputs. The exogenous level of expertise of such buyers may be high. Thus the producer-goods buyer may be responsive only to more costly and higher quality information sources, such as personal selling and technical publications, and media may be effective only if their content emphasizes technical information. However, it is the balance of these buyer and product factors which

14. With varying attribute bundles across buyers, the provision of information about attributes rather than about products follows logically.

determines the producer-goods buyer's strategy for gathering information, and this balance will vary markedly across the range of products the buyer purchases.

Consider a purchasing agent buying two products: one a major input to the production process of his firm, the other paint for the company's sign. The perceived benefits of making an informed choice for the former will greatly exceed those of the latter. For the former, the purchasing agent is likely to engage in the prototypical extensive information-gathering process associated with industrial buyers. For the other, the purchasing agent may behave much like a consumer, relying on less costly information sources. In fact, the household buyer may make a more informed choice about a paint purchase, which often represents a substantial part of his budget, than a purchasing agent for whom paint represents an insignificant part of his budget. In each case, the proportion of the buyer's purchasing budget expended on a product influences the buyer's desire to make an informed choice.[15]

The process of gathering information about producer goods is complicated by the fact that other individuals in the firm besides the purchasing agent typically contribute to brand choice. While the purchasing agent engages in the negotiations, personnel with expertise in the particular area for which the purchased product is intended (manufacturing, engineering, and so on) will strongly influence, if not determine, the brand chosen.[16] This is most generally true for high-cost, nonroutine purchases; for routine purchases the purchasing agent is typically the sole buyer. In the presence of multiple choosers, the information-gathering strategy for each chooser must be weighted by that chooser's influence in the decision. Seller sales-promotion strategies must similarly be directed toward all individuals influencing the choice.[17]

15. Esposito and Esposito (1971) found advertising to be a significant determinant of profitability in producer goods. This result, inconsistent with the informed-buyer model of industrial purchasing, is readily explained by my argument.

16. This split of the purchase decision is routinely described in the textbooks about industrial marketing.

17. The split purchase decision also occurs in household buying. Marketing studies have demonstrated that the husband and wife both influence most durable goods purchase decisions and that their relative influence varies markedly among products. See E. Wolgast (1958) and *Sales Management,* April 1975. Since the husband's and wife's opportunity cost of time, level of expertise and subjective displeasure in gathering information from the various sources may differ, my analysis of information equilibrium must allow for these differences as well as the relative influence of husband and wife in purchase. See Engel et al. (1973), p. 411, for a study which finds different information gathering behavior by husbands and wives for given products.

Information Equilibrium over Time

The focus thus far has been largely static. Purchase frequency affected the perceived risks of making a poor brand choice and experience was posited as an information source, but no attention has as yet been given to the dynamic nature of choice. The buyer is engaged in a continuous process of learning and forgetting about brand choices. He is continuously absorbing (to some degree) inexpensive-to-obtain forms of information, such as media advertising, about a multitude of products and brands. As he repeatedly purchases a given product, his experience with brands he has purchased builds, and the information he has gathered for each purchase decision to some degree cumulates.

Thus for those products which the buyer purchases more than once, we must examine the consequences of his learning over time. Buyers will not engage in costly forms of information gathering unless they perceive the possibility of purchase. We can focus our attention, then, on the buyer's accumulation of information from inexpensive sources, on the effect of his experience with brands he actually purchased, and on the retention of the information he gathered when making his previous purchase decision on the product. The key to this process of accumulating information is, of course, the nature of information decay. Before I examine the decay process, however, it should be noted that the nature of the product will influence the rate of accumulation of information. Some attributes, especially technical performance features and those bound up in externalities in consumption, are difficult to accumulate information about even through repeated purchase. Hence the rate of accumulation of information will vary across products.

Information accumulating from experience with the brand of the product previously purchased may have little impact on subsequent information gathering if the experience was unfavorable. The buyer has learned not to purchase the disappointing brand but still faces the same information-gathering problem for repurchase (minus one brand). Bad experiences, then, are likely to change the information-gathering process only if brands are few or sampling of brands has been extensive. Good experiences, conversely, may markedly change the information-gathering process unless the buyer has reason to expect that another brand will come to be superior.

Information from experience, as well as information gathered for previous choices, decays to the extent that conditions in the market change. New brands, brand changes, model changes, and marketing (packaging, display, distribution process, and so on) changes render old information and experience obsolete, leading the buyer to perceive the need to gather new information, since he can no longer assume that his old preference ranking of brands remains valid. Changes in the buyer himself over time, which increase his desire to make an informed choice or which change his ranking of product attributes, also reduce the value of past information. Experience with a product (for example, stereo equipment) may enhance a buyer's sophistication with its use and shift his ranking of attributes (thus this information source may be partly self-destructive).

The final mechanism by which information decays is through forgetting. The buyer continuously forgets prior purchase information, and much of the information that he continuously receives from low-cost sources. Some amount of forgetting may be exogenously determined and a basic human trait. But forgetting may also be in part an endogenous, rational process of discarding information of low expected usefulness that occupies storage space. For example, the buyer's forgetting may depend on his expected likelihood of being in the market in the future coupled with his desire to make an informed choice. If the buyer expects to be in the market again shortly and perceives the need to make an informed choice, information may depreciate very slowly. Conversely, even if the buyer expects to be in the market soon, he is likely to forget very quickly if he puts little weight on making an informed choice. From the accumulation and decay of information we can derive some propositions for the steady-state information-gathering strategy in a dynamic process of interbrand choice. First, the longer the period between purchases of a product, the less likely it will be that repeated choice affects information gathering. For goods purchased infrequently, the quality of experience erodes, and the buyer is likely to go through successive rounds of information gathering. Thus infrequent purchase makes successive purchase decisions more difficult, as well as its previous role in increasing the risk of a poor decision. Second, the more product and marketing changes in the market, the less the information-gathering strategy will change from the initial purchase to subsequent purchases, since product and marketing changes impede the buyer's learning process. Several studies, for example, M. A. Alemson (1970), have found that advertising is correlated with the rate of new brand introduction in individual product markets. This result is consistent with the buyer's responsiveness to increased information in changing markets. Third, the more the buyer desires to make an informed choice (for example, for an expensive product), the less is the information accumulation process likely to affect his information gathering behavior in subsequent purchases because the perceived depreciation of information will be weighted heavily. He may be more attentive to low-cost information sources to which he is exposed and he will repeatedly reconsult the more expensive information sources for each purchase.

In a given product market, the buyer's information-gathering strategy may change over time because of accumulation. When a product is first introduced, buyers are unaware that the product exists. Buyers making their initial purchase decisions for a product are choosing to allocate a portion of their income to a new product, at the expense of known substitutes. Since they have no experience with the product, buyers seek to learn the nature of the product and its use, and their unfamiliarity with it makes the relative merits of competing brands of less interest to them. Buyers will seek information sources which inform them of the product's use (physical demonstration) and about the benefits they can obtain from its purchase relative to substitutes.[18] As experience with the product accumulates buyers will become familiar with these attributes. Their desired attribute ranking will likely mature, then, and they will desire information about the relative performance of brands rather than about the product per se. We would expect the information-gathering strategy to change over time as more and more buyers of a given product became experienced buyers. A key aspect of the market for information, then, is the proportion of buyers who are first-time or new buyers of the product.[19]

Specifying Equilibrium of Information

While my concern has thus far been conceptual, the model presented has important empirical implications which reveal pitfalls in previous research which I can usefully describe briefly here. The equilibrium I have described is the outcome of a complex set of factors and is difficult to specify empirically. Since a large number of product and buyer characteristics interact to yield the buyer's information-gathering strategy, we face the constant danger of mismeasurement. For example, product price directly influences the desire of the buyer to make an informed choice. But product price is also a rough proxy for frequency of purchase and for the complexity of the product (its attribute set). Peter Doyle (1968) predicts that low unit price will be associated with high advertising, since the buyer will not desire information from other sources. His regression of unit price on advertising rates is inconclusive, however, because he does not control for the other influences on buyer

18. For example, with recreational vehicles the buyers will be interested in why recreational vehicles are a superior use of their expenditures on leisure over sports equipment, conventional vacations, and so on.

19. This is another dimension along which buyers in a given market may vary.

information-seeking behavior which low price may proxy. Nelson (1970, 1974) employs a similarly partial approach. Nelson views information as coming from physical inspection (which he calls search) or experience with the product. While this distinction usefully reflects my observation that different attributes are important for different products and that information sources differ in their ability to provide information about given attributes, Nelson fails to recognize that these sources of information both appear in every buyer's information portfolio and that they are two elements in a complex range of information sources. Nelson's classification of durable goods as goods where experience is the dominant influence on choice is based on his view that search will not uncover the highly technical characteristics of these typically complex goods. Yet this flies in the face of copious evidence that buyers shop heavily for durables. It contradicts the effect of infrequent purchase on the relevance of the buyer's experience and the buyer's imperfect ability to evaluate his experience. And it reflects Nelson's omission of a mechanism by which the buyer's desire to make an informed choice affects his information-gathering behavior. Such a mechanism would suggest that the high cost and longevity of durables would lead the buyer to demand a greater total quantity of information and to seek information from costly information sources such as salesmen and technical publications about the technical characteristics of durables. The buyer would rationally do so despite the difficulty in getting information about these characteristics, rather than relying on experience as Nelson posits. Nelson's view that advertising must be factual and informative for search goods (where the buyer can make his own inspection and verification), and is only influential in providing information that the brand is advertised in experience goods (where the buyer is assumed to be able to test the product conclusively by its use), assumes implausibly that the buyer is able to judge the quality of brands accurately in relation to the attributes that enter his utility function. Nelson's view of advertising in experience goods also makes no distinction between low-priced goods for which no other costly information sources are consulted and high-priced goods for which advertising is only one in a portfolio of sources.

### The Seller's Choice of a Portfolio of Sales Promotion Devices

The seller faces a market composed of buyers with information-gathering strategies determined from the equilibrating process described above. In this section I investigate the process by which the seller devises an optimum portfolio of sales-promotion devices, under the assumption that the seller ignores the reactions of competing firms. I will relax that assumption in the next section. For simplicity I will assume that all buyers facing the seller arrive at identical information equilibria.

The equilibrating process of the composite group of buyers of a given product determines the responsiveness of the buyer to the various information sources. Buyer responsiveness determines the total net revenue to the seller to the quantity of messages from each information source. The revenue responsiveness of messages from each information source is derived from the buyer's information-gathering strategy and the weight he places on information from each information source he consumes. The buyer responsiveness to information from the various sources becomes a key input to the seller's choice of an optimum marketing strategy. Marketing strategy encompasses decisions about expenditures on all information-providing sources plus other elements of sales promotion such as packaging, distribution methods, product changes, and new brand introductions. As I explained in the previous chapter, all these elements of marketing strategy are interrelated and thus jointly set by the seller. I will initially be concerned with setting the seller's optimal information-providing strategy and later discuss how this interacts with choices about other elements of selling strategy.

The rational seller would expend resources on each sales promotion device to the point where the marginal revenue productivity of an additional dollar spent on each device equaled its cost. While the marginal productivity of the last dollar spent on each sales promotion device would be equal, the shape of the relationship between total net revenues and dollar outlays and hence the total amount spent on each device would be proportional to the responsiveness of the buyer (and thus the seller's demand curve) to that device. Our framework for buyer information equilibrium allows us to translate this self-evident proposition into operational terms.

The seller's problem in determining his optimum portfolio of sales promotion devices would be relatively easy if he could simply derive his strategy from the buyer's information responsiveness. However, the seller's problem is greatly increased in complexity by three slippages in the process. First, the seller has imperfect knowledge about the buyer's optimization process. Thus the seller's view of the buyer's responsiveness is probabilistic. Second, the seller cannot directly influence all the buyer's information sources and, consequently, faces competing supplies of information. The seller directly sets the level of advertising and influences the salesman's presentation but has only indirect influence (at best) over other sources. The information sources controlled by the seller have their own unique cost/quality characteristics from the buyer's viewpoint, as determined by the buyer's information gathering process. These characteristics define the influence of seller-controlled information sources over the buyer vis-à-vis competing information sources, and hence the seller's decision to invest in providing them to the buyer.[20] Third, the buyer responds to messages from the various information sources to which he is exposed. The seller, though, expends dollars on sales promotion which are converted through the production functions of the respective information dissemination devices into messages to prospective buyers. Since the marginal conditions outlined above relate to dollar productivities, the relationship between resources expanded on a sales promotion device and messages to prospective buyers (the *efficiency* of the sales promotion device) will be an important determinant of the cost effectiveness of alternative sales promotion devices and a determinant of the optimal portfolio. This is illustrated in the following expression:

$$\frac{\text{Total net revenue from promotion device}}{\text{Total dollar outlay on promotional device}} = \left(\frac{\text{Total net revenue}}{\begin{array}{c}\text{Number of}\\\text{messages before}\\\text{potential buyers}\end{array}}\right)\left(\frac{\begin{array}{c}\text{Number of}\\\text{messages before}\\\text{potential buyers}\end{array}}{\begin{array}{c}\text{Dollar outlay on}\\\text{promotional device}\end{array}}\right)$$

Low message responsiveness can be offset by high efficiency and vice versa.

The Efficiency of Sales Promotion Devices

The efficiency of a sales promotion device is determined by the ratio of dollar outlays on the device to messages before potential buyers. This can be divided into two components, the unit cost of a message and the leakage between the receivers of the message and potential buyers:

$$\left(\frac{\begin{array}{c}\text{Number of}\\\text{messages before}\\\text{potential buyers}\end{array}}{\begin{array}{c}\text{Dollar outlays on}\\\text{promotional device}\end{array}}\right) = \left(\frac{\begin{array}{c}\text{Total number of}\\\text{messages sent}\end{array}}{\begin{array}{c}\text{Dollar outlays on}\\\text{promotional device}\end{array}}\right)\left(\frac{\begin{array}{c}\text{Number of}\\\text{messages before}\\\text{potential buyers}\end{array}}{\begin{array}{c}\text{Total number of}\\\text{messages sent}\end{array}}\right)$$

The cost per message of a salesman making a selling presentation to an individual customer exceeds that of the cost per reader of providing an advertisement read by thousands of individuals. The greater the

20. The seller-controlled sources may indirectly influence other sources such as advice from friends.

dollar cost per receiver of the message, the greater the responsiveness to that message required for the benefits of the message to exceed its cost. Thus as the unit cost of products varies, the efficiency of information source varies. The unit cost per receiver of messages from the various information sources is largely invariant across products, since it is imbedded in the technology of the information source.[21] While the message cost per receiver is unaffected by the product, however, the leakage of messages to receivers who are not potential buyers varies markedly across products. For some information sources messages are received only by potential buyers. For others, the messages are received by large proportions of nonbuyers and this proportion varies across products.

Three factors strongly influence the leakage of messages to nonbuyers: breadth of market, homogeneity of market, and purchase frequency. Breadth of market refers to the proportion of all buyers who purchase the product and the geographic distribution of these buyers. Virtually all households purchase food items, while only a fraction of these purchase camera equipment. Homogeneity of market refers to the ease with which buyers can be identified and categorized. Jewelry buyers are concentrated among upper-income households while cosmetics buyers, though primarily women, are more randomly distributed by income and other socioeconomic variables. Geographic buyer distribution could also be looked upon as an element of market homogeneity.

Outlays on the various information sources lead to messages placed before buyer groups of different scope. The salesman calls on or is visited by only potential buyers and delivers his message directly to these potential buyers. Media advertising, on the other hand, delivers its message to all the readers, listeners, or watchers of the media. Each medium—television, radio, newspapers, and magazines—has an audience with different characteristics, and some proportion of the messages will be delivered to other than potential buyers. The efficiency of a given medium for a product depends on the mapping between the potential buyers of a product and the medium's audience. National television advertising places messages before a large national audience. If a large proportion of consuming households are buyers of a product, television advertising may involve few wasted messages (leakage). If only a fraction of households buy a product, however, television may be an inefficient way to reach them, and media with a more specialized audience

---

21. The exception is selling presentations where the length of the presentation and the quality of the salesman may vary across products, and hence the message cost. These factors can be adjusted for in computing a normalized selling message across products and pose no special difficulty for the analysis.

may be more cost effective. The breadth of the market for a product relative to the coverage of the various media determine their cost per message placed before potential buyers of the product.

The homogeneity of the market for a product reflects the degree to which potential buyers can be identified and reached via specialized media. If most potential buyers of camera equipment subscribe to photography and travel magazines, for example, they may be efficiently reached using these media.[22] A seller in a market with narrow market breadth but no common traits on which to reach potential buyers with specialized media may be faced with an adverse ratio of dollars to messages, however.

Frequency of purchase affects the efficiency of an information source by proxying the proportion of buyers of a product who are not in the market during a given period. Messages will have the greatest impact on potential buyers in the market for purchase. If a product is purchased relatively infrequently, a large proportion of eventual buyers will not be in the market at any given time. Thus even if most households purchase toasters, for example, messages directed toward all households will be an inefficient way to reach households which are in the market in the period. Unless there is some way to identify those buyers whose toasters are wearing out, this inefficiency may be inevitable.[23] Frequency of purchase thus interacts with breadth and homogeneity of market to define each media's leakage in reaching potential buyers of a product.[24]

Each product will face a different set of ratios of dollar outlays to messages placed before potential buyers for each information source. National television advertising will generally be very efficient, especially for products with broad markets. Personal selling is generally inefficient, but this may be offset by high buyer responsiveness in some products. Assuming all other things are equal, we can derive a number of illustrative propositions about how efficiency of sales promotion devices

22. The homogeneity of the market defines opportunities for the creation of specialized media.

23. A new product innovation in toasters may cause buyers to replace their toasters before they are worn out. Thus product changes may alter the media efficiency function.

24. This role of frequency of purchase is different from its effects on the buyer information equilibrium and is illustrative of the difficult identification problems inherent in empirical testing of information models. Other product and buyer characteristics relevant to determining the information responsiveness of buyers may also proxy breadth or market and other efficiency determining market traits. Low unit price, for example, is associated empirically with broad markets; purchase frequency, while reducing the perceived need for an informed choice and hence the buyer's likelihood of reliance on advertising also makes advertising relatively more efficient. Separating these effects will be difficult empirically.

determines the portfolio of devices chosen as the nature of the market for the product varies. As the market for a product becomes broader, and the product is more frequently purchased, the more dollars will be spent on advertising relative to other sales-promotion devices. A given dollar outlay on advertising will have greater average productivity in such markets. As the market becomes narrower, purchase frequencies decline and the market becomes less homogeneous, and more will be spent relatively on personal selling.[25]

### Indirect Seller Control of Information Sources

The seller controls directly only media advertising and sometimes personal selling. In most consumer goods, however, personal selling is accomplished by the retailer because it is inefficient for the manufacturer to reach potential buyers by means of personal selling. The manufacturer can only influence the promotion of his brand by retailer salesmen indirectly through margins paid to the retailer, persuasion of retailers by the manufacturer's sales force, and exclusive-dealing arrangements.[26] In Chapters 2 and 3 I identified situations where the retailer gains bargaining power from his influence as an information source. These are situations in which personal selling and retailer reputation are important information sources to the buyer. The manufacturer's choice of distribution strategies will reflect this importance of retailer personal selling, as will his allowances for retailer margins and his promotional payments to retailers.

The seller's influence over advice from friends is indirect if not absent. Where this source of information is important, advertising may attempt to utilize it via testimonials from satisfied customers. Their prevalence in many product advertisements perhaps reflects the widespread importance of advice from friends as an information source.

25. A number of authors have identified advertising as a source of information to the buyer and have argued that differences in advertising reflect either differences in the cost of putting a given amount of information before buyers across markets (Else, 1966) or differences in the efficiency of advertising in disseminating information (Telser, 1964). (Nelson [1970, 1974] treats advertising as a source of information but fails to note its differing efficiency across markets.) While examining the seller supply problem in converting dollars to messages placed before buyers, neither author combines this with the responsiveness of buyers to messages. Conversely, those authors that relate the incidence of advertising to the buyers demand for information (Comanor and Wilson, 1974, give by far the most comprehensive statement) do not combine this with the differing technical efficiency of advertising in placing messages before potential buyers in different product markets.

26. Included in margins would be such things as free displays, shelf stocking, and cooperative advertising funds provided to retailers.

The Interaction of the Seller's Choice of Information Sources and Other Elements of Marketing Strategy

A seller seeks to differentiate his product to shift favorably the demand curve he faces. If the buyer's choice depends on ranking of product attributes based on their contribution to his utility, the seller has the incentive to shift this ranking in ways that further his interests. For example, the seller has the incentive to increase the weight the buyer places on externalities if this increases the perceived risk of a poor brand choice and thereby enhances the influence of information the sellers provide through advertising or in general enhances the seller's ability to differentiate his product. Buyer experience with products and information accumulation over subsequent purchases of a product may affect the set of attributes which the buyer ranks highly in his choice. If experience and information accumulation tend to shift the basis of choice towards price, making the product less differentiated, the seller acting under uncertainty may have the incentive to engage in offsetting sales promotion devices. For example, if attributes bound up in externalities are difficult to accumulate information about the seller has the incentive to emphasize these. Finally, I have assumed so far that the array of brands facing the buyer is given. The buyer's demand for information is affected by product innovation and thus the seller's optimum portfolio of information devices depends on the level of product innovation in the market. But product innovation can also be a strategy variable set by the seller.

The rapid introduction of new brands and brand improvements by an existing seller in low-priced nondurable consumer goods has often been looked on as an anomaly. Product differentiation is posited to be a goodwill asset built up over time. Why, then, do sellers scrap that asset and introduce new brands, often competing with their existing brands? One reason may be that a market where a high rate of brand turnover is occurring is more difficult to enter, since residency in the market requires parallel new brand introduction accompanied by expensive advertising campaigns. There are other reasons flowing from our model, however. New brand introduction and brand improvements nullify experience. They may thus keep the buyer's basis of choice away from price and allow continually heavy media advertising that would elicit a negative reaction if it provided no information perceived as new by the buyer. The most useful brand improvements from the seller's viewpoint would be those that involved hidden features (for example, hexachloraphine) that are difficult to evaluate. This prediction is consistent with casual observation. Brand turnover for these purposes would be unwise where the buyer viewed the purchase as important, because it would increase the buyer's perceived risk in purchasing the now unfamiliar product. Yet in products where well-informed decisions are made, styling changes and brand improvements which can be evaluated by the buyer may aid the seller by nullifying experience and preventing the product from becoming a homogeneous commodity.[27]

### Market Influences on Seller's Sales-Promotion Equilibrium

Based on the model presented in the previous section, one can envision each seller in a market calculating his optimal portfolio of sales-promotion expenditures. However, the presence of existing and potential competitors in the market will affect this choice. In this section I will hold constant the product and buyer characteristics that determine the responsiveness of buyers to the various information sources and their cost in placing messages before buyers, and focus on the market factors that alter the seller's portfolio of sales-promotion expenditures from that which a single seller would choose. There are three major market influences on sales promotion equilibrium: market power in adjacent stages, entry barriers, and market rivalry.

Market Power in Adjacent Stages

The model of manufacturer-retailer interaction in Chapter 2 implied bargaining power at the retail stage. Media advertising directed toward the ultimate buyer was seen to improve the manufacturer's position vis-à-vis the retailer, as did manufacturer persuasion of retailers through margins, personal selling and promotional subsidies. Improving the manufacturer's bargaining relation with the retail stage, then, provides a direct motivation for altering the manufacturer's sales promotion strategy. Advertising, for example, may be increased beyond the point at which its marginal effect on demand equals its cost if the increased advertising raises manufacturer profits because of an improved bargaining position.

Entry Barriers

I have argued earlier (as have many others) that advertising and other forms of sales promotion provide barriers to the entry of new firms in a market. If sales-promotion outlays enhance barriers to entry, they will rationally be increased beyond the point at which their influence on demand equals their cost.[28] If different sales-promotion de-

27. The number and variety of brands in a market have their own exogenous determinants, such as the nature of technology and the buyers' utility space. The endogeneity of product introduction and turnover within the constraints of these elements is an important example of the interrelationship of firm strategy variables.

28. This process of investment in entry barriers depends on the nature of the

vices affect entry barriers asymmetrically, then the link between sales-promotion and entry barriers will affect the distribution as well as the level of sales-promotion outlays.

## Market Rivalry

The most complex market influence on sales-promotion equilibrium is the rivalry among competing sellers. As the degree of mutual dependence recognized among sellers changes, competition in sales promotion alters their sales-promotion portfolios. The existence of competing messages may also change the responsiveness of the buyer to messages of the individual seller. While I cannot survey the literature on this topic here,[29] I present my own analysis of the sales promotion-rivalry linkage and discuss a number of empirical studies relating advertising to concentration in light of the analysis.

As oligopoly tightens (concentration increases), how might one expect rivalry among sellers to affect levels of sales promotion? The analysis of Edward Chamberlin and William Fellner suggests that increasing concentration and the associated increase in mutual dependence recognized will lead to a shift in the nature of competition away from price and towards non-price means, notably sales promotion.[30] Price cutting is subject to rapid and easy imitation and is particularly destabilizing; its potential for driving down industry-wide profits with no offsetting improvements in the seller's market position make it a form of competition sellers seek to avoid.

This general relationship between concentration and sales promotion, however, leaves open the important question of whether advertising rivalry will continue to increase as industry concentration increases further. If recognition of mutual dependence led to control of price competition, its continued increase should be accompanied by consensus on advertising rates. Such consensus is particularly difficult to achieve, however, because the consensus required is difficult to measure and enforce. The effect of advertising on demand is hard to measure relative to that of a price cut. The response to the latter is immediate, while the response to the former takes time in which other market parameters change. This uncertainty involves not only the effects of the firm's own advertising campaigns but those of rival sellers. Unlike a price cut, a competitive advertising campaign is difficult to retaliate against. Finding out about rival sellers' changes in advertising is more difficult than find-

---

oligopolistic consensus in the market and other factors. See R. E. Caves and M. E. Porter, "From Entry Barriers to Mobility Barriers."

29. For such a survey, see Fergusen (1974), chapter 5. See also Greer (1971).

30. Fellner (1941) pp. 183–197; Doyle (1968), pp. 410–411.

ing out about price changes. A significant time lag may occur before the advertising change of a seller can be matched. Unlike a price cut, a successful advertising campaign may be hard to imitate. Since firms face the possibility of devising an advertising campaign that yields durable benefits, it will be difficult for them to agree ahead of time on discounting future gains and limiting advertising outlays, especially given the difficulties in detection and enforcement of the consensus.

Because of uncertainties involved in advertising competition, F. M. Scherer (1970) argues that Cournot-like reaction functions are not unreasonable to assume. Whether or not this is true, the difficulty of reaching advertising consensus should lead risk-averse firms to continue to compete on advertising even when concentration levels are high. But the form of the relationship is unclear; advertising could stay the same with increasing concentration, or increase. P. K. Else (1966) and Alemson (1970) argue that advertising competition operates according to a ratchet effect analogous to the kinked demand curve model. Given the uncertainties and retaliation lags, sellers will match increases in rival's advertising outlays but will not match decreases. This effect, if it holds, would contribute to the elevation of advertising levels even in the presence of high concentration.

When the level of concentration becomes very high, Douglas Greer (1971, following Bain, 1952) suggests that mutual dependence recognized will finally increase to the point where it leads to the reduction of advertising rivalry. Thus Greer argues that the relationship between advertising and concentration will be nonlinear, becoming negative at very high levels of concentration.[31]

There is ample reason to suspect, then, that market rivalry affects advertising levels, although the form of the relation is left extremely uncertain by the theory. This must be kept in mind in a review of the empirical studies of the advertising-concentration relation.

Statistical Studies of the Advertising-Concentration Link

There have been a large number of empirical tests of the relation between advertising and concentration. Many of their results seem contradictory [32] but a close examination in light of our information model can contribute to reconciling their differences. Lester Telser (1964, 1969) and Doyle (1968) test the simple linear relationship between advertising and concentration, including no other control variables,

31. Several authors (Greer, 1971; Kaldor, 1949–50) posit a relationship between advertising and concentration with the causality reversed. Advertising enhances entry barriers, which lead over time to concentration.
32. These studies are surveyed in Fergusen (1974), chapter 5.

across broad samples of consumer goods industries. Their results are remarkably consistent. Both find little, if any, relation between advertising and concentration. My analysis concurs that the relation between advertising and concentration is most uncertain in form. Thus the linearity of Doyle and Telser's models may account for part of the nonsignificance of their results. A more fundamental problem, however, is their failure to control for the multitude of other factors which affect the buyer's responsiveness to advertising information and the efficiency of advertising as an information source from the seller's viewpoint. Across a broad sample of industries, the variation in these factors would likely swamp the partial effect of concentration on advertising and thus nonsignificance of the partial relation is not surprising.

Greer (1971) argued that the impact of concentration on advertising varied across industries, as well as that the relation was nonlinear. Greer divided consumer goods into three classes based on the "product characteristics generally agreed to be relevant to optimal advertising expenditures" before he tested the advertising-concentration relationships.[33] Greer's class I was primarily (though not exclusively) composed of what I have termed convenience goods, class II primarily of nonconvenience goods. Class III had no systematic tendencies. Greer found the nonlinear relation between advertising to sales and concentration which he hypothesized for classes I and II but very weak results for class III.[34] Greer's product classes I and II captured in a rough way some of the ideas discussed above about the efficiency of advertising outlays and the differences in the buyer's responsiveness across products to information from the various sources embodied in the convenience-nonconvenience distinction. Convenience goods are typically priced lower and purchased more frequently, are sold to nearly all households regularly, and the low power of the retailer enhances the payout to advertising. Nonconvenience goods, on the other hand, are higher (but more variably) priced, less frequently purchased, and sold to varying segments of households. Partially controlling for differences in efficiency and buyer responsiveness, the advertising-concentration relationship became weakly visible.

In a study which has appeared contradictory with other work, H. Michael Mann, J. A. Henning, and J. W. Meehan, Jr., found a strong positive relationship between advertising and concentration.[35] This appears to conflict sharply with the Telser, Doyle and, to a lesser, degree,

33. Greer (1971), p. 24.
34. The $R^2$ of the relation for Class I was substantially higher. A later note by Mann, Henning, and Meehan (1973) casts doubt on the significance of the nonlinear (though not the linear) part of the relation.
35. Similar results with a similarly defined sample are found in Cable (1972).

the Greer results. The answer to this dilemma can be found, however, by looking carefully at Mann's sample and statistical methods. Mann's sample consisted of 14 industries, all but one convenience items, and all but three or four high advertising industries. Although several of the industries were regional or local, Mann's advertising data was taken solely from the leading two to four firms, all of which were national.

Mann's criteria for selecting these firms was that they "did not produce in regulated industries, employed advertising as the principal means of sales promotion, and were not highly diversified." [36] Implicitly, however, Mann's choice of sample controlled quite well for the efficiency of advertising and relatively well for many of the factors affecting the buyer's responsiveness to advertising. In addition, the use of data from national firms minimized the problems with the use of the advertising/sales ratio to be discussed below. Mann's $R^2$ values varied from .35 to .52 with his best data sample; hence his control was still imperfect. However, his sample control did correspond more closely to the theoretical principles given above than any of Greer's product classes.[37] Many determinants of the seller's choice of advertising controlled for the relation between advertising and concentration comes to the surface.[38] Taken together, the statistical studies of the relation between advertising and concentration tend to support my model of the seller's choice of sales promotion strategies. The inability to obtain a significant advertising-concentration relation across a broad sample of consumer industries suggests that the effect of concentration is small relative to the other factors proposed.

### Sales Promotion Outlays and Performance

Given the portfolio of sales-promotion devices adopted by rival sellers, what is their effect on market performance? If sales-promotion outlays affect market power, providing the seller with an additional motive to engage in sales promotion, important questions arise for public policy. A number of authors, Telser (1964), Nelson (1970, 1973), have argued that advertising and other forms of sales promotion are information which benefits the buyer by improving his choice of products. While this is undeniably true to some degree, concurrence that sales promotion informs buyers does not end the controversy about

36. Mann et al. (1967), p. 352.

37. Greer's Class I was the closest, and thus it is not surprising that Greer obtained his highest $R^2$ there.

38. A series of comments and replies to Mann's study appeared in the *Journal of Industrial Economics*, 18. 1 (November 1969). These articles focus on statistics and sampling and ignore the substantive issues explaining the success of Mann's regression.

whether it is desirable socially as these authors seem to argue. If sales promotion also enhances the market power of sellers, the adverse effects on performance of market power due to sales promotion must be weighed against the information benefits of sales promotion to determine the direction of the net social effect of sales promotion outlays.

In examining the effects of sales promotion on market power previous empirical work has framed the question more narrowly by focusing on the relation between advertising and market power, taking no account of other forms of sales-promotion outlays. But all industries engage in sales promotion, while only some engage in substantial advertising: extensive selling via a sales force occurs in most, if not all, producer goods industries and in many consumer goods industries. The discussion in Chapter 2 suggested that manufacturer selling efforts toward the retailer can influence the manufacturer-retailer bargain (hence market power). So may sales force selling in general, as may other sales-promotion efforts. If all forms of sales promotion have equivalent effects on market power, then we may be socially indifferent among them and our concentration on advertising is misdirected. The importance of the relative influence of alternative sales-promotion devices on market power also extends to the relative influence of different advertising media. If the reduction in one form of sales promotion or advertising medium is associated with increases in another, asymmetry among them has important implications for policy toward sales promotion.

One must then take a wider view of the effect of sales promotion on market power than merely looking at advertising, treated homogeneously. In view of the attention placed on advertising and its empirical importance, I will first reexamine the theoretical link between advertising and performance, proposing an amended version of this relation. In the process, I will briefly explore how this link varies among advertising media. Finally I will examine some of the effects of other forms of sales promotion on market power.

Advertising and Performance: A Reexamination

The established theoretical link between advertising and performance is articulated by Bain (1956) and more recently by William Comanor and Thomas Wilson (1967, 1974). This theory postulates that advertising erects barriers to entry of new firms, and hence elevates profitability. In approaching the question of advertising's (and sales promotion generally) effect on performance it is important to note the change in perspective from that of the first part of this chapter. Here we focus on imperfections in the supply of advertising information which yields existing firms systematic advantages over their potential rivals, or on the effects of advertising on the competitive rivalry among going firms, not on how advertising affects buyer demand.

The essence of the established argument linking advertising and entry barriers is as follows. Advertising may increase entry barriers in three ways. First, advertising expenditures by existing firms create brand preferences which must be overcome by potential entrants. Advertising costs for new entrants will be higher than for established firms, since entrants must overcome the brand preferences developed by existing firms. The difficulty of doing so increases as the entrant's market share goals increase, since increasingly more loyal consumers must be convinced to switch sellers. Existing firms have the advantage of having been first. This effect results in an absolute cost advantage for existing firms, which is independent of the other links between advertising and entry barriers below.

Second, economies of scale of two sorts occur in advertising. First, a threshold effect exists which leads to increasing effectiveness of advertising messages per unit of output as output expands. This threshold effect results from the fact that a certain level of repetition of advertising messages must be reached before the benefits of advertising are realized. The expenditure on advertising to develop this repetition must be borne by any firms desiring to be successful in the market. Large firms, then, have the advantage of distributing this expenditure over a greater output. Comanor and Wilson (1967) cite a study by Leonard Weiss showing that the smaller auto producers spent over twice as much per unit on advertising as Ford and General Motors as evidence of this effect. The second economy of scale in advertising results from a decline in the unit cost per advertising message as the amount of advertising used increased. This could result for two reasons. First, the unit cost of a given advertising medium might decline with volume purchased due to media pricing schedules. Recent evidence suggests that this may be true with television.[39] Second, some forms of advertising of equal

---

39. Comanor and Wilson (1974), pp. 53–61, present the most recent evidence on this point. This issue has been the focus of active debate between those who believe advertising affects market power and those who do not. For examples of the latter see Fergusen (1974) and Schmalensee (1972). The resolution of this issue may not be very important to the impact of advertising on market power. The discussion of it has been straitened by the consistent assumption of both sides that all television advertising messages are of equal quality. However, it seems clear that messages on more popular prime-time shows are more effective than messages on also-rans, because they reach a larger audience and may require the buyer to experience less disutility in their absorption. If larger advertisers have preferential access to the better programs, this serves to produce media purchasing economies. Another important point in the debate is whether or not the media are able to

quality have lower costs per message (notably network television) and size makes the use of these media possible. These two sources of economies of scale lead to an economies-of-scale barrier to entry in the usual way.[40]

The final mechanism through which advertising is postulated to affect barriers to entry is through the mechanism of absolute capital requirements. The requirement that the entrant advertise means a larger pool of funds is necessary for entry into the industry. The use of capital for advertising investment is particularly risky, since advertising does not result in a tangible asset that can be liquidated in the event of failure. Hence the need for advertising strongly increases capital-requirement barriers to entry. In practice it is possible to look at the two other links between advertising and entry barriers as absolute capital requirements barriers. Absolute cost advantages of existing firms and the scale effects noted both mean that the potential entrant, to be successful, must expend added capital: to overcome buyer inertia and to reach threshold advertising levels and achieve media message economies. Hence both other components increase the absolute capital requirements for successful entry.

This theoretical link can be improved in several ways. It is instructive to begin by reviewing the conditions required for allocative performance to diverge from the competitive norm. The ability of firms in an industry to sustain rates of return in excess of normal is dependent on two interdependent factors. Barriers to entry allow price to be elevated above the long-run competitive price without erosion from the entry of new firms, and create potential excess return. Whether this potential is realized depends on the character of rivalry within the industry and between the firms in the industry and adjacent stages of production. The ability of firms within the industry to agree tacitly to suppress certain forms of rivalry, notably price, determines the degree to which the price is held at the above-normal price and the potential rate of return achieved. In addition, the rate of return in consumer goods manufacturing is dependent upon the rivalry between the manufacturing and retail stages.[41]

---

extract the rents incident to their advertisements through higher prices. Recent evidence suggests that media markets are highly competitive despite typically small numbers of sellers, arguing that they cannot retain these rents [Roberts (1975), p. 104]. Also arguing against extraction is the fact that the rents resulting from a given advertisement vary by advertiser, making them very difficult to capture.

40. See Bain (1956), pp. 53–113.

41. More generally, the concept of rivalry extends to rivalry with suppliers and customers. For convenience, I will treat rivalry with adjacent stages as a separate category here.

Advertising affects performance in three ways: through its impact on entry barriers (entry barrier effect); through affecting the relative power between stages (manufacturer and retailer); and through its influence on the pattern of rivalry within the industry (rivalry effect). The entry barrier effect of advertising follows from the ability of advertising to create or raise entry barriers and hence the limit price, as was discussed earlier. The other two advertising-performance links require more explanation, since they have not been emphasized in previous work.

Chapter 2 analyzed the bargaining relationship between manufacturer and retailer. In convenience goods, advertising directed toward the ultimate buyer was seen to be the primary basis for manufacturer power vis-à-vis the retailer. In nonconvenience goods, advertising performed the same function but was less influential due to the influence of the retailer on product differentiation. Thus the manufacturer has an incentive to advertise directly to the consumer (rather than use means of promotion utilizing or dependent on the retailer) to increase his bargaining power vis-à-vis the retailer. Advertising is important in gaining access to retail distribution and in allowing the manufacturer to extract concessions from the retailer (the manufacturer's threat of withholding his product is meaningful if the manufacturer had developed loyalty with the ultimate buyer).

Advertising's ability to confer power to the manufacturer against the retailer depends on its success in influencing the buyer's choice. To some extent, then, the effect of advertising on bargaining power is collinear with its effect on rivalry within the industry. However, recall the discussion of interindustry strategy differences in Chapter 4. Advertising's effect on bargaining power may shift the choice of the firm's marketing strategy away from strategies utilizing the retailer and enhance the use of advertising in such strategies, especially in cases where retail structure is conducive to retailer power. In any event, the notion of advertising's effect on bargaining adds a useful dimension to the theory of the link between advertising and performance.

The rivalry effect of advertising on performance follows from the often noted observation that advertising can lead to product differentiation, which lowers cross price elasticities of demand for individual firms within an industry.[42] Advertising, by reducing price elasticity, limits the effectiveness of price rivalry and thus reduces the incentive for firms to engage in it. Hence the ability of firms in the industry to agree to maintain price at the limit price determined by entry barriers is improved. While the bulk of attention has been placed on advertising's

42. See Bain (1956), pp. 114–115, for example; also Comanor and Wilson (1967) p. 425.

effect on entry barriers, then, these other two links between advertising and performance are important as well.

The rivalry effect of advertising, because it has received little attention in the literature on advertising, deserves further discussion.[43] Advertising is indeed an important source of entry barriers. The rivalry effect of advertising is not contingent, however, on entry barriers created specifically by advertising. Rather, the rivalry effect of advertising improves the chances for the industry to attain the limit price determined by its collective entry barriers from all sources: advertising, production scale effects, capital requirements, and so on. This includes entry barriers not usually specified in statistical studies such as patents, special raw materials advantages, and the like. This observation has some interesting implications for empirical work. Although from industry to industry the mix of entry barriers is likely to vary, the rivalry effect of advertising will remain stable, since it interacts with collective entry barriers. Hence the advertising coefficient is likely to be highly significant and make a large contribution to explaining variations in rate of return, probably more so than any other coefficient. This is reinforced by the property that the rivalry effect of advertising will show up empirically even if entry barrier variables important in a given industry are omitted in empirical specifications. That the rivalry effect is not contingent on the inclusion of all relevant entry barriers has the effect of further increasing the likely significance of the advertising variable. Since it is relatively easy to think of industries where important entry barriers are omitted in the usual specifications (for example, cigarettes and photographic equipment), this effect may be an important one.

To expand further on rivalry effects of advertising, it will be necessary to recall the earlier discussion of the determinants of the incidence of advertising as a form of sales promotion. Since advertising's ability to influence product differentiation is central to the rivalry effect, it becomes obvious that one must deal with the differential impact of advertising outlays on buyer behavior across industries predicted by our

---

43. Bain (1956) suggests that advertising may also allow sellers to maintain different prices (p. 115), and he includes product differentiation as a separate structural variable. He does not, however, make the transition between the change in the character of rivalry this suggests and performance across industries. Comanor and Wilson (1969) point out that advertising "may influence competitive relationships among established firms" (p. 87). The balance of their article demonstrates, however, that what they meant by this was the relationship between large and small firms within an industry. Schmalensee (1972), p. 217, states that advertising can be used to exploit preexisting entry barriers. He later incorrectly argues that advertising must directly affect entry barriers also if this is to be true (pp. 217–218).

model. The earlier discussion suggests that a dollar of advertising outlay will not be equally effective across industries in developing product differentiation and influencing buyer choice. Specifically, for nonconvenience goods I predicted on efficiency and buyer responsiveness grounds that a dollar of advertising outlay would on average produce less of an increment to product differentiation than in convenience goods.[44] Advertising dollar outlays are not comparable between industries unless the product and market characteristics which determine the productivity of advertising are controlled.

The entry barrier effect of advertising on performance appears to sidestep this problem. Advertising creates entry barriers by increasing scale economies and absolute capital requirements, which are related to the dollar outlays on advertising prevailing in the industry and not their productivity. Thus the effectiveness of a dollar of advertising outlay in creating entry barriers would appear to be constant across industries. However, market and product characteristics do matter. Consider the buyer inertia effect, which leads to absolute cost advantages for existing firms. I have argued above that a given level of advertising expenditure does not lead to the same degree of product differentiation across industries. This would suggest that the degree of buyer inertia (or differential advantage of existing firms) corresponding to a given level of advertising expenditure would not be constant across industries. For a given level of advertising, the extra expenditure the entrant must make to overcome these differential advantages would be less in nonconvenience goods than with a convenience good, since the consumer retains more price sensitivity and is willing to shop around with nonconvenience goods. Thus the potential for a given level of advertising to elevate entry barriers would be greater in convenience goods than in nonconvenience goods.

### The Threshold Effect of Advertising

The information equilibrating process has implications for the threshold effect of advertising on entry barriers as well. For a given industry, Comanor and Wilson argue a threshold level of advertising is required to make advertising productive in influencing choice. While my information framework yields a consistent prediction, Comanor and Wilson do not clearly distinguish the fact that this threshold level of advertising refers to the consumer and not to the firm. The relevant threshold is measured in terms of advertising messages (of a given level of quality) per consumer household. The threshold, therefore, has nothing to do

---

44. This is true although the marginal dollar of outlay yields equal effects across markets.

with either the firm's unit or dollar sales, and this is the crux of its effect. The extreme importance of the advertising as an entry barrier results from the fact that the potential entrant must spend a comparable or greater amount on advertising per consuming household than existing firms, no matter what its scale.[45] If advertising media were such that the entrant could direct his advertising outlays solely to a group of consumers corresponding in size to his expected sales, then the amount the entrant need spend on advertising would be a constant proportion of the entrant's sales no matter what those sales were. Advertising, in these circumstances, would pose a problem only insofar as the volume of messages the entrant would have to place before each buyer would exceed those of existing firms, necessitating a somewhat large outlay per dollar of sales. But assume conversely that the only cost-effective advertising medium available was national television where messages reached all households. If the existing firms were spending $x$ dollars on advertising, the entrant would be required to spend at least $x$ dollars on advertising as well regardless of his sales. It follows directly from this that the important factor in determining the scale effects of advertising is not so much the repetition threshold but rather the segmentability of the cost-effective advertising media in the industry, as determined via the information equilibrium. If the important media are local (newspapers, spot television) then the entrant can enter one local market at a time and compete effectively. If the important media are national, however (network television, national magazines), the potential entrant faces very substantial barriers to entry.[46]

## The Advertising-Performance Link across Advertising Media

Different advertising media vary in productivity across markets depending on the responsiveness of buyers to information on them in the market and on the efficiency of the media in reaching potential buyers in that market. Both of these factors are in large part exogenous from the sellers' viewpoint. Assuming firms in the market select the media of highest productivity for their market, does the media selected have implications for the advertising-market power link? My argument suggests

45. The entrant firm may choose not to achieve parity in advertising, but the theory in Chapter 4 suggests that doing so will place him in a different strategic group from going firms, with different potential for profits.

46. Fergusen (1974), chapter 5, and Schmalensee (1972), chapter 7, miss the point in arguing that media pricing policies are the key justification for advertising's link to entry barriers. As I have argued, the modified threshold effect and the impact of buyer inertia are far more central. See also Porter (1976) for a discussion of media rate structures.

that it does, and hence the choice of media will be influenced in part by the differential effect of media on market power.

In terms of the capital requirements and absolute cost advantage effects of advertising, there is no reason to suspect that outlays of different media will lead per se to differences in their impact on performance. The importance of the threshold effect (as amended), however, will vary markedly across media. The key to the threshold effect is the indivisibility of media. National television, national radio, and national newspaper supplements and magazines are highly indivisible. If a firm seeks to use these media, outlays will result in messages directed nationally. Local or regional television, radio, and magazines, and especially local newspapers, are quite divisible, on the other hand. The firm can direct its advertising outlays at a particular city or region. It has the option of entering small markets rather than being forced to enter a large market.

Thus the more indivisible the media used in a market the greater the impact of given advertising outlays on market power. Existing firms, then, have the incentive to use media as indivisible as possible, other things being equal.[47]

### Other Forms of Sales Promotion and Performance

As in the case of advertising, sales promotion outlays will affect performance if they affect rivalry within the industry, the relative power of adjacent stages or entry barriers. The arguments are analogous to those presented earlier and need not be repeated here. It is clear that any form of sales promotion which enters into the buyer's information equilibrium will affect performance to some extent. Such outlays on sales promotion enhance product differentiation and hence affect intraindustry rivalry. All outlays will similarly have some impact on bargaining power. If they are directed toward the ultimate buyer they enhance the loyalty of the buyer to the seller and hence his power vis-à-vis intermediate stages. If the sales promotion outlays are directed toward the intermediate stages (for example, manufacturer selling of retailers) they directly influence the bargaining relation between them. Thus when measuring the rivalry and bargaining power effects of sales promotion on performance, all forms of sales promotion should be included.

The analysis of the effects of other forms of sales promotion on entry barriers is somewhat more complex. After having discussed the link

---

47. Since this study was completed I have extended this discussion of the asymmetrical effects of the media on market power and verified them empirically. See Porter (1976).

between advertising and entry barriers, the conditions which dictate whether other forms of sales promotion affect entry barriers are evident. The form of sales promotion must be subject to imperfections in supply, such as significant threshold effects or reductions in unit costs as its volume increases. These scale economies must be associated with significant capital requirements. As a result of these factors potential entrant firms must face a cost disadvantage in overcoming the buyer loyalties to existing sellers due to the sales promotion device.

The three primary forms of seller sales promotion other than media advertising are direct mail advertising, promotion and selling via a sales force.[48] Direct mail advertising involves few apparent fixed costs, and since it is directed toward buyers individually it is difficult to ascertain serious imperfections in its supply. Promotional outlays, since they can generally be restricted to retail outlets selling the product and tied to the level of sales in those outlets, offer little apparent potential for providing advantages to existing sellers. Selling via a sales force, however, may be another story.

Establishing a sales force involves fixed costs, though they may not be high relative to variable costs. The number of salesmen and the associated overhead costs can be related to the firm's volume of sales. There may be economies of scale in sales force selling, however. The cost of selling a product with low sales per outlet may be very sensitive to volume changes. Because of the requirement that the salesman travel to the customer, a salesman covering a smaller geographical area may make more sales visits per day, resulting in a lower cost per salesman message. Also, salesman-customer relationships, since they are interpersonal, may be subject to substantial buyer inertia. The use of wholesalers representing multiple sellers to perform the direct selling task in some industries is an indication that such economies may be substantial for some products.[49] If, as our analysis in Chapter 3 suggests, the wholesaler is an inferior substitute for the manufacturer's own salesforce, the availability of the option of using a wholesaler may not offset these scale economies. Thus in the same way that advertising's effect on entry barriers depends on the medium, selling by salesmen may substantially lead to entry barriers in some (though not all) industries.

It is unlikely that scale economies in sales force selling are generally as large as those in media advertising, and thus sales promotion using

48. In consumer goods, the sales force sells to the retail stage. Promotion commonly refers to outlay such as point-of-purchase displays and literature.

49. The analysis of the incidence of intermediate channels of distribution in Chapter 3 suggests some factors which would identify industries with economies of scale in direct selling via a sales force.

this vehicle may have less of an impact on entry barriers. Failure to include measures of expenditure on sales force, then, may not be a serious omission in measuring the effect of sales promotion on entry barriers, though it is in measuring the rivalry and bargaining effects. However, whether or not the preoccupation with advertising in the industrial organization literature is happily justified remains an empirical question.[50] The analysis here suggests that the relationship between sales promotion in its various forms and market performance is not a general one, and that by examining the various forms of sales promotion we can identify those industries where sales promotion will be significant. These differences in the effects of sales promotion on performance across firms of sales promotion and industry situations offer more promise in extending our understanding of the effects of sales promotion than do the similarities.

50. If sales force selling is an important form of selling outlays in leading to market power, its measurement raises difficult problems suggested in the last section. Salesmen engage in both selling and physically distributing their product in some industries. We need a way of separating the two.

# 6

## Convenience Goods, Nonconvenience Goods, and Performance

Chapters 2–5 of this study have developed a general theory of the link between structure and performance in consumer goods industries. This theory can be used to formulate a large number of hypotheses subject to empirical testing. Chapters 6 and 7 report the results of a series of empirical investigations based on my theory, which can be divided into three major areas. The first, making up the core results of the study, partitions consumer goods industries into convenience and nonconvenience groups and investigates the structure-performance link in the two groups. These tests will be the subject of this chapter. The second area of empirical investigation tests a series of hypotheses about the effect of strategy variations within industries on industry performance. Finally, the third investigates the effect of retail structure on the performance of manufacturing industries. The tests performed in the empirical section of this study cover only a subset of the hypotheses suggested by my analysis. However, it will be argued that the tests performed capture the major implications of our model, and that the results support them strongly.

**Convenience Goods, Nonconvenience Goods, and Performance: Theory**

Chapter 2 set forth a basic distinction between consumer goods sold through convenience outlets and those sold through nonconvenience outlets. The importance of this distinction was reinforced in the discussions of intraindustry strategic variation (Chapter 4) and the link between advertising and performance (Chapter 5). Thus a test of the structure-performance relation across consumer goods industries, utilizing the convenience-nonconvenience distinction, will constitute the core result of this study. Before discussing the procedures used in making this test and the results obtained it is useful to collect and summarize briefly the implications of my theory for the convenience-nonconvenience dichotomy. The overall implication of the theory is that the link between structure and performance should be fundamentally different for the two groups.

Chapter 2 focused on the effect of the characteristics of retail outlets on performance in manufacturing. The convenience-nonconvenience distinction is important in several major ways. It signals a fundamental difference in the characteristics of demand for the product. Convenience goods are purchased without shopping, and the influence of the retailer on the purchase decision is small. The retailer's contribution to the differentiation of the product is small, although it may be relatively large for weakly differentiated convenience items. Hence advertising is the dominant form of product differentiation. Not only is the consumer responsive to advertising, but advertising provides the key to the relationship between manufacturer and retailer. The consumer's loyalty due to advertising is a major basis for the manufacturer's bargaining power vis-à-vis the retailer. Because the retailer is relatively unable to influence the consumer's purchase decision, he has no effective bargaining threat besides withholding shelf space by refusal to stock a product. Yet the consumer's loyalty due to advertising reduces the credibility of this threat. The retailer's power is low against a heavily advertised convenience good. Advertising holds the key to gaining access to distributive channels, which was identified as a key component of entry barriers in consumer goods industries.

For nonconvenience goods, the consumer's desire to shop and obtain more extensive product information, and the retailer exerts a relatively large influence on his purchase decisions. The power of the retailer is higher vis-à-vis the manufacturer in these industries, other things being equal. Advertising is no longer the key element of product differentiation; it ceases to dominate the consumer's decision to purchase or to define the relationship between manufacturer and retailer. Because the retailer's own sales efforts can substantially offset the effects of advertising, the manufacturer's persuasion of the retailer becomes more important. Although advertising still enhances the manufacturer's power vis-à-vis the retailer and assists the manufacturer in gaining access to distribution channels, its effect is weaker, and the importance of enlisting the retailer's support remains. In addition, gaining access to distribution is eased somewhat by the reduced need for intensive geographic market coverage. But to increase market share the manufacturer must supplement advertising with increased efforts to persuade retailers.

In general, the power of the nonconvenience retailer will be greater and manufacturer's profit lower, other things being equal. Advertising is likely to be a much more significant variable for convenience goods. Advertising proxies the relative power of manufacturer and retailer. In addition, advertising captures the essence of product differentiation in convenience goods. (Other forms of product differentiation are relatively unimportant.) The usual practice in industrial organization research of employing advertising as the sole measure of product differentiation is likely to be quite successful.[1] For nonconvenience goods, however, other factors are of relatively great importance to product differentiation. First, product design and technical characteristics are likely to take on greater importance when the consumer engages in extensive shopping and comparison.[2] Second, nonadvertising selling efforts by the manufacturer (manufacturer persuasion of the retailer) are crucial. Hence advertising is likely to be a less significant structural variable in nonconvenience good industries. More fundamentally, however, the standard industrial organization model is likely to explain relatively less of the cross-industry variation in profits in view of the great importance of omitted variables: technical product characteristics, nonadvertising selling outlays, and other proxies for retailer power. Since there is no *a priori* basis for believing that these omitted variables are significantly correlated with any of the included variables in the standard model, their absence is likely to introduce substantial noise into that model, tested across nonconvenience industries.

The convenience-nonconvenience partitioning also provides an indirect test of our hypotheses regarding intraindustry strategic variation. For nonconvenience goods, the theory suggests that the opportunities for economically important strategic variation exceed those in convenience goods. This difference reinforces the conclusion above that advertising is a weaker variable for nonconvenience goods, because the

1. For expository convenience, I will term the basic model used by Comanor and Wilson (1967) and others the standard industrial organization model. While there are nontrivial differences among the models used by various authors, they all test across broad samples of industries unadjusted for differences in buyer characteristics.

2. Across industries this occurs in two ways. First, the more complex the product the more important the retailer becomes in selling. Second, technical characteristics divert the product choice away from price.

pattern of strategies adopted and thus the group structure will vary across industries and advertising is not equally important for every pattern. It further suggests a large potential unexplained variance for nonconvenience goods. As the pattern of intraindustry strategic variation (group structure) changes across industries so does performance (via the direct and indirect effects), holding other structural variables constant. In contrast with convenience goods, the wide potential for variations in strategy for producers of nonconvenience goods implies a generous scope for the influence of historical, managerial, and random factors. Hence omission of proxies for strategic variation from the model should affect our ability to explain profits only slightly in convenience goods but severely in nonconvenience goods. Thus unexplained variance will be much greater for nonconvenience goods.

Finally, the expanded link between advertising and performance presented in Chapter 5 provides some additional implications of sorting industries into convenience and nonconvenience groups. First, the model suggests that a given level of advertising outlays will have less effect on performance in nonconvenience than in convenience goods, for reasons going beyond the difference in relative manufacturer power. This argument suggests that the advertising coefficient will be different as between convenience and nonconvenience goods: unlike the earlier arguments it does not imply a lower level of significance of the advertising variable for nonconvenience goods.

**Structure of the Test**

The model provides a clear mandate for the partitioning of consumer goods into convenience and nonconvenience goods when we test the effect of structure on performance. A sample of 42 consumer goods industries was used for the test. Its composition, the sources of data, definitions of the variables and their methods of construction are described in detail in the Technical Appendix. The dependent variable for the study was net profit after taxes as a percent of stockholders' equity. Six basic structural variables were taken over from previous statistical studies: seller concentration, minimum efficient scale of plant as a percent of industry output, growth rate of demand, absolute capital requirements for production, advertising, and a dummy variable for regional submarkets.

Using data on the distribution of industry sales by class of retail outlet, described in the Appendix, the 42 consumer goods industries were grouped into 19 convenience goods and 23 nonconvenience goods industries. Table 6–1 lists the industries in the sample and their classification. An industry's product was classified a convenience good if the

TABLE 6-1.   Forty-two Consumer Goods Industries

| IRS number | Industry | Convenience/ Nonconvenience |
|---|---|:---:|
| 2010 | Meat products | C |
| 2020 | Dairy products | C |
| 2030 | Canned and frozen foods | C |
| 2040 | Grain mill products | C |
| 2050 | Bakery products | C |
| 2060 | Sugar | C |
| 2070 | Confectionary and related products | C |
| 2082 | Beer | C |
| 2084 | Wine, Brandy | C |
| 2085 | Liquor | C |
| 2086 | Soft drinks | C |
| 2091 | Vegetable and animal oil | C |
| 2110 | Cigarettes | C |
| 2110 | Tobacco | C |
| 2712 | Periodicals | C |
| 2715 | Books | C |
| 2830 | Drugs | C |
| 2841 | Soap | C |
| 2842 | Perfumes, cosmetics, toilet preparations | C |
| 2250 | Knit goods | NC |
| 2270 | Carpets | NC |
| 2310 | Men's clothing | NC |
| 2330 | Women's clothing | NC |
| 2380 | Miscellaneous apparel and accessories | NC |
| 2510 | Household furniture | NC |
| 2850 | Paint | NC |
| 3010 | Tires | NC |
| 3140 | Footwear | NC |
| 3198 | Leather and finishing | NC |
| 3260 | Pottery and related products | NC |
| 3420 | Cutlery, hand tools, and general hardware | NC |
| 3520 | Farm machinery and equipment | NC |
| 3630 | Household appliances | NC |
| 3650 | Radio and television equipment | NC |
| 3691 | Electric lighting and wiring equipment | NC |

Table 6-1.   (continued)

| IRS number | Industry | Convenience/ Nonconvenience |
|---|---|---|
| 3711 | Motor vehicles | NC |
| 3830 | Optical, medical, and ophthalmic goods | NC |
| 3860 | Photographic equipment and supplies | NC |
| 3870 | Watches and clocks | NC |
| 3910 | Jewelry | NC |
| 3920 | Toys and sporting goods | NC |
| 3991 | Costume jewelry | NC |

majority of its sales were made through convenience outlets and similarly for nonconvenience industries.[3] Convenience outlets were defined, following the model, as those outlets where little or no sales assistance was provided with sale and high locational density of outlets signals that convenience is a dominant factor in consumer buying behavior. A determination of these characteristics was made based on data giving the number of establishments in SMSA's per retail outlet class, on data giving the salesperson expense as a per cent of gross margin, and on direct observation. Other outlet types were designated as nonconvenience. Most cases were quite unambiguous.[4] In the empirical tests those industries where some ambiguity existed in classification were alterna-

3. In practice, for all but three industries (books, tires, and photo equipment) the percent of convenience industry output sold through outlets classified as nonconvenience and vice versa was negligible. The sensitivity of the results to changes in the classification of these industries is discussed below.

4. The ambiguity centered primarily on the classification for drug stores. Drug stores are unambiguously convenience outlets based on the locational density criterion. The problem occurred with respect to the sales assistance criterion. Although it is clear that drug stores are convenience outlets of toiletries, cosmetics, and other nondrug items, there is some question at least about their classification for drug items. Bowman (1952) and Palamountain (1955) implicitly argue this by asserting that druggists influence strongly the consumer's purchase of health oriented items.

With ethical drugs this is clearly not the case. The druggist merely fills the prescription. For over-the-counter health items, however, the druggist potentially can be important and it was to these items that Bowman and Palamountain must have been referring. It appears, however, that their reasoning is dated. The bulk of over-the-counter drug sales are widely advertised items such as pain killers, cold remedies, and so on. Here, unlike 20 years ago, the druggist exerts little influence and the consumer in any event will not shop around. The conclusion is, then, that drug stores are convenience outlets for drugs as they clearly are for perfumes, cosmetics, and toilet preparations.

tively excluded and reclassified. In no case did the results change materially. Hence the original partitioning between convenience and nonconvenience industries is maintained throughout the study.

There are two potential ways to incorporate the partitioning in a test of structure-performance relations. One is to run separate regressions for the convenience goods and the nonconvenience goods samples. The other involves the use of dummy variables to allow each independent variable to take on a different value for each set of data.[5] The latter alternative, however, is ruled out by the model. The use of dummy variables in a single regression requires the assumption that the variance of the error term is the same for all observations in the pooled data set.[6] The model, on the other hand, strongly suggests that the variance of the error term will be greater for nonconvenience goods. If the sole difference in the model in the two samples were the error variance, we could estimate the error variances in the two samples and use these to make a pooled test. However the theory further suggests that the model itself is different in the two subsamples. Estimating a separate equation for each data set incorporates the alternative assumption that the variance of the error term is constant within each group but not across groups, and allows the appropriate model and specification of variables to vary across groups. These latter assumptions are congenial to the model, and separate regressions are computed for each data set throughout the study.[7]

Before proceeding to our empirical results, it is necessary to respond to recent criticism of single equation structure-performance tests including advertising, such as those I performed. Criticism of such tests revolves around two issues.[8] First, it is argued that advertising is improperly measured as an expense when it has a lasting effect and therefore should be treated as an asset. This measurement error leads to a spurious positive relation between advertising and profits. Second, it is argued that advertising is not an exogenous but an endogenous vari-

5. Formally, the first method involves estimating an equation of the form
$$Y_b = B_o + B_1 X_b$$
separately for each data set. The alternative involves a single equation of the form
$$Y_c = b_o + a_o D + B_1 X_c + a_1 (D \cdot X_c)$$
across the pooled data, $D$ taking on the value of 1 for convenience goods and 0 for nonconvenience goods.

6. See Rao and Miller (1971), pp. 90–93.

7. This argument also has relevance to hypothesis testing across the convenience and nonconvenience samples.

8. A number of authors have participated in this criticism. Leading and recent summaries are found in Ferguson (1974) and Schmalensee (1972). The most recent defense is contained in Comanor and Wilson (1974).

able, itself determined by industry concentration and even profitability. Therefore the proper methodology for testing the structure-performance relation is one utilizing a simultaneous equation model.

The first criticism raises an empirical question. The proposed mismeasurement depends on the presence of ever increasing advertising outlays—in the steady state there would be no mismeasurement. Thus we would expect the empirical significance of the mismeasurement to be small. Two recent studies have employed different methods of correcting for the asset character of advertising in structure-performance tests across consumer goods industries (Comanor and Wilson, 1974, chapter 8; John Siegfried and Weiss, 1974).[9] In both cases, correction for the effects of the investment character of advertising made no significant change in the basic advertising-profitability relation. In view of these consistent findings that the problem has little empirical significance, I did not attempt to correct for the investment character of advertising here.

The second criticism has also been tested in recent empirical investigations. Comanor and Wilson (1974, chapter 7) and John Vernon and R. E. Nourse (1973) both estimate simultaneous equation models with advertising as an endogenous variable. Both find that advertising's causal relation to profitability continues to hold, with Comanor and Wilson reporting that the coefficient of advertising's effect on profits actually increases in the simultaneous equation model (p. 163). The failure of the simultaneous equation model to affect the single equation results is consistent with the theory presented in Chapter 5, which argues that the impact of concentration and any impact of profits on advertising will be overshadowed by the effects of the buyer information gathering process and the technology of alternative information sources, both of which are intrinsic to the product. In view of the difficulties raised by simultaneous equation estimation, I will take these consistent results as a justification for retaining a single equation format. In any case, I would not expect the results to be biased, since there is no reason to suspect that any reverse causality would be different as between the convenience and nonconvenience samples.

### Results

The pioneering statistical research on structure-performance relations in consumer-goods industries is reported in a 1967 paper by Comanor

9. An earlier study by Bloch (1971), which yields contradictory results, is countered in the latter paper.

and Wilson, later updated by Frances Esposito and Lewis Esposito.[10] Comanor and Wilson's study will, therefore, provide a standard of comparison for my results. The initial tests utilized a model substantially identical to that used by Comanor and Wilson.

Table 6–2 gives the results of multiple regression analysis of all 42 consumer goods industries in the sample. The results in Table 6–2 are quite similar to those obtained by Comanor and Wilson and even more so to those of Esposito and Esposito.[11] The magnitudes of the coefficients and the levels of significance are substantially the same as Comanor and Wilson's, as is the overall proportion of the variance in profitability explained. The similarity of my results to Comanor and Wilson's, despite the 7 year separation in the period covered by the data, lends strong support to the stability of the structure-performance relations inherent in the model. The similarity also provides evidence that the reverse causality between advertising and profits suggested by some is doubtful.[12] The only important difference between my results and earlier studies is in the concentration variable. My results indicate a higher level of significance for the concentration variable, in addition to a persistent negative sign.[13] Comanor and Wilson, Esposito and Esposito, and recently K. D. Boyer find a negative sign in comparable runs, but its significance level is somewhat lower in some cases.[14]

Tables 6–3 and 6–4 present corresponding sets of regression equations for the convenience goods and nonconvenience goods samples, respectively. The results are striking. For the convenience goods sample, the model yields a corrected $R^2$ of .81 as compared with .48 for the entire sample, using the lead equations for comparison. The $t$ value of the advertising variable increases dramatically, while the $t$ values of the other variables hold relatively steady despite the halving in degrees of

10. Comanor and Wilson (1967); Esposito and Esposito (1971). Comanor and Wilson used data for the period 1957–59, while Esposito and Esposito's data was for the period 1963–65. Comanor and Wilson (1974) contains the same results.

11. Hereafter, consequently, I will make comparisons primarily to Comanor and Wilson's results. Since Esposito and Esposito's data served as the core for my data (see the Technical Appendix), the similarity of my results to those of Esposito and Esposito is to be expected.

12. For a discussion see Comanor and Wilson (1967), p. 436–437.

13. In my equations a continuous eight-firm concentration ratio outperformed both the continuous four-firm concentration ratio and a dichotomous concentration variable based on Kaysen and Turner's 70 percent eight-firm concentration ratio cut-off. Therefore, only equations with the eight-firm concentration ratio are reported. There will be an extensive discussion of the concentration ratio results below.

14. Boyer (1974), p. 545. Boyer's model, as he notes, omits important structural traits and therefore must be treated with less confidence.

TABLE 6-2. Multiple Regression Equations Explaining Profit Rates: All Consumer Goods Industries
(n = 42)

| Intercept | Eight-firm concentration ratio | Minimum efficient scale | Advertising/ sales | Growth | Regional dummy | Absolute capital requirements | $R^2$ | Corrected $R^2$ |
|---|---|---|---|---|---|---|---|---|
| 54.34[b] (2.08) | -.50154[b] (1.926) | .01677[c] (1.673) | .52339[a] (3.703) | .02128[b] (1.725) | 17.037 (.975) | .0007433[a] (2.970) | .553[a] | .477 |
| 67.81[a] (3.068) | -.38188[c] (1.664) | .01129[c] (1.362) | .50968[a] (3.627) | .02093[b] (1.699) | | .0007142[a] (2.876) | .541[a] | .477 |
| 46.31[b] (1.734) | | .005660 (.666) | .44907[a] (3.185) | .02534[b] (2.011) | 1.1598 (.073) | .0005025[b] (2.235) | .506[a] | .437 |
| 70.43[a] (2.835) | -.25082 (1.150) | | .52629[a] (3.634) | .01780[c] (1.429) | .61985 (.042) | .0006898[a] (2.712) | .517[a] | .450 |
| 88.72[a] (5.131) | -.57837[b] (2.195) | .01386[c] (1.365) | .62966[a] (4.819) | | 16.164 (.901) | .0009843[a] (4.615) | .515[a] | .448 |
| 101.0 (2.015) | -.46355[b] (2.015) | .008692 (1.040) | .61499[a] (4.756) | | | .0009529[a] (4.540) | .504[a] | .451 |

Note: Figures in parentheses are t values. The significance of the regression coefficients is tested using a one-tail t test and the significance of the coefficients of multiple determination is tested using the F test.

[a] Coefficient is significant at the 99 percent level.
[b] Coefficient is significant at the 95 percent level.
[c] Coefficient is significant at the 90 percent level.

TABLE 6-3. Multiple Regression Equations Explaining Profit Rates: Convenience Good Industries
(n = 19)

| Intercept | Eight-firm concentration ratio | Minimum efficient scale | Advertising/ sales | Growth | Regional dummy | Absolute capital requirements | $R^2$ | Corrected $R^2$ |
|---|---|---|---|---|---|---|---|---|
| 51.72[c] (1.718) | −.63223[a] (2.622) | .01499[c] (1.526) | .59122[a] (5.146) | .02596[b] (1.945) | 9.6922 (.698) | .001763[a] (2.675) | .876[a] | .813 |
| 61.37[b] (2.340) | −.58308[a] (2.580) | .01057[c] (1.437) | .60016[a] (5.363) | .02364[b] (1.880) | | .001918[a] (3.156) | .871[a] | .821 |
| 10.74 (.346) | | .01440 (1.217) | .51713[a] (3.854) | .03994[a] (2.793) | −.94 (.059) | .001150[c] (1.549) | .804[a] | .729 |
| 14.65 (.452) | −.40346[c] (1.474) | .02665[a] (2.495) | .54961[a] (3.977) | .03680[a] (2.448) | 22.250[c] (1.403) | | .801[a] | .725 |
| 81.32[a] (3.363) | −.62377[a] (2.465) | | .62281[a] (5.249) | .016583[c] (1.347) | −3.9717 (.356) | .0002209[a] (3.563) | .852[a] | .794 |

TABLE 6-3. (continued)

| Intercept | Eight-firm concentration ratio | Minimum efficient scale | Advertising/sales | Growth | Regional dummy | Absolute capital requirements | $R^2$ | Corrected $R^2$ |
|---|---|---|---|---|---|---|---|---|
| 102.6[a] (6.244) | −.83008[a] (3.446) | .006506 (.671) | .71697[a] (6.851) |  | 4.3149 (.288) | .002178[a] (3.170) | .836[a] | .774 |
| 105.4[a] (8.211) | −.80074[a] (3.796) | .004737 (.653) | .71695[a] (7.087) |  |  | .002236[a] (3.524) | .835[a] | .788 |
| 9.381 (.472) |  | .01486[b] (1.750) | .51558[a] (4.076) | .04025[a] (3.146) |  | .001128[b] (1.813) | .804[a] | .748 |
| 80.68[a] (3.455) | −.65650[a] (2.875) |  | .62307[a] (5.423) | .01602[c] (1.355) |  | .002192[a] (3.662) | .850[a] | .807 |
| 108.2[a] (9.117) | −.80253[a] (3.879) |  | .70893[a] (7.199) |  |  | .002330[a] (3.843) | .830[a] | .796 |
| 59.29[b] (1.940) | −.26509 (.972) |  | .59632[a] (3.847) | .02336[c] (1.483) |  |  | .706[a] | .648 |

*Note:* Figures in parentheses are *t* values. The significance of the regression coefficients is tested using a one-tail *t* test and the significance of the coefficients of multiple determination is tested using the *F* test.

[a] Coefficient is significant at the 99 percent level.
[b] Coefficient is significant at the 95 percent level.
[c] Coefficient is significant at the 90 percent level.

TABLE 6-4. Multiple Regression Equations Explaining Profit Rates: Nonconvenience Good Industries
$(n = 23)$

| Intercept | Eight-firm concentration ratio | Minimum efficient scale | Advertising/ sales | Growth | Absolute capital requirements | $R^2$ | Corrected $R^2$ |
|---|---|---|---|---|---|---|---|
| 77.38[b] (1.969) | .15305 (.244) | −.001317 (.155) | .22419 (.336) | .008886 (.340) | .0005110 (1.159) | .347 | .155 |
| 77.76[b] (2.068) | .12534 (.346) | | .21851 (.341) | .009190 (.371) | .0005193[c] (1.289) | .347[c] | .202 |
| 88.55[a] (4.195) | .16218 (.266) | −.0030369 (.133) | .35244 (.657) | | .00060095[b] (1.746) | .342[c] | .196 |
| 91.62[a] (4.519) | .25464 (.435) | −.002377 (.106) | | | .0005342[c] (1.649) | .327[c] | .220 |
| 90.39[a] (5.814) | .096044 (.278) | | .34930 (.669) | | .00062830[b] (2.336) | .342[c] | .238 |
| 83.94 | | | .32779 (.603) | .007319 (.310) | .0005968[b] (1.823) | .342[c] | .239 |

Note: Figures in parentheses are $t$ values. The significance of the regression coefficients is tested using a one-tail $t$ test and the significance of the coefficients of multiple determination is tested using the $F$ test.
[a] Coefficient is significant at the 99 percent level.
[b] Coefficient is significant at the 95 percent level.
[c] Coefficient is significant at the 90 percent level.

freedom.[15] For the convenience goods sample, the standard industrial organization model yields a very good fit indeed.

For the nonconvenience sample, however, the model performs quite
badly. The corrected $R^2$ of the model drops substantially to .16 in equation 1 (.24 for the best specification) indicating a very large proportion
of the variance in profits unexplained. The overall significance level of
the model is low. Advertising loses all significance and the magnitude of
its coefficient drops markedly. Similarly, the growth variable loses significance, and the concentration and scale variables perform poorly.[16]
The only variable retaining marginal significance is the measure of absolute capital requirements. The standard error of the estimate for the
nonconvenience sample is 2.8 rate of return percentage points versus
1.5 for the convenience sample.[17]

### Tests for Equivalence of Coefficients

These results lend strong confirmation to the model, and so it is instructive to analyze them in greater detail. Because the values of the
regression coefficients appear quite different, it is desirable to test the
null hypothesis that the regression coefficients are the same for the two
data sets. The simple $F$ test available for this purpose does not apply
here because the residual variance is strikingly different between the two
data sets, and the $F$ test assumes that the variance of the error term is
the same across both data sets. Alternative tests using the *estimated*
variance are available, but these promise no improvement over the simple $F$ test in showing that the coefficients are indeed different, because

15. When interpreting these results in the context of other industrial organization research it is important to remember the adage that if one has enough degrees
of freedom, anything is statistically significant. Many recent studies, where the
number of degrees of freedom is in the hundreds, are properly considered in this
light.

16. The low significance of the scale economies and concentration variables may
be due to collinearity as discussed below.

17. The means and standard deviations of selected sample characteristics are as
follows

|  | Convenience | | Nonconvenience | |
|---|---|---|---|---|
|  | Mean | Standard deviation | Mean | Standard deviation |
| Profit | 10.8% | 3.4% | 10.8% | 3.0% |
| Advertising to sales | 4.7% | 3.7% | 2.1% | 1.2% |
| Advertising interaction (identified below) | .1344D07 | .3068E07 | .1468D06 | .2118E06 |

using an estimated variance would further discount the results in the nonconvenience sample.[18]

In view of this difficulty a formal test was abandoned. The importance of the conclusion about advertising to my analysis motivated, however, an ad hoc procedure for testing this coefficient. The advertising coefficients in the lead equations in Tables 6–3 and 6–4 were compared using a one-tailed *t* test, as were the simple averages of the advertising coefficients of all equations presented in Tables 6–3 and 6–4 respectively. In both cases it was possible to reject the null hypothesis that the advertising coefficient for convenience goods was equal to the value of coefficient for nonconvenience goods at the 99 percent level of significance. This adds some additional confidence that these coefficients are significantly different.

It was possible to construct a test of the equality of variances in the two samples by adapting a procedure suggested by S. M. Goldfeld and Richard Quandt (1965). The residual sums of squares (*RSS*) in the two samples are independent and are distributed as chi-square. Therefore, $RSS_i/n$ are distributed as chi-square, where $n$ is the number of degress of freedom. We can construct an $F$ statistic by forming the quotient of $RSS/n$ for the two samples, which allows a test of the null hypothesis that the variances in the convenience and nonconvenience sample are the same.

Applying this test to equation 2 in Table 6–3 and equation 1 in Table 6–4, I was able to reject the null hypothesis that the variances were the same at the 99 percent level of significance. The applicability of the test depends on the variance of the dependent variable, since greater residual variance may simply be associated with greater variance in the dependent variable. The means and standard deviations of rate of return on equity in the two samples are as follows:

|  | Convenience goods | Nonconvenience goods |
|---|---|---|
| Mean | 10.80% | 10.80% |
| Standard deviation | 3.40% | 3.02% |

The means are the same; however, the variance in rate of return is actually less in nonconvenience goods. This strengthens the power of the test.

18. Several simple $F$ tests were made. It was not possible, however, to reject the hypothesis that the coefficients were the same across the two data sets, for individual coefficients or for the entire model. This is to be expected in view of the large residual variance in the nonconvenience sample.

Intercorrelations among Structural Variables

Table 6–5 presents the simple correlations between profit and the independent variables in the model. The simple correlations confirm the sharp differences between the two samples, primarily a dramatic decrease in the coefficient of the advertising variable and a reversal in the sign of the correlation between profits and concentration. In addition, capital requirements are significantly more correlated with profits in nonconvenience goods. The correlation coefficients for the full sample of consumer goods industries appear to be the result of an averaging process across the two very different subsamples.

The pattern of collinearity among the independent variables also differs greatly between samples as shown in Table 6–6, which also gives the multiple correlation coefficient among concentration, scale economies, and capital requirements. Comanor and Wilson and Esposito and Esposito cite this coefficient as evidence that collinearity among the three variables is high. Making the convenience-nonconvenience partitioning, the coefficient is seen to be markedly higher for nonconvenience goods.

In the nonconvenience goods sample, the regression coefficient for the concentration ratio is positive. Although the significance of the coefficient is low, this sign is confirmed by the correlation analysis. The very high degree of collinearity among the concentration, scale economies, capital requirements, and growth variables offers a partial explanation for the very low significance levels of these coefficients in the noncon-

TABLE 6-5.   Simple Correlation Coefficients of Profit and Market Structure Variables for Convenience Goods, Nonconvenience Goods and All Consumer Goods

| Market structure variable | Correlation with profits | | |
|---|---|---|---|
| | Convenience goods | Non-convenience goods | All consumer goods |
| Eight-firm concentration ratio | −.23 | .39 | .10 |
| Economies of scale | .05 | .08 | .07 |
| Absolute capital requirements | .29 | .56 | .42 |
| Growth | .64 | .47 | .55 |
| Advertising/sales | .77 | .06 | .48 |

TABLE 6-6.   Correlation Coefficients Among Market Structural Variables in the Convenience and Nonconvenience Samples[a]

| Market structure variable | Simple correlations | | | | |
|---|---|---|---|---|---|
| | Eight-firm concentration ratio | Minimum efficient scale | Capital require-ments | Growth | Advertising/ sales |
| *Convenience goods* | | | | | |
| Eight-firm concentration ratio | 1.000 | | | | |
| Minimum efficient scale | .094 | 1.000 | | | |
| Capital requirements | .448 | .238 | 1.000 | | |
| Growth | −.374 | .372 | −.034 | 1.000 | |
| Advertising/sales | .034 | −.107 | .047 | .500 | 1.000 |
| *Nonconvenience goods* | | | | | |
| Eight-firm concentration ratio | 1.000 | | | | |
| Minimum efficient scale | .724 | 1.000 | | | |
| Capital requirements | .504 | −.016 | 1.000 | | |
| Growth | .383 | −.023 | .664 | 1.000 | |
| Advertising/sales | .299 | .406 | −.179 | .265 | 1.000 |

[a] Multiple correlation coefficients for concentration, scale economies, and capital requirements: convenience goods .448; nonconvenience goods .889; all consumer goods .611.

venience sample. The advertising variable, however, is not strongly correlated with the other variables and hence this explanation for its poor performance does not apply.

In the convenience sample, collinearity is less serious than in the nonconvenience sample. The sign of the regression coefficient for concentration is negative, however, and the coefficient is quite significant. The negative sign matches that of the simple correlation coefficient. Since the sign of the regression coefficient and the simple correlation coefficient are positive for nonconvenience goods, it appears that the negative coefficient for concentration in the all consumer goods sample is due to the convenience good industries.

Comanor and Wilson suggest that the partial effect of concentration may be unimportant when introduced with other structural variables and note the collinearity between concentration and other variables.[19] Thus collinearity may be a possible explanation for the negative concentration coefficient in the convenience sample. My results, however, suggest that this explanation does not hold.[20] In the nonconvenience sample where collinearity is extremely high, the sign of the concentration coefficient is positive. In the convenience sample collinearity is relatively low while the coefficient of concentration remains negative and more significant. Hence it appears necessary to seek additional explanations for this puzzling result.

The Partial Effect of Concentration on Profits

My results provide some evidence relating to the question of whether the partial effect of concentration is important or whether concentration is largely explained by other variables. Comanor and Wilson take the latter view. Esposito and Esposito's results suggest the opposite. Esposito and Esposito report equations omitting separately and together variables measuring scale economies and capital requirements.[21] In the equation that omits capital requirements, the sign of the concentration variable changes from negative to positive, the coefficient of concentration becomes less significant, and the explanatory power of the equation decreases. With scale economies alone omitted, concentration becomes more significant but the coefficient remains negative and stable, and corrected $R^2$ does not change. When both are omitted, the concentration coefficient reverses sign from negative to positive and becomes slightly more significant, and the corrected $R^2$ falls.

These results are consistent with the hypothesis that collinearity between scale economies and concentration makes the concentration coefficient marginally less significant in the sample of Esposito and Esposito. The behavior of the equation when the capital requirements variable is omitted suggests, however, that the negative concentration coefficient is not the result of multicollinearity and that concentration is an important variable on its own. If collinearity were causing the negative sign, omitting capital requirements would make concentration more rather than less significant. That the concentration coefficient reverses in sign and the corrected $R^2$ falls suggests the presence of omitted variable bias in the concentration coefficient in those equations without capital

19. Comanor and Wilson (1967), p. 431.
20. As do Esposito and Esposito's (1971); see below.
21. Esposito and Esposito (1971), p. 347.

requirements. The bias in a regression coefficient where there is an omitted variable can be expressed as follows: [22]

$$E(\tilde{B}_1) = B_1 + B_2 b_{21}$$

where $\tilde{B}_1$ = the coefficient in the misspecified model
$B_1$ = coefficient in the true model
$B_2$ = coefficient of omitted variable
$b_{21}$ = regression coefficient of the included variable with the omitted variable

Since concentration and capital requirements are positively correlated and the sign of the capital requirements coefficient is positive, omitting capital requirements will produce a positive bias in the concentration coefficient. This is consistent with the shift in the concentration coefficient from negative to positive. Collinearity between the two variables probably contributes to the relatively low significance of the concentration coefficient. The stability of the negative sign of the concentration variable and its independent partial effect on profits are reinforced, however, by this argument.

My results reinforce the independent effect of concentration implied by Esposito and Esposito's results but suggest that this is due largely to the effect of concentration in the convenience sample. Table 6–7 presents multiple regression equations explaining profits for the convenience and nonconvenience samples which omit scale economies and capital requirements. In the convenience sample, omitting these variables provides an even stronger illustration of omitted variable bias; the concentration coefficient becomes less negative and less significant. In the nonconvenience sample, however, the classic symptoms of multicollinearity occur. As technical entry barriers (scale economies and capital requirements) are omitted, concentration becomes greatly more significant.

Perhaps a more interesting test of the partial influence of concentration is the ability of other structural variables to explain concentration. Table 6–8 presents regressions of concentration as the dependent variable on the other structural variables in the model. In the nonconvenience sample concentration is substantially explained by the technical entry barrier variables; scale economies and plant capital requirements. In the convenience sample, however, these variables explain very little of the variation in concentration. Capital requirements, the regional dummy variable and demand growth (with the expected negative sign)

---

22. See Rao and Miller (1971), pp. 61–63. In the absence of collinearity the biased coefficient will be a more efficient estimate. That it is not in Esposito and Esposito's results suggests that collinearity is also a problem.

TABLE 6-7. Multiple Regression Equations Explaining Profit Rates: Tests for Collinearity Through Omitting Collinear Variables

| Intercept | Eight-firm concentration ratio | Minimum efficient scale | Advertising/ sales | Demand growth | Regional dummy | Absolute capital requirements | $R^2$ | Corrected $R^2$ |
|---|---|---|---|---|---|---|---|---|
| | | | *Convenience goods* | | | | | |
| 14.65 (.452) | -.40346[c] (1,474) | .02665[b] (2.495) | .54961[a] (3.977) | .036799[b] (2.448) | 22.250[c] (1.403) | | .801[a] | .725 |
| 58.40[b] (1,875) | -.25645 (.819) | | .59620[a] (3.716) | .023507[c] (1.427) | -.9609 (.064) | | .706[a] | .623 |
| | | | *Nonconvenience goods* | | | | | |
| 44.21[c] (1.626) | .57747 (1.125) | -.010761 (.474) | -.18786 (.330) | .02700 (1.280) | | | .295 | .139 |
| 42.77[c] (1.616) | .38476 (1.255) | | -.30192 (.598) | .03252[b] (1.887) | | | .286 | .174 |

*Note:* Figures in parentheses are *t* values. The significance of the regression coefficients is tested using a **one-tail** *t* test and the significance of the coefficients of multiple determination is tested using the *F* test.

[a] Coefficient is significant at the 99 percent level.
[b] Coefficient is significant at the 95 percent level.
[c] Coefficient is significant at the 90 percent level.

TABLE 6-8. Multiple Regression Equations Explaining Concentration

| Units of eight-firm concentration | Intercept | Minimum efficient scale | Absolute capital requirements | Regional dummy | Growth | Advertising to sales | $R^2$ | Corrected $R^2$ |
|---|---|---|---|---|---|---|---|---|
| | | | Convenience goods | | | | | |
| Natural units | 49.23[a] (7.295) | -.0004983 (.058) | .001320[b] (1.958) | | | | .200 | .100 |
| Natural units | 23.41[c] (1.500) | .01039 (1.039) | .0007107 (1.023) | 26.347[b] (1.809) | | | .344 | .212 |
| Natural units | 66.70[a] (3.648) | | .0009979[a] (1.669) | 15.972[c] (1.456) | -.02347[b] (2.061) | .11922 (.984) | .460[b] | .306 |
| Natural units | 64.82[b] (2.189) | .0009366 (.083) | .0009694[a] (1.368) | 16.817 (1.101) | -.02291[c] (1.678) | .11718 (.915) | .461[b] | .253 |
| Natural units | -44.97 (1.187) | (log)[d] 5.5143 (1.230) | (log) 8.6978[b] (2.599) | | | | .336[b] | .253 |
| Log units | 2.299[a] (3.466) | (log) .080851 (1.029) | (log) .15132[b] (2.581) | | | | .322[b] | .237[e] |
| Natural units | 164.0 (1.153) | (log) 3.373 (.707) | (log) 8.7546[a] (2.652) | | (log) -27.212[a] (1.491) | (log) .49037 (.109) | .437[c] | .276 |

TABLE 6-8. (continued)

| Units of eight-firm concentration | Intercept | Minimum efficient scale | Absolute capital requirements | Regional dummy | Growth | Advertising to sales | $R^2$ | Corrected $R^2$ |
|---|---|---|---|---|---|---|---|---|
| *Nonconvenience goods* | | | | | | | | |
| Natural units | 32.09[a] (10.976) | .03251[a] (7.140) | .0004138[a] (5.028) | | | | .790[a] | .769 |
| Natural units | 26.33[b] (1.962) | .03070[a] (5.730) | .0004113[a] (3.056) | | .001781 (.182) | .17639 (.713) | .801[a] | .757 |
| Natural units | −41.42[a] (4.866) | (log) 6.6816[a] (5.142) | (log) 7.7093[a] (7.465) | | | | .855[a] | .840 |
| Natural units | −90.79 (1.279) | (log) 6.8639[a] (4.555) | (log) 7.3384[a] (6.121) | | .00928 (.697) | −.39580 (.100) | .859[a] | .827 |
| Log units | 1.788[a] (9.510) | (log) .16183[a] (5.639) | (log) .16070[a] (7.046) | | | | .855[a] | .840[e] |

*Note:* Figures in parentheses are $t$ values. The significance of the regression coefficients is tested using a one-tail $t$ test and the significance of the coefficients of multiple determination is tested using the $F$ test.

[a] Coefficient is significant at the 99 percent level.
[b] Coefficient is significant at the 95 percent level.
[c] Coefficient is significant at the 90 percent level.
[d] Independent variables entered in logarithmic form are shown by including (log) above the coefficient.
[e] $R^2$'s are not directly comparable with other equations, since the dependent variable is introduced in logarithmic form.

are all relatively significant. Yet even in the best equation the corrected $R^2$ is .31 compared to .84 in the nonconvenience sample. Thus it appears that the results of Comanor and Wilson stem largely from nonconvenience industries.

These results reinforce my earlier conclusion that the characteristics of convenience and nonconvenience goods are fundamentally different. While concentration appears to follow exogenous technical entry barriers in nonconvenience goods, these exert only minor influence in convenience goods where concentration appears to have a significant partial effect. Additional evidence of this property of the convenience sample is to be found in Table 6–3 where dropping the concentration variable worsens the fit significantly and decreases $R^2$.

Analysis of Residuals and Alternative Functional Forms

To conclude my analysis of the basic results, the residuals in the convenience and nonconvenience samples were examined in view of the heteroscedasticity observed in previous studies. In addition, alternative functional forms were tested. Comanor and Wilson find that small industries have larger residuals; Esposito and Esposito find that the more highly concentrated industries have larger residuals.[23] In view of these results the residuals from the lead equations in the convenience and nonconvenience samples were plotted against each of the suggested variables. The residuals did increase for smaller industries and more concentrated industries in the convenience sample. In the nonconvenience sample no discernable pattern was evident at all with regard to either variable, perhaps because of the presence of important omitted structural traits.

Weighted regressions were computed for all consumer goods, convenience goods and nonconvenience goods using both the weighting variables previously suggested. The weighted regressions for the convenience sample are shown in Tables 6–9 and 6–10; these are potentially significant in view of the pattern observed in the residuals. In none of the weighted regressions did the results change significantly from the linear results. In all cases $R^2$ increased, but this is inherent in the weighting procedure.[24] As is evident in Tables 6–9 and 6–10, the coefficient for the concentration ratio remained negative and stable.

23. Comanor and Wilson (1967), pp. 435–436; Esposito and Esposito (1970), pp. 349–351.

24. The dangers of indiscriminate use of the weighting procedure was clearly illustrated in the nonconvenience sample. Although none of the coefficients increased in significance and the plotting of residuals uncovered no heterosedastic pattern, the $R^2$ obtained jumped from .2 to .8.

TABLE 6-9. Multiple Regression Equations Explaining Profit Rates for Convenience Goods: Weighted Regressions Using Industry Size as the Weighting Variable

| Intercept | Eight-firm concentration ratio | Minimum efficient scale | Advertising/ sales | Growth | Regional dummy | Absolute capital requirements | $R^2$ |
|---|---|---|---|---|---|---|---|
| 53.877[b] (2.025) | −.63391[a] (2.682) | .012266 (1.235) | .56605[a] (5.486) | .027592[b] (2.407) | 6.4353 (.447) | .0018934[a] (3.769) | .943[a] |
| 59.012[b] (2.539) | −.59144[a] (2.822) | .009243 (1.313) | .56921[a] (5.708) | .02705[b] (2.450) | | .001968[a] (4.285) | .942[a] |
| 69.173[a] (3.078) | −.59539[a] (2.771) | | .58640[a] (5.785) | .02260[b] (2.097) | | .002097[a] (4.559) | .934[a] |
| 8.7501 (.479) | | .0095287 (1.106) | .45520[a] (4.080) | .04426[a] (3.930) | | .001421[a] (2.790) | .906[a] |

*Note:* Figures in parentheses are $t$ values. The significance of the regression coefficients is tested using a one-tail $t$ test and the significance of the coefficients of multiple determination is tested using the $F$ test.

[a] Coefficient is significant at the 99 percent level.
[b] Coefficient is significant at the 95 percent level.
[c] Coefficient is significant at the 90 percent level.

TABLE 6-10. Multiple Regression Equations Explaining Profit Rates for Convenience Goods: Weighted Regressions Using Eight-firm Concentration as the Weighting Variable

| Intercept | Dichotomous eight-firm concentration ratio | Minimum efficient scale | Advertising/ sales | Growth | Regional dummy | Absolute capital requirements | $R^2$ |
|---|---|---|---|---|---|---|---|
| 7.3047 (.333) | −16.550[c] (1.395) | .016947[b] (1.969) | .51566[a] (4.658) | .04096[a] (3.997) | 3.5154 (.343) | .0018741[a] (2.796) | .958[a] |
| 6.7326 (.434) | | .015667[b] (2.491) | .48904[a] (4.554) | .04341[a] (4.697) | | .001774[a] (2.904) | .951[a] |
| 41.486[a] (2.791) | −16.438 (1.253) | | .55503[a] (4.613) | .03043[a] (3.151) | −10.21 (1.228) | .002116[a] (2.905) | .945[a] |
| 12.436 (.802) | −16.155[c] (1.417) | .01494[b] (2.451) | .52037[a] (4.907) | .03976[a] (4.279) | | .001957[a] (3.240) | .958[a] |
| 3.5487 (.157) | | .01689[b] (1.894) | .48573[a] (4.318) | .04420[a] (4.275) | 2.1232 (.201) | .0017212[b] (2.513) | .951[a] |

*Note:* Figures in parentheses are $t$ values. The significance of the regression coefficients is tested using a one-tail $t$ test and the significance of the coefficients of multiple determination is tested using the $F$ test.

[a] Coefficient is significant at the 99 percent level.
[b] Coefficient is significant at the 95 percent level.
[c] Coefficient is significant at the 90 percent level.

The significance of the coefficients in the convenience model was improved slightly, the growth variable showing the greatest improvement.[25]

To complete a general analysis of the results various alternative functional forms were tested. Theory is not clear with regard to the issue of functional forms. It is possible to argue, as Weiss does, a multiplicative relation between concentration and entry barriers.[26] Plausible arguments also suggest that individual entry barriers depend on the values of other barriers (suggesting a multiplicative relation). Alternatively, it can be argued that overall barriers are all that counts, and thus the relationship is additive. A further problem is that many of the structural variables are already in ratio form ($A/S$, growth, $MES$). Hence a logarithmic transformation may be redundant.

My sentiments lie with the linear model in view of the lack of a clear theoretical mandate to the contrary. This is generally supported by the tests with log-log form, semi-log form, and various attempts to transform subsets of the structural variable in the model.[27] In no case was the pattern of results changed. In the convenience goods sample the linear form was consistently superior to all transformed equations. The negative concentration coefficient was insensitive to all transformations. In the nonconvenience sample, the log-log form and the semi-log form performed marginally better, primarily because of a slight improvement in the significance of the capital requirements and growth variables. These results are shown in Table 6–11. It is evident, however, that the improvement in explained variance was minor.[28]

### Summary and Implications

Closer analysis of the results has reinforced the striking differences between the convenience and nonconvenience samples. These differences are not affected by weighting or changes in functional forms. Nor are they sensitive to reclassification of industries which may be controversial for one reason or another. The results give strong confirmation to my theory. The standard industrial organizational model is very successful in explaining profits for convenience goods and the advertising variable is highly significant and importantly adds to explained

25. No change in the pattern of the results was observed in weighted regressions for the nonconvenience sample. The coefficients of all variables except capital requirements remained nonsignificant.

26. Weiss (1972), pp. 376–378.

27. A possibility attempted was to enter entry barrier variables in log form and variables measuring rivalry in linear form, and vice versa.

28. The shift in sign for the concentration coefficient is probably explained by collinearity. At any rate the significance level remains low.

TABLE 6-11. Multiple Regression Equations Explaining Profit Rates: Double Log and Semilog Functional Forms

| Units of profit rate | Intercept | Eight-firm concentration ratio (log) | Minimum efficient scale (log) | Advertising/ sales (log) | Growth (log) | Absolute capital requirements (log) | $R^2$ | Corrected $R^2$ |
|---|---|---|---|---|---|---|---|---|
| | | | *Convenience goods* | | | | | |
| Logarithmic | 1.996 (1.003) | −.42594[b] (2.386) | .083033[c] (1.498) | .16737[a] (3.218) | .31501[c] (1.367) | .12255[b] (2.622) | .737[a] | .636[d] |
| Natural | −399.6[c] (1.722) | −20.666 (1.080) | 10.283[c] (1.568) | 17.173[a] (3.024) | 57.042[b] (2.177) | 6.4953[c] (1.580) | .733[a] | .630 |
| | | | *Nonconvenience goods* | | | | | |
| Logarithmic | 2.509[c] (1.379) | −.23868 (.891) | .02488 (.434) | −.003752 (.038) | .30661 (1.189) | .09229[b] (1.782) | .340 | .147[d] |
| Natural | −195.7 (.894) | −30.453 (.945) | 4.1847 (.606) | −2.4334 (.203) | 43.171[c] (1.391) | 11.933[b] (1.918) | .392 | .213 |
| Natural | −235.3 (1.178) | | | | 39.794[c] (1.407) | 6.9300[b] (2.137) | .354[a] | .290 |

*Note:* Figures in parentheses are $t$ values. The significance of the regression coefficients is tested using a one-tail $t$ test and the significance of the coefficients of multiple determination is tested using the $F$ test.

[a] Coefficient is significant at the 99 percent level.

[b] Coefficient is significant at the 95 percent level.

[c] Coefficient is significant at the 90 percent level.

[d] $R^2$'s are not directly comparable with other equations since the dependent variable is introduced in logarithmic form.

variance. The model is quite weak in explaining profits for nonconvenience goods and the coefficient of the traditional advertising variable is much smaller and not significant. These results are in accord with my theoretical prediction that advertising is not as important in nonconvenience goods as it is in convenience goods, and that substantial noise is introduced into the model by misspecification of the advertising variable, omitted product differentiation variables, and intraindustry strategic variation in nonconvenience goods.

It seems clear that previous empirical work in consumer goods industries (and in all-industry structure-performance testing as well) has mixed two very different samples. The results obtained in previous structure-performance tests represent a curious averaging of these two diverse groups. As notable examples, the significance of $A/S$ is due entirely to the convenience sample while the relationship between concentration and other structural variables is due to a great extent to the nonconvenience sample. These results reflect the dominance of advertising over the technical sources of entry barriers in convenience industries suggested by the theory. The danger that this suggests in using the results of previous work to interpret and analyze specific industries is clear.

### Extensions of the Empirical Model

The results presented above have emphasized the model tested by Comanor and Wilson. Several extensions of this basic model are possible, however, and are indicated in view of the poor performance in the nonconvenience goods sample and the puzzling negative coefficient for the concentration ratio in the convenience sample. In addition, Chapter 5 suggests some modifications in the specification of the advertising variable. These extensions, not all of which were successful, are reported below.

#### Deflated Growth Rates and the Growth-Profits Relation

The industry growth in demand variable used in the equations presented above measures industry growth in dollar sales over the seven year period from 1958–65.[29] An alternative specification of the growth variable is to measure real growth over the period.

While the industry growth variable is a common hill on the landscape of structure-performance studies, surprisingly little attention has been given to its theoretical underpinnings. There are a number of interpretations of the growth-profits relation. One posits that high growth implies difficulty in adjusting capacity. High growth industries will have

---

29. This type of measure, with varying time periods, is used in all known studies incorporating a demand growth variable.

insufficient capacity and prices and profits will be bid up.[30] R. E. Caves has pointed out that imperfect adjustment may in part be due to growth different from expectations rather than growth per se. High but anticipated growth may still imply high profits, however, in the face of capital market imperfections and long lead times for building capacity.

Another hypothesis linking growth to profits is that growth effectively reduces barriers to entry. This would imply a negative growth-profits relation. A third hypothesis is that growth affects market rivalry. High growth may blunt the tendency toward competition for market share within an industry, since firms can maintain their shares and still increase in size. Formally, this argument also assumes that firms have some desired or satisfactory rate of growth. But this desired rate of growth may be due to internal constraints on growth such as management or capital, as well as to managerial utility maximization.[31] The growth-rivalry hypothesis would predict a positive relation between growth and profits.

While I have not exhausted the possible growth-profits hypotheses, it is apparent that they yield inconsistent sign predictions. The results of empirical testing with the growth variable have unanimously found its impact on profits to be positive, however. The distinction between real growth and nominal growth may allow us to begin to discriminate between the leading hypotheses predicting the observed positive relation.[32]

Real growth would seem to be the appropriate measure of industry growth under the capacity adjustment hypothesis, since the constraints on capacity clearly reflect growth in units sold rather than dollar sales. Dollar growth may be the more appropriate measure of growth for the rivalry hypothesis. If investors and management are primarily judging performance in terms of dollar sales, then the posited blunting of market share competition which accompanies high growth is appropriately proxied by dollar sales growth. Casual observation suggests that dollar sales are seldom translated in real sales by the financial community, except sporadically during the recent period of high inflation rates. On the other hand, internal constraints to growth may be most properly proxied by real growth.

Table 6–12 represents regression equations substituting real growth, constructed in the manner detailed in the Technical Appendix, for nominal growth. These results support the nominal growth hypothesis. For

30. See Hall and Weiss (1967), p. 323.
31. See Penrose (1959) for a discussion of internal constraints to growth.
32. The positive empirical relation could of course reflect the net effect of causal forces in both directions.

TABLE 6-12. Multiple Regression Equations Explaining Profit Rates: Results Incorporating Real Growth in Demand

| Intercept | Eight-firm concentration ratio | Minimum efficient scale | Advertising/ sales | Real growth in demand | Regional dummy | Absolute capital requirements | $R^2$ | Corrected $R^2$ |
|---|---|---|---|---|---|---|---|---|
| *Convenience goods* | | | | | | | | |
| 72.62[b] (2.597) | −.69778[a] (2.732) | .01153 (1.131) | .63981[a] (5.433) | .017185 (1.307) | 4.1918 (.287) | .001930[a] (2.777) | .857[a] | .785 |
| *Nonconvenience goods* | | | | | | | | |
| 80.27[b] (2.259) | −.15598 (.249) | −.002681 (.114) | .27062 (.439) | .006676 (.294) | | .0005344 (1.273) | .346 | .153 |

*Note:* Figures in parentheses are *t* values. The significance of the regression coefficients is tested using a one-tail *t* test and the significance of the coefficients of multiple determination is tested using the *F* test.

[a] Coefficient is significant at the 99 percent level.
[b] Coefficient is significant at the 95 percent level.
[c] Coefficient is significant at the 90 percent level.

both convenience and nonconvenience goods, the real growth variable is less significant and $R^2$ declines (for comparison see the results presented in Tables 6–3 and 6–4). This effect is most noticeable in convenience goods where growth is an important variable.

Nonhousehold Sales

The classification of industries as consumer goods industries is based on the majority of industry sales. Many consumer goods industries, however, sell a significant portion of their output to other manufacturers, government, and institutions. The nature of such nonhousehold buyers[33] is different from the consumer buyers, although it is difficult to generalize regarding these buyers and to formulate unambiguous hypotheses about how they are likely to affect performance. On the one hand, it may be argued that the nonhousehold buyer is akin to the industrial purchasing agent, buying carefully and in relatively large quantities. This would suggest that, since all other conditions of supply (in the model) are constant, sales to nonhouseholds would be less profitable. Industries such as sugar and optical and medical goods would serve as prototypes for this hypothesis. On the other hand, the nature of most goods where the majority of sales are to the household is such that they are a minor input to the production process of other manufacturers (paint, electric lighting, tires). Hence the nonhousehold buyer would behave in much the same way as the household buyer, perhaps purchasing with even less care, since the items would represent such a small part of total purchases. This would argue that nonhousehold sales would be equally or more profitable to household sales. The cost savings of larger size orders from nonhousehold buyers might accrue to the manufacturer as well, at least offering more bargaining latitude with such buyers. These arguments would suggest that in addition to the straightforward bargaining implications, the extent of nonhousehold sales may also indicate something about the nature of the product. In producer goods, technical product characteristics play a major part in the purchase decision. The consumer, however, is in general not as able to assess technical characteristics as the industrial buyer. His behavior is more heavily influenced by advertising and other selling activities.[34] Those industries with large nonhousehold sales tend to be those where technical characteristics which might be of great importance to the nonhousehold buyer are present; in any case the argument suggests that the nonhousehold buyer will value technical characteristics more than household buyers.

33. Consumers will be used synonymously with households.
34. This may be optimal, given search and information costs.

At the very least including a measure of nonhousehold sales will control for a spurious element in the structure-performance relation. However, one can perhaps be more systematic in predicting the expected sign of the variable. The regression plane in consumer goods industries is dominated by the influence of advertising. To the extent that technical characteristics and nonadvertising (and unmeasured) selling expenditures lead to a rate of return higher than that which the pure consumer goods industry with the measured level of advertising would earn, the profits for industries with substantial nonhousehold sales will be understated.[35]

Data were available in the 1958 Census of Manufacturers to allow the construction of a series showing percent of nonhousehold sales.[36] This data was apparently unavailable in 1963, although it appears to have been tabulated in 1967. Despite the apparent lack of 1963 figures, however, the percent of nonhousehold sales was felt to be a relatively stable characteristic over time, certainly within the tolerance of the data (see the Technical Appendix). There are two apparent alternatives for testing with this data. One is to introduce the percent of nonhousehold sales as a separate structural variable. The other is to adjust the advertising variable. The latter alternative is based on the following argument. If advertising is primarily influential over and directed toward household buyers, then the ratio of advertising to sales should be adjusted to remove from the denominator nonhousehold sales. The problem with this is that nonhousehold sales may not yield the same rate of return as household sales, in fact I have argued that they will not in general. It may be most correct then, when adjusting $A/S$, to also include the percent nonhousehold sales as a separate variable.

Table 6–13 presents the results of tests incorporating both these alternative formulations. The simple correlation between the percent nonhousehold sales and profits is $-.07$ in convenience goods and $+.25$ in nonconvenience goods. The variable is not importantly correlated with other structural variables in the model. The percent nonhousehold sales performs very well as a structural variable. In the convenience goods sample it is significant and positive. The introduction of the variable improves the fit of the regression equation, most coefficients gaining markedly in significance. The overall $R^2$ increases from .813 to .854. In contrast, the adjusted advertising variable offers no improvement over the unadjusted version, while introducing it together with

35. Of course it could go the other way, although my arguments suggest this direction of bias.
36. Construction of the series is detailed in the Technical Appendix.

TABLE 6-13. Multiple Regression Equations Explaining Profit Rates: Results Incorporating Percent Nonhousehold Sales and Adjusted Advertising to Sales Ratio

| Intercept | Eight-firm concentration ratio | Minimum efficient scale | Advertising/ sales | Adjusted advertising/ sales | Growth | Regional dummy | Absolute capital requirements | Percent non-household | $R^2$ | Corrected $R^2$ |
|---|---|---|---|---|---|---|---|---|---|---|
| *Convenience goods* | | | | | | | | | | |
| 49.89[b] (1.869) | −.65615[a] (3.066) | .01275[c] (1.453) | .63197[a] (6.094) | | .02540[b] (2.189) | 3.6704 (.290) | .002006[a] (3.367) | .93531[b] (2.069) | .910[a] | .854 |
| 51.34[c] (1.701) | −.60514[b] (2.515) | .014483[c] (1.467) | | .55409[a] (5.124) | .02606[b] (1.994) | 7.5452 (.540) | .001802[a] (2.721) | | .875[a] | .812 |
| 49.04[c] (1.759) | −.62134[b] (2.797) | .01259[c] (1.372) | | .58129[a] (5.757) | .02648[b] (2.196) | 2.2192 (.168) | .002013[a] (3.233) | .82537[c] (1.760) | .902[a] | .840 |
| (log)[d] −404.5[b] (2.117) | (log) −31.700[b] (1.872) | (log) 9.6245[b] (1.878) | (log) 17.858[a] (3.705) | | (log) 58.342[a] (2.688) | | (log) 10.723[b] (2.410) | (log) 6.7472[c] (1.475) | .821[a] | .732 |

TABLE 6-13. (continued)

| Intercept | Eight-firm concentration ratio | Minimum efficient scale | Advertising/ sales | Adjusted advertising/ sales | Growth | Regional dummy | Absolute capital requirements | Percent non-household | $R^2$ | Corrected $R^2$ |
|---|---|---|---|---|---|---|---|---|---|---|
| | | | | *Nonconvenience goods* | | | | | | |
| 51.60[c] | −.47201 | .015492 | −.71247 | | .03285 | | .0005905[c] | 1.0831[b] | .489[c] | .298 |
| (1.363) | (.734) | (.667) | (.114) | | (1.246) | | (1.463) | (2.112) | | |
| 84.15[b] | .0014309 | −.0009220 | | .49829 | .003428 | | .0006602[c] | | .380 | .197 |
| (2.249) | (.002) | (.040) | | (1.008) | (.147) | | (1.541) | | | |
| 52.64[c] | −.47438 | .015128 | | −.002253 | .031733 | | .0006052[c] | 1.0826[b] | .489[c] | .297 |
| (1.352) | (.738) | (.651) | | (.042) | (1.188) | | (1.506) | (1.850) | | |

*Note:* Figures in parentheses are *t* values. The significance of the regression coefficients is tested using a one-tail *t* test and the significance of the coefficients of multiple determination is tested using the *F* test.

[a] Coefficient is significant at the 99 percent level.
[b] Coefficient is significant at the 95 percent level.
[c] Coefficient is significant at the 90 percent level.
[d] Independent variables entered in logarithmic form are shown by including (log) above the coefficient.

percent nonhousehold sales yields improvement but less than that obtained by introducing the percent of nonhousehold sales alone.

In the nonconvenience sample, percent nonhousehold sales is again positive and quite significant. The fit of the entire equation is greatly improved: the overall corrected $R^2$ jumps from .155 to .298. The introduction of the percent nonhousehold sales variable causes both the concentration coefficient and the advertising coefficient to become negative. Neither of these coefficients is significant, however, and the fact that the extreme collinearity is present in the nonconvenience sample leads to the *a priori* expectation of unstable coefficients. The adjusted advertising to sales ratio performs somewhat better than the unadjusted ratio in the nonconvenience sample, yet the improvement of $R^2$ is small. As in the convenience sample, the best specification appears to be one including the percent nonhousehold sales as a separate structural variable.

In the convenience sample, the results appear to support the hypothesis that the consumer goods regression plane underestimates the market power of industries with substantial nonhousehold sales. In convenience goods, the two industries with the highest percentage of nonhousehold sales are grain mill products and (by far the most important) sugar. In both cases the residuals from the lead equation in Table 6–3 indicate that the standard model underestimates rate of return (sugar is the convenience good industry with the largest residual). Reestimating the model with percent nonhousehold sales in both cases all but eliminates the residual. In the nonconvenience sample, 10 industries have substantial nonhousehold sales. Of these, the standard model underestimates rate of return in 6; overestimates in 2 and is quite close in 2. Of the 6 underestimates, 4 are substantially improved and 2 remain about the same when percent household sales is introduced. Of these latter 2, one is photo equipment where general observation would suggest that one basis for the underestimate may be the failure to include the effect of patent protection. The two industries with large nonhousehold sales for which the standard model overestimated rate of return are tires and optical/medical goods. In both cases extremely powerful nonhousehold buyers may be bargaining down rate of return.[37] Inclusion of the percent nonhousehold sales variable has little or no effect on the residuals in these two industries.

Specification of Advertising

Chapter 5 presented a series of arguments which suggested that, in addition to manufacturer-retailer effects, the impact of a dollar of ad-

---

37. In tires these buyers are the motor vehicle producers, in optical/medical goods they are licensed optemetrists, opticians, and medical personnel.

vertising outlay on performance was different in convenience and non-convenience goods. Testing the two samples separately would, in theory, incorporate this notion. Indeed the performance of the advertising variable is dramatically different in the two samples. A further important reason for the low significance of the advertising variable in the non-convenience sample is suggested by the arguments in Chapter 5, namely that the variation in the factors determining the efficiency of advertising and the buyer's responsiveness to it seem to be greater in nonconvenience goods. This would introduce yet another element of noise into the advertising-profits relation.

*Specifying advertising as a structural variable.* Virtually all empirical work (with one known exception) has utilized the advertising to sales ratio $(A/S)$ to measure advertising as a structural variable.[38] The theory in Chapter 5 suggests that there is little theoretical basis for the use of $A/S$ alone to measure the effect of advertising on performance, although practically it is justified in some cases. $A/F$ is, as Comanor and Wilson recognize, an appropriate variable for measuring the absolute capital requirements and economies-of-scale barriers to entry which arise from advertising. The relationship of $A/F$ to absolute capital requirements is obvious. The capital requirements barriers due to advertising are dependent on the total outlays required by the firm in the same way as capital requirements for production are. The economies of scale barrier due to advertising consists of a threshold effect, as modified in Chapter 5, and economies in purchasing media of given quality or in purchasing differing quality media. The ability to obtain media economies of both types clearly relates to the total advertising outlay which is made by the firm. The operation of the threshold effect is through the essentially fixed cost of advertising required regardless of scale where media are indivisible. Clearly the total outlay on advertising captures the threshold concept, while the use of $A/S$ understates this threshold by assuming implicitly that media are divisible. If the entrant can utilize local or regional media and enter one market at a time, this may be possible. In the case where the entrant must utilize regional or

38. Comanor and Wilson (1967), p. 428, construct in addition to $A/S$ a second variable; advertising per firm for the largest firms accounting for 50 percent of industry sales $(A/F)$. Comanor and Wilson discuss their specifications as follows (p. 428): "It is useful to examine the absolute volume of advertising expenditures by existing firms as well as the advertising-sales ratio. The latter variable probably provides a good indication of the absolute cost disadvantage of the new entrant at small scales of entry, but it is likely to be a less accurate index of the economies of scale and absolute capital requirements effects of advertising." In their empirical results, Comanor and Wilson find $A/S$ a superior variable to $A/F$ in all specifications.

national media, the threshold effect is severe and $A/S$ alone fails to capture it.

As a measure of advertising capital requirements and economies of scale, $A/S$ can actually be misleading. Consider two firms with equal $A/S$ and assume one is in the appliance industry, the other producing watches and clocks. Because the unit price of appliances is so great, a 2 percent $A/S$ for an appliance firm may represent $10 million in threshold advertising outlays (or capital requirements) while 2 percent $A/S$ for a watch company may represent but $1 million in advertising outlays. Unless the large firms in all industries are the same size, which is clearly not empirically the case, $A/S$ will understate advertising barriers for the industries with relatively large leading firms.

Comanor and Wilson assert that $A/S$ provides a good indication of the absolute cost disadvantages facing the potential entrant. Although $A/S$ may capture some of this effect, the relevant figure based on theory would seem to be the total advertising outlay required to overcome the advantage of existing firms or the difference between $A/S$ for existing firms and $A/S$ for the potential entrant. That $A/S$ is approximately equal in the two industries is not necessarily suggestive of the difficulty of a potential dairy products producer in raising $100,000 to overcome buyer inertia relative to a potential motor vehicle producer raising $20 million. Comanor and Wilson's view here is apparently linked to Doyle's assertion that $A/S$ shows the share of resources the firm spends on advertising.[39] Somehow the $100,000 required by the dairy should loom as large as the $20 million required by the auto producer because both represent an equal share of resources. Perhaps this is partially correct. But that shakedown advertising losses in a large industry of $20 million are a small percent of sales is small comfort to the potential entrant who must finance entry. To the extent that the size of advertising as a proportion of sales proxies the cost advantage due to advertising scale economies, $A/S$ is an appropriate measure. As we have seen, however, $A/S$ is not fully satisfactory for these purposes. Perhaps the ideal measure of advertising is the absolute volume of advertising required to establish a minimum viable position in the industry, which implies a nontrivial market share, plus some measure of the cost disadvantage. Hence theory suggests some combination of $A/F$ and $A/S$.

I have thus far considered the measurement of advertising entry barriers and focused on conventional entry theory. My expanded view presented in Chapter 5 identified further important effects of advertising on performance through the rivalry effect and through its impact on

39. Doyle (1968), p. 395.

bargaining power. I have also presented some extensions of the concept of advertising induced entry barriers. The choice of a structural variable measuring advertising must encompass these new ideas as well.

In measuring the rivalry effect of advertising, $A/F$ once again appears to be the most appropriate structural measure. As I have argued earlier, advertising's impact on product differentiation depends on the advertising messages received by the relevant consumers. The effectiveness of these messages depends in turn on the consumer's responsiveness to advertising information. Advertising dollars are not equally effective in influencing product differentiation across industries. The base figure for measuring advertising's effect on product differentiation is clearly total advertising outlay per firm. This must then be corrected for differences in relevant geographic market size and breadth, media segmentability, the nature of the product, and so on. That market size is important can be seen with the following example. Compare a dairy serving a small region to a national producer of cosmetics. The dairy presumably uses local and regional media. If both firms spend an identical amount of advertising, the outlay per relevant household would be considerably greater for the dairy, since its denominator would be the number of households in the region, while the cosmetic firm's would be the number of households nationally. An analogous problem occurs when, though geographic market size is similar, media segmentability varies.[40]

As a first step, we can utilize the convenience/nonconvenience dichotomy to control for differences in advertising's efficiency and differences in the buyer responsiveness function. Even doing this, however, problems remain due to the local and regional industries. This will not be a problem in nonconvenience industries because no nonconvenience industries are substantially regional or local. Among convenience goods, however,

---

40. The problems in the use of $A/S$ are illustrated in studies by Doyle and Else. Doyle (1968) finds that $A/S$ is strongly negatively related to industry sales and unit product price (p. 407). Else (1966) also finds $A/S$ to be strongly and negatively related to sales (p. 95). Industries with large sales, then, have lower $A/S$. But this has little to do with barriers. Rather, it reflects the problems from relating advertising to sales rather than to the household. There is no reason why an industry with twice the sales and spending twice as much on advertising as another industry should be considered equal to the industry in terms of the effects of advertising.

If the relevant concept is adjusted total advertising outlay per household, then, assuming the adjustments for advertising's efficiency and the nature of the product do not vary systematically with industry sales, advertising to sales is quite likely to decrease with industry sales. Yet this has little to do with advertising barriers or advertising's effect on product differentiation.

many industries are strongly local or regional. This not only will affect the use of $A/F$ to capture the rivalry effect of advertising, but it will also cloud the use of $A/F$ to measure entry barriers under certain conditions. If all firms in a local or regional industry are not local or regional, then $A/F$ data taken from perhaps the few national firms in the industry will overstate capital barriers and the threshold effect to the extent that nonnational firms are important in the industry.[41]

The problem of segmentability of media also survives the dichotomization into convenience and nonconvenience industries. If, based on the nature of their products and buyers, some industries utilize more locally or regionally segmentable media, then for these industries advertising barriers to entry will be overstated. Many such industries will be local or regional, which makes them self-correcting. However, those other industries where use of segmentable media such as newspapers, local radio, and local television is heavy require correction. It may be possible to compute the percentage advertising budget spent on national television, or on national television and magazines, to introduce as a correcting variable. (This problem is again probably less significant for nonconvenience goods.)

For convenience goods, the problem of differing market size remains; the use of $A/F$ in convenience goods is compromised. One possible way to adjust for this is to return to $A/S$. Among convenience goods, variations in unit price and purchase frequency are relatively small across products, thus differences in the size of leading firms are probably less than in nonconvenience goods. Firm sales may be a good index of "nationalness" or market size. Thus $A/S$ may, in convenience goods, correct for some of the measurement problems in $A/F$. In addition, there is some independent justification for the use of $A/S$ as noted above.

This discussion suggests that both $A/S$ and $A/F$ are the appropriate measures of advertising. $A/F$ would *a priori* seem to have the dominant effect, though some combination of $A/F$ and $A/S$ would be optimal. Measurement problems, however, compromise the use of $A/F$ in convenience goods. There $A/S$ alone may be the superior measure. The biases in using $A/S$ alone are least serious in convenience goods as well. In nonconvenience goods, $A/F$ is relatively free of measurement problems and should exert a powerful influence, and some combination of $A/F$ and $A/S$ should prove optimal.

Comanor and Wilson tested advertising per firm across their sample

41. Weiss (1972) makes the interesting point that in local and regional industries, the more differentiated firms tend to have wider market areas, the disadvantage in transport costs being overcome by the product differentiation advantage.

of 41 consumer goods industries, finding it generally weaker than the advertising to sales ratio.[42] This result is not surprising given our theory. The problems with advertising per firm in convenience goods are severe. As the results above indicate, the significance of advertising to sales in all consumer goods industries sample is almost solely due to the convenience goods industries. Hence testing advertising per firms over all consumer goods industries would mix greatly unequal groups and the performance of the variable would be likely to suffer.

*Tests of alternative specifications.* The theory provides a clear mandate for testing specifications including advertising per firm separately in the convenience and nonconvenience samples. In view of this advertising per firm was tested in the two samples, as well as two specifications of the joint effect of $A/F$ and $A/S$. The first specification was simply including both $A/F$ and $A/S$ in the regression model. The second was an interaction variable which was the product of advertising to sales $(A/S)$ and advertising per firm $(A/F)$. This is termed *advertising interaction.*

Tables 6–14 and 6–15 present correlation matrices and multiple regression equations incorporating the alternative specifications of the advertising variable. The results are striking. I will first discuss the performance of advertising per firm. With regard to the simple correlation analysis, $A/F$ is much less correlated with profit than $A/S$ in the convenience sample as expected. In the nonconvenience sample, however, $A/F$ is much more correlated with profits. These results carry over to the multiple regression equations shown in Table 6–15. In the convenience sample, $A/F$ proves to be a far inferior variable to $A/S$ as expected. In the nonconvenience sample, however, $A/F$ produces a dramatic improvement in the fit of the model. (Corrected $R^2$ jumps from .16 to .52). $A/F$ is highly significant in all specifications. The results thus strongly support the theoretical appropriateness of $A/F$ in nonconvenience goods.

Introducing $A/F$ leads to severe collinearity problems in the nonconvenience good sample, however. As is evident from Table 6–13, $A/F$ is highly correlated with concentration, capital requirements and to a lesser extent with growth and economies of scale. The multiple correlation coefficient between $A/F$ and these variables is .88. Concentration, scale economies, and capital requirements are also highly intercorrelated in the nonconvenience sample. Hence the nonconvenience equa-

---

42. Comanor and Wilson (1967), p. 431. I tested advertising per firm over the entire sample of 42 consumer good industries and obtained very similar results to those reported by Comanor and Wilson.

TABLE 6-14. Correlation Coefficients Among Market Structure Variables Incorporating Alternative Specifications of the Advertising Variable

| Measure of advertising | Profit | Eight-firm concentration ratio | Minimum efficient scale | Advertising/sales | Advertising per firm | Growth | Regional dummy | Absolute capital requirements | Percent non-household |
|---|---|---|---|---|---|---|---|---|---|
| *Convenience goods* | | | | | | | | | |
| Advertising/sales | .773 | | | | | | | | |
| Advertising/firm | .273 | .268 | .051 | .491 | | .062 | .058 | .199 | −.033 |
| Interaction | .340 | .237 | −.032 | .565 | .972 | .147 | .103 | .105 | −.009 |
| *Nonconvenience goods* | | | | | | | | | |
| Advertising/sales | .064 | | | | | | | | |
| Advertising/firm | .741 | .740 | .366 | .053 | | .550 | | .778 | .228 |
| Interaction | .647 | .737 | .677 | .423 | .803 | .361 | | .330 | .278 |

*Note:* Multiple correlation of advertising per firm with eight-firm concentration ratio, minimum efficient scale, growth, and absolute capital requirements: .878[a]

[a] Coefficient is significant at the 99 percent level.

TABLE 6-15a.  Multiple Regression Equations Explaining Profit Rates Incorporating Alternative Specifications of the Advertising Variable

| Intercept | Eight-firm concentration ratio | Minimum efficient scale | Advertising/ sales | Advertising/ firm | Advertising interaction | Growth | Regional dummy | Absolute capital requirements | Percent non-household | $R^2$ | Corrected $R^2$ |
|---|---|---|---|---|---|---|---|---|---|---|---|
| | | | | | | *Convenience goods* | | | | | |
| 3.329 (.070) | −.46186 (1.127) | .02351c (1.440) | | .0002831 (1.223) | | .05932a (3.195) | 19.304 (.827) | .0012316 (1.116) | | .645b | .468 |
| 52.90c (1.702) | −.60838b (2.416) | .01459c (1.439) | .62959a (4.612) | −.00009174 (.563) | | .02431b (1.783) | 8.6404 (.599) | .001816b (2.650) | | .879a | .302 |
| .7920 (.016) | −.46368 (1.095) | .02278 (1.345) | | .0002842 (1.188) | | .06046a (3.127) | 16.842 (.683) | .0013267 (1.146) | .42180 (.482) | .625c | .432 |
| 51.38b (1.897) | −.62542a (2.848) | .01212c (1.360) | .68474a (5.623) | −.0001220 (.856) | | .02386b (2.009) | 2.0167 (.156) | .002086a (3.418) | .97480b (2.119) | .917a | .850 |
| 13.22 (.280) | −.50883 (1.277) | .022923c (1.452) | | | .0000030785c (1.566) | .05586a (3.053) | 7.560 (.780) | .001401 (1.313) | | .669b | .530 |
| 10.73 (.219) | −.50971 (1.237) | .02229c (1.357) | | | .0000030723c (1.512) | .05697a (2.989) | 15.197 (.639) | .001492 (1.333) | .40383 (.478) | .676c | .469 |

TABLE 6-15a.  (continued)

*Nonconvenience goods*

| Intercept | Eight-firm concentration ratio | Minimum efficient scale | Advertising/ sales | Advertising/ firm | Advertising interaction | Growth | Regional dummy | Absolute capital requirements | Percent non-household | $R^2$ | Corrected $R^2$ |
|---|---|---|---|---|---|---|---|---|---|---|---|
| 91.81[a] (3.285) | -.33695 (.693) | -.009920 (.552) | | .0032566[a] (3.643) | | .010584 (.653) | | -.0003247 (.930) | | .631[a] | .522 |
| 102.7[a] (4.064) | -.46375 (.997) | -.001693 (.109) | | .002762[a] (3.858) | | .0059147 (.385) | | | | .612[a] | .526 |
| 81.26[a] (2.678) | -.53230 (.998) | -.002379 (.121) | | .002790[a] (2.704) | | .01807 (.992) | | -.0001424 (.353) | .43654 (.918) | .649[a] | .518 |
| 110.6[a] (8.691) | -.55402[b] (1.830) | | | .002899[a] (4.771) | | | | | .29905 (.894) | .623[a] | .564 |
| 97.37[a] (3.167) | -.37751 (.748) | -.011347 (.609) | .25288 (.493) | .003264[a] (3.568) | | .004983 (.243) | | -.0002371 (.595) | | .636[a] | .500 |
| 85.19[b] (2.452) | -.53895 (.980) | -.003791 (.179) | .13960 (.259) | .002832[a] (2.633) | | .014378 (.610) | | -.0001087 (.250) | .40138 (.789) | .651[b] | .488 |
| 113.9[a] (4.324) | -.19897 (.466) | -.030143 (-1.739) | | | .0014049[a] (4.514) | -.005341 (.352) | | .0003893[c] (1.541) | | .701[a] | .613 |
| 98.88[a] (3.633) | -.51347 (1.117) | -.018590 (1.015) | | | .00012440[a] (3.917) | .0061721 (.376) | | .0004924[b] (1.951) | .57908[c] (1.530) | .739[a] | .641 |

*Note:* Figures in parentheses are *t* values. The significance of the regression coefficients is tested using a one-tail *t* test and the significance of the coefficients of multiple determination is tested using the *F* test.

[a] Coefficient is significant at the 99 percent level.
[b] Coefficient is significant at the 95 percent level.
[c] Coefficient is significant at the 90 percent level.

TABLE 6-15b. Nonconvenience Sample: Log Forms with Advertising Interaction Variable

| Units of profit | Intercept | Eight-firm concentration ratio (log) | Minimum efficient scale (log) | Advertising interaction (log) | Growth (log) | Absolute capital requirements (log) | Percent non-household (log) | $R^2$ | Corrected $R^2$ |
|---|---|---|---|---|---|---|---|---|---|
| Log units | .7690 | −.29586 | .03271 | −.022633 | .55222[b] | .10047[b] | .11728[b] | .499[b] | .311 |
| | (.418) | (1.184) | (.653) | (.647) | (2.161) | (2.032) | (2.249) | | |
| Natural units | −338.1[b] | −36.773 | 4.7610 | −2.6135 | 69.066[b] | 13.016[b] | 12.856[b] | .511[b] | .328 |
| | (1.683) | (1.189) | (.768) | (.603) | (2.183) | (2.126) | (1.991) | | |

*Note:* Figures in parentheses are $t$ values. The significance of the regression coefficients is tested using a one-tail $t$ test and the significance of the coefficients of multiple determination is tested using the $F$ test.

[a] Coefficient is significant at the 99 percent level.
[b] Coefficient is significant at the 95 percent level.
[c] Coefficient is significant at the 90 percent level.

tion is plagued by serious estimation problems. This is evident in the negative signs for concentration, scale economies, and capital requirements, and the low significance levels of these variables despite their strong simple correlation with profit. The strength of $A/F$ is unmistakable, however.[43] Thus the price of a correctly specified advertising variable may be the inability to sort out the effects of other variables in the model, although these problems existed with $A/S$ as well.

The results with the advertising interaction variable alleviate some of the estimation problems and strongly support my theoretical prediction that both $A/F$ and $A/S$ are important. In the convenience good sample, introducing both $A/F$ and $A/S$ separately produces no improvement. The advertising interaction variable (the product of $A/F$ and $A/S$) performs very poorly. Both these results are expected from my theory. The results are not altered by testing with alternative function forms.

In the nonconvenience sample, introducing $A/S$ with $A/F$ again yields no improvement over the specification with $A/F$. However, the advertising interaction variable is highly significant and produces a major increase in corrected $R^2$ (.518 to .641). The advertising interaction variable yields greatly superior results to those with advertising per firm alone. As is seen from Table 6–14, the interaction variable is still highly correlated with scale economies and concentration. However, it is less correlated with growth and much less correlated with capital requirements. In the equations with the advertising interaction variable, capital requirements become positive and significant, supporting my earlier argument that collinearity led to the negative capital requirements coefficients when $A/F$ was introduced. The advertising interaction variable, then, reduces the problems of estimation.[44] A further result is that the percent nonhousehold sales remains quite significant and positive when the advertising interaction variable is in-

43. $A/F$ was tested using the log-log and semilog functional forms. In both cases, $A/F$ was not significant and the $R^2$ obtained were approximately those attained using $A/S$. This is an interesting result. Since $A/S$ is in ratio form already, log transformation does not greatly affect its performance in regressions. Yet $A/F$ is strongly affected. This is a powerful argument for the linear influence of the advertising variable.

44. The second part of Table 6–15 gives regression equations testing the model with alternative functional forms. As with the results shown in Table 6–11, growth and capital requirements become more significant. However, advertising interaction performs very poorly. In addition, advertising per firm is not significant when introduced in log forms. These results are not shown. These results in conjunction with those presented in Table 6–11 argue strongly for the linear specification of advertising as a structural variable.

cluded, further suggesting the appropriateness of the percent nonhousehold variable.[45]

The results obtained with alternative specifications of the advertising variable provide support for my theory of the effect of advertising on performance, as well as the arguments regarding the appropriate empirical specification of the advertising variable. It is of interest also to consider how the results relate to the basic convenience-nonconvenience partitioning. Comparing advertising variables in the two samples is now no longer quite so straightforward, since their specifications are different. However, a few observations are possible. The advertising interaction variable is not nearly as significant in the nonconvenience sample as $A/S$ in the convenience sample, even when both are regressed by themselves against profits.[46] The $R^2$ of $A/S$ regressed alone against profits in the convenience sample, and the partial $R^2$ of $A/S$ in the full model greatly exceed those of advertising interaction in the nonconvenience model. Thus although a properly specified advertising variable tests strongly in the nonconvenience sample,[47] its explanatory power does not appear to approach that of advertising in the convenience sample. This is in accord with my theory. In addition, while careful specification has made a major impact, the unexplained variance in the nonconvenience sample continues to greatly exceed that in the convenience sample, as does the standard error of the estimate. For the convenience sample, with percent nonhousehold sales included, the standard error of the estimate is 1.34 rate of return percentage points. In the nonconvenience sample with the advertising interaction variable and percent nonhousehold sales included, the standard error is 1.80 percent.

## Concentration in Convenience Good Industries

In the results presented above, the puzzling negative coefficient of the concentration variable in convenience good industries has remained negative and quite significant. This result was insensitive to weighting, alternative functional forms and the addition of new variables and alternate specifications. All the more vexing is the negative simple correlation between concentration and profits in convenience good industries. These results are contrary to the most sacred of established

45. The percent nonhousehold sales reduced somewhat in significance when advertising per firm was included in the model.

46. These latter results are not presented.

47. It would be surprising if it did not test strongly. Recall the discussion in Chapter 5 which suggests that advertising, because it operates on performance both through a rivalry and an entry barrier effect, would *a priori* appear to test more significantly than other structural variables.

doctrine in industrial organization. Therefore it is appropriate to consider the various possible explanations for the negative coefficient and construct further tests to attempt to identify its cause.

*Measuring concentration in regional and local industries.*      There are a large number of possible explanations, perhaps the simplest of which is measurement error in the concentration ratio. This could take on several dimensions but the most potentially important would seem to be error resulting from the regional or local character of some industries. The regional dummy is admittedly a crude correction for regional and local industries. Since the great majority of regional and local industries are convenience good industries and a fair percentage of convenience good industries have local or regional elements, the failure of the regional dummy variable to adequately adjust for market scope may lead to the negative coefficient for concentration in convenience goods which is not present in nonconvenience goods. Regional industries with high profits and high true concentration but low measured concentration would tend to bias the coefficient to be negative.

To attempt to correct for this, I was able to construct adjusted concentration ratios based on data contained in an article by David Swartzman and Joan Bodoff.[48] Swartzman and Bodoff first identified local or regional industries using conventional sources, like Carl Kaysen and Donald Turner (1959), in conjunction with the 1963 Census of Transportation Commodity Transportation Survey, the latter showing average commodity shipment distances.[49] With the industries so identified, Swartzman and Bodoff calculated weighted average four-firm concentration ratios using Census Bureau regional or SMSA concentration data depending on whether the industry was regional or local. I aggregated Swartzman and Bodoff's four-digit adjusted concentration ratios to the three-digit level for use in my tests.

A study by Weiss also addresses the problem of the geographic size of markets.[50] Weiss developed several indexes for geographic market size, all based on the distance products are shipped as reported in the 1963 Census of Transportation. However, Weiss's assertion that this index (or the concept of the geographic market it is based upon) is meaningful for the measurement of industry structure or use in anitrust enforcement is misleading. Weiss asserts that "The geographic market will be defined in this paper as the set of locations from which *plants* supply or could profitably supply a given consuming point. This seems

48. Swartzman and Bodoff (1971).
49. Swartzman and Bodoff (1971), p. 343.
50. Weiss (1972).

to correspond to the market concept used in enforcing the anti-merger law." [51] (Emphasis added.) It is true that all regional or local industries have short average shipment distances. However, the converse does not hold. A national firm may find it advantageous to decentralize production, locating plants in different parts of the country. If most firms in an industry did this, which would seem likely, average shipment distances would fall. However, unless each firm had a plant in each region or locality, this fall in the average shipment distance would say nothing about the relevant competitors in the market. The number of firms which happened to have plants in a specified area would not correspond to the number of competitors in the national market. Yet the national competitors set prices and engage in rivalry nationally. Weiss's index of geographic market size is thus selectively biased in the downward direction and thus it can overstate the appropriate adjustment to national concentration ratios. For this reason it was rejected in favor of Swartzman and Bodoff's index which seemed more theoretically sound.[52]

The magnitude of the adjustments made to the concentration ratio and the industries affected are reported in the Technical Appendix. Unfortunately, Swartzman and Bodoff's data only covered four-firm and not eight-firm concentration ratios. Since results with four-firm concentration ratios have not been presented above, the presentation of results of my tests with the adjusted four-firm concentration ratio include an equation with the unadjusted four-firm concentration ratio for comparative purposes. Tables 6–16 and 6–17 present simple correlation coefficients and multiple regression equations incorporating the adjusted

TABLE 6-16.    Simple Correlation Coefficients of Profit Rate with Alternative Specifications of the Concentration Ratio

| Convenience goods | | Nonconvenience goods | |
|---|---|---|---|
| Eight-firm concentration ratio | −.231 | Eight-firm concentration ratio | .387 |
| Four-firm concentration ratio | −.203 | Four-firm concentration ratio | .469 |
| Adjusted four-firm concentration ratio | −.214 | Adjusted four-firm concentration ratio | .492 |

51. Weiss (1972), p. 245.
52. A similarly inappropriate index was used by Rhoades in a recent paper. See Rhoades (1973), p. 154.

TABLE 6-17. Multiple Regression Equations Explaining Profit Rates Results Incorporating the Adjusted Four-firm Concentration Ratio

| Intercept | Four-firm concentration ratio | Adjusted four-firm concentration ratio | Minimum efficient scale | Advertising/sales | Advertising/firm | Advertising interaction | Growth | Regional dummy | Absolute capital requirements | Percent non-household | $R^2$ | Corrected $R^2$ |
|---|---|---|---|---|---|---|---|---|---|---|---|---|
| | | | | | Convenience goods | | | | | | | |
| 47.64c (1.626) | -.75512b (2.628) | | .01630c (1.656) | .60470a (5.206) | | | .02539b (1.940) | 8.533 (.621) | .001743b (2.659) | | .876a | .814 |
| 45.44c (1.749) | -.78095a (3.056) | | .014110c (1.603) | .64537a (6.142) | | | .02537b (2.192) | 2.4792 (.197) | .0019819a (3.337) | .92858b (2.051) | .910a | .853 |
| 73.25b (1.350) | | -.71101b (2.130) | .01484c (1.423) | .63719a (4.886) | | | .02135c (1.402) | -9.55515 (.652) | .001542b (2.274) | | .860a | .790 |
| 55.39b (1.980) | | -.65360b (2.129) | .01917b (2.441) | .61282a (5.017) | | | .02579b (1.939) | | .001307b (2.325) | | .855a | .799 |
| 43.93c (1.594) | | -.63634b (2.181) | .01979 (2.649) | .63230a (5.420) | | | .02898b (2.222) | | .001361b (2.545) | .75535c (1.555) | .879a | .819 |
| 71.57b (1.972) | | -.72891b (2.439) | .01267 (1.316) | .67674a (5.573) | | | .02135c (1.532) | -15.951 (1.150) | .001764a (2.785) | .90025b (1.816) | .892a | .824 |

TABLE 6-17. (continued)

| Intercept | Four-firm concentration ratio | Adjusted four-firm concentration ratio | Minimum efficient scale | Advertising/sales | Advertising/firm | Advertising interaction | Growth | Regional dummy | Absolute capital requirements | Percent nonhousehold | $R^2$ | Corrected $R^2$ |
|---|---|---|---|---|---|---|---|---|---|---|---|---|
| | | | | | *Nonconvenience goods* | | | | | | | |
| 73.64[b] (1.919) | .40270 (.529) | | .006056 (.266) | .16984 (.253) | | | .009123 (.352) | | .0003861 (.768) | | .355 | .166 |
| 68.03[b] (1.737) | | .60550 (.733) | -.01009 (.451) | .13620 (.205) | | | .009591 (.373) | | .0002927 (.578) | | .369 | .181 |
| 87.30[a] (3.180) | -.22040 (.369) | | -.01463 (.836) | | .003180[a] (3.495) | | .009808 (.599) | | -.0003339 (.894) | | .623[a] | .513 |
| 77.92[b] (2.541) | -.38683 (.597) | | -.009416 (.493) | | .002807[a] (2.659) | | .01565 (.849) | | -.0001761 (.404) | .34669 (.730) | .635[a] | .498 |
| 77.83[b] (2.494) | | -.28996 (.414) | -.012025 (.622) | | .002790[a] (2.628) | | .01468 (.794) | | -.002091 (.466) | .32873 (.672) | .631[a] | .493 |
| 97.86[a] (3.571) | -.54032 (.971) | | -.02230 (1.303) | | | .0001281[a] (3.958) | .004565 (.280) | | .0005255[b] (1.797) | .53013[c] (1.430) | .734[a] | .635 |
| 99.12[a] (3.529) | | -.52444 (.869) | -.02355 (1.373) | | | .0001285[a] (3.930) | .003929 (.240) | | .0005192[c] (1.694) | .53551[c] (1.401) | .731[a] | .631 |

*Note:* Figures in parentheses are $t$ values. The significance of the regression coefficients is tested using a one-tail $t$ test and the significance of the coefficients of multiple determination is tested using the $F$ test.

[a] Coefficient is significant at the 99 percent level.
[b] Coefficient is significant at the 95 percent level.
[c] Coefficient is significant at the 90 percent level.

four-firm concentration ratio.[53] In the convenience sample, the adjusted four-firm concentration ratio remains negatively correlated with profit, and its regression coefficient remains negative and quite significant in all equations. Curiously, the adjusted four-firm concentration ratio performs somewhat worse than the unadjusted ratio, both in terms of significance level and contribution to explained variance. In the nonconvenience sample, the adjusted four-firm concentration yields identical if not slightly poorer performance than the unadjusted ratio.

In view of the major adjustments made to the concentration ratio in the convenience sample, it is of interest to see whether one can explain variations in adjusted concentrations in the convenience sample more successfully than I was able to explain variations in unadjusted concentration. The lower $R^2$ in explaining concentration in the convenience sample may have been due to the misspecified concentration variable used. Table 6–18 presents a regression of the adjusted four-firm concentration on the other variables in the model. Comparing this to the results in Table 6–8, the overall explained variance is somewhat improved. However, growth remains the dominant explanatory variable, and advertising increases in significance. Thus the substitution of the adjusted concentration ration reinforces the differences between the convenience and nonconvenience samples.

My results with the adjusted four-firm concentration ratio in the convenience sample, as well as the general results presented earlier in Table 6–3 offer some implications about the nature of regional industries. Comanor and Wilson note the relatively high significance level of the regional dummy variable in their tests and also suggest that it appears to have an independent effect in addition to correcting the concentration variable.[54] Esposito and Esposito report quite weak results for the regional dummy variable. My overall results are more in accord with the latter. In Table 6–3 the significance level of the regional dummy variable is low and in the absence of the concentration ratio the variable loses all significance.[55] My results differ from both studies reported above in that they test the regional dummy in the convenience

53. If the adjusted four-firm concentration ratio corrects for regionality it should be entered into the equations without a regional dummy. The results presented, which test this specification as well as one with both the adjusted four-firm concentration ratio and the regional dummy, have some interesting implications for the separate effect of the regional dummy beyond its effect on concentration.

54. Comanor and Wilson (1967), p. 433.

55. This reasoning is apparently the criteria used by Comanor and Wilson to discern independent effect of the regional dummy. In their results, the regional dummy remained significant and stable even in the absence of the concentration variable.

TABLE 6-18. Multiple Regression Equation Explaining Adjusted Four-firm Concentration in Convenience Goods

| Units of concentration | Intercept | Minimum efficient scale | Absolute capital requirements | Regional dummy | Growth | Advertising | $R^2$ | Corrected $R^2$ |
|---|---|---|---|---|---|---|---|---|
| Natural units | 70.39[a] (4.551) | .006592 (.998) | .0002744 (.567) | | −.02213[b] (2.223) | .14878[c] (1.509) | .413[c] | .245 |

Note: Figures in parentheses are t values. The significance of the regression coefficients is tested using a one-tail t test and the significance of the coefficients of multiple determination is tested using the F test.

[a] Coefficient is significant at the 99 percent level.
[b] Coefficient is significant at the 95 percent level.
[c] Coefficient is significant at the 90 percent level.

sample, which for reasons discussed above, constitutes a more valid test.

The results with the adjusted four-firm concentration ratio shed some additional light on the influence of regionality. They suggest an independent effect of the regional dummy. Adjusting the concentration ratio removes, by definition, the influence of regionality from this variable. In Table 6–17 the results of estimating the model with the adjusted four-firm concentration ratio and the regional dummy excluded and then included are shown. Where the adjusted four-firm concentration ratio is included, the regional dummy becomes negative and more significant, especially when the percent nonhousehold sales variable is included (see Table 6–13).[56]

This suggests a reason why the regional dummy is not significant in earlier runs. The expected effect of the regionality on concentration would normally be that it increased effective concentration, with a positive effect on rate of return. In the convenience sample, however, concentration has a negative influence on rate of return. In addition, the regional dummy appears to have a separate negative effect. In view of these conflicting effects, it is not surprising that the regional dummy introduced in the usual way has low significance.

My theory provides a clear justification for the negative effect of the regional dummy separate from its effect on concentration. The discussion in Chapter 5 suggests that the importance of advertising in creating entry barriers rests heavily on media segmentality. Since local and regional industries typically utilize local and regional (and hence more segmentable) media, we would expect advertising barriers to be lower in these industries, other things being equal. Thus regional industries would have lower return for given levels of the other structural variable, a prediction consistent with the negative coefficient obtained.[57]

*Marginal concentration.* The results obtained with the adjusted four-firm concentration ratio failed to affect the negative and significant concentration coefficient which characterized earlier tests. A second alternative explanation for the negative coefficient is the effect of marginal concentration. If high eight-firm or four-firm concentration was associated with high concentration in the second four firms, and high marginal concentration importantly increased rivalry (with a downward effect on profits), then concentration could appear with a negative sign.

56. The overall explained variance is lower. However, including the regional dummy improves $R^2$ in the model including the adjusted concentration ratio.

57. In empirical work this effect would normally be obscured by the impact of mismeasured concentration.

The mechanism for increased rivalry would be greater equality among leading firms and the next four firms.[58]

An unbiased test of this explanation for the negative concentration coefficient is unfortunately somewhat difficult. There are constraints on the value which the marginal concentration ratio can take for various values of the four-firm concentration ratio.[59] As a quick test of the effect of marginal concentration I chose to ignore this constraint. The results are presented in Table 6–19. Four-firm concentration remains negative and significant. Marginal concentration enters with a negative sign and is not significant. The statistical relationship based on the constraints on the maximum value of the concentration ratio would suggest a negative sign for marginal concentration if the relationship between concentration and profits were positive.[60] If the relationship between concentration and profits is negative, the predicted statistical relationship would be positive. The negative sign obtained (and the negative simple correlation between marginal concentration and profits) suggest that the true effect of marginal concentration is to reduce profit but that marginal concentration does not explain the negative four-firm concentration coefficient.

In the nonconvenience sample, marginal concentration enters with a negative sign (and negative simple correlation with profits) which may or may not be purely a statistical artifact. It is interesting that the sign of the four-firm concentration ratio flips in the nonconvenience equations including the advertising interaction variable. This provides some additional justification for my earlier assertion that collinearity is responsible for the negative concentration sign in some tests in the non-convenience sample.

*Heteroscedasticity.* Another possible explanation for the negative concentration coefficient may be suggested by the pattern of residuals observed in the convenience sample but not in the nonconvenience sample. It was found that in the convenience sample the residuals tended to decrease with industry size and with decreasing concentration. Table 6–20 presents a correlation analysis of the relationship between industry size, concentration, and profits. Though industry size is positively correlated with profits in both samples, it is negatively related to concentration in the convenience sample and positively related to concentration in the nonconvenience sample. This is yet another striking difference between the two groups of industries. The more puzzling result is the positive association of concentration and industry size in

58. For a statement of this hypothesis see R. A. Miller (1967).
59. Collins and Preston (1969), pp. 275–276.
60. Collins and Preston (1969), pp. 275–276.

TABLE 6-19. Multiple Regression Equations Explaining Profit Rates: Results Incorporating Marginal Concentration Ratios

| Intercept | Four-firm concentration ratio | Marginal concentration (C8–C4) | Minimum efficient scale | Advertising/sales | Advertising/firm | Advertising interaction | Growth | Regional dummy | Absolute capital requirements | Percent nonhousehold | $R^2$ | Corrected $R^2$ |
|---|---|---|---|---|---|---|---|---|---|---|---|---|
| | | | | *Convenience goods* | | | | | | | | |
| 49.82c (1.554) | −.70482b (1.889) | −.29514 (.226) | .01570c (1.484) | .59923a (4.854) | | | .02528b (1.853) | 9.1627 (.628) | .001758b (2.561) | | .876a | .840 |
| 48.30c (1.690) | −.71921b (2.166) | −.36294 (.312) | .01338c (1.410) | .63883a (5.722) | | | .02525b (2.079) | 3.225 (.242) | .002001a (3.212) | .93294b (1.973) | .911a | .840 |
| | | | | *Nonconvenience goods* | | | | | | | | |
| 82.20a (2.093) | .83700 (.950) | −2.4038 (1.011) | .001221 (.051) | .02059 (.030) | | | .01315 (.502) | | .00005117 (.085) | | .394 | .167 |
| 97.56a (3.440) | .14119 (.214) | −.21324 (1.216) | −.008547 (.476) | | .003129a (3.483) | | .01054 (.653) | | −.005673 (1.365) | | .655a | .523 |
| 114.1a (4.184) | −.17610 (.276) | −.28114 (1.644) | −.02996c (1.644) | | | .0001399a (4.054) | −.00526 (.335) | | .0003769 (1.045) | | .701a | .589 |
| 98.99a (3.535) | −.37542 (.599) | −1.0716 (.620) | −.016897 (.866) | | | .0001195a (3.345) | .007186 (.418) | | .00041473 (1.193) | .60402c (1.524) | .741 | .620 |

*Note:* Figures in parentheses are $t$ values. The significance of the regression coefficients is tested using a one-tail $t$ test and the significance of the coefficients of multiple determination is tested using the $F$ test.

[a] Coefficient is significant at the 99 percent level.

[b] Coefficient is significant at the 95 percent level.

[c] Coefficient is significant at the 90 percent level.

TABLE 6-20.  Simple Correlation Coefficients of Industry Size with Concentration and Profits

|  | Eight-firm concentration ratio | Four-firm concentration ratio | Profit |
|---|---|---|---|
|  | *Convenience goods* | | |
| Industry size | −.166 | −.429 | .411 |
|  | *Nonconvenience goods* | | |
|  | .419 | .555 | .501 |

nonconvenience goods.[61] In any case, if industry size is negatively correlated with concentration and positively correlated with profit, but concentration is actually positively correlated with profit, then the effects of industry size may make the relationship between concentration and profits negative. Table 6–21 tests industry size as a structural variable. The negative concentration coefficient in the convenience sample remains unchanged. In the nonconvenience sample, industry size enters with a curious negative coefficient but is not significant.

Incorporating the adjusted four-firm concentration ratio, the results with industry size and my findings with respect to the specification of advertising, I can update the earlier analysis of the ability of other structural variables to explain concentration. The updated results are shown in Table 6–22. In the convenience sample industry size is a significant and negative influence on concentration. However, the general pattern of results is unchanged in the convenience sample. There I am unable to explain concentration to a great extent, while in the nonconvenience sample the explained variance is quite high.

*Growth-concentration interaction.*   A final hypothesis for the negative partial effect of concentration on profits in the convenience sample is the interaction between growth and concentration. Growth was the most important variable explaining concentration in convenience goods (Table 6–8), entering with a negative sign. This negative growth-concentration relation is reinforced in a paper by W. G. Shepherd (1964) for a broad sample of industries. Furthermore, it is apparent from Table 6–3 that omitting the growth variable from the model always makes the negative concentration-profits coefficient more negative and significant.

The interaction between growth and concentration may take on several forms. High growth may blur the concentration-profit relation if

61. Motor vehicles, a very large industry, is undoubtedly an influence.

TABLE 6-21. Multiple Regression Equations Explaining Profit Rates: Results Incorporating Industry Size as a Structural Variable

| Intercept | Eight-firm concentration ratio | Minimum efficient scale | Advertising/sales | Advertising interaction | Growth | Regional dummy | Absolute capital requirements | Percent non-household | Industry size | $R^2$ | Corrected $R^2$ |
|---|---|---|---|---|---|---|---|---|---|---|---|
| *Convenience goods* | | | | | | | | | | | |
| 32.88 (1.043) | −.52071[b] (2.066) | .019574[c] (1.772) | .61864[a] (5.925) | | .02600[b] (2.241) | 5.5127 (.432) | .001272[c] (1.358) | .90023[b] (1.988) | .001325 (1.014) | .919[a] | .854 |
| *Nonconvenience goods* | | | | | | | | | | | |
| 99.95[a] (3.616) | −.51887 (1.113) | −.02029 (1.084) | | .0001160[a] (3.398) | .008406 (.496) | | .001159 (1.245) | .65268[c] (1.647) | −.002460 (.745) | .748[a] | .631 |

*Note:* Figures in parentheses are *t* values. The significance of the regression coefficients is tested using a one-tail *t* test and the significance of the coefficients of multiple determination is tested using the *F* test.

[a] Coefficient is significant at the 99 percent level.
[b] Coefficient is significant at the 95 percent level.
[c] Coefficient is significant at the 90 percent level.

TABLE 6-22. Multiple Regression Equations Explaining Concentration: Updated Results

| Form of concentration ratio | Intercept | Minimum efficient scale | Advertising/ sales | Advertising/ firm | Advertising interaction | Growth | Regional dummy | Absolute capital requirements | Industry size | R² | Corrected R² |
|---|---|---|---|---|---|---|---|---|---|---|---|
| *Convenience goods* | | | | | | | | | | | |
| Adjusted four-firm | 70.39[a] (4.551) | .006592 (.998) | .14878[c] (1.509) | | | -.02213[b] (2.223) | | .0002744 (.567) | | .413[c] | .245 |
| Adjusted four-firm | 87.92[a] (3.784) | .0006151 (.069) | .16886[c] (1.680) | | | -.02615[b] (2.441) | -12.112 (1.010) | .0005520 (.992) | | .455 | .246 |
| Adjusted four-firm | 74.18[a] (5.116) | -.0002373 (.033) | .13444[c] (1.464) | | | -.01692[c] (1.750) | | .0009707 (1.614) | -.001828 (1.808) | .531[c] | .350 |
| Adjusted four-firm | 102.3[a] (4.883) | -.01121 (1.224) | .16203[b] (1.868) | | | -.02187[b] (2.323) | -18.791 (1.753) | .001574 (2.428) | -.002282 (2.343) | .626[b] | .439 |
| Eight-firm | 82.08[a] (2.996) | -.01324 (1.105) | .10899 (.961) | | | -.01778[c] (1.444) | 8.809 (.628) | .002195 (2.590) | -.002735 (2.148) | .610[b] | .416 |
| *Nonconvenience goods* | | | | | | | | | | | |
| Eight-firm | 25.26[b] (1.791) | .03155[a] (5.239) | .19222 (.746) | | | .001417 (.140) | | .0002462 (.498) | .006348 (.347) | .803[a] | .745 |
| Eight-firm | 24.31[b] (1.981) | .02807[a] (4.950) | | .0005444 (1.316) | | .004786 (.616) | | .0002010 (1.238) | | .814[a] | .772 |
| Eight-firm | 23.65[b] (1.796) | .02858[a] (4.386) | | .0005414 (1.272) | | .004792 (.599) | | .0001208 (.246) | .0003032 (.173) | .814[a] | .759 |
| Eight-firm | 26.49[b] (2.016) | .02812[a] (4.074) | | | .00001464 (.870) | .003608 (.433) | | .0003400[a] (2.979) | | .804[a] | .760 |

*Note:* Figures in parentheses are *t* values. The significance of the regression coefficients is tested using a one-tail *t* test and the significance of the coefficients of multiple determination is tested using the *F* test.

[a] Coefficient is significant at the 99 percent level.
[b] Coefficient is significant at the 95 percent level.
[c] Coefficient is significant at the 90 percent level.

high growth promotes entry of new firms, as has been demonstrated statistically.[62] In my data, concentration ratios are available only for the beginning year of the period under study (1963) and other data series are three-year averages. In high growth industries, measured concentration overstates true concentration if new entrants reduce the collective market share of the leading firms, whereas in low growth industries there is no such bias. Thus the coefficient of the (disequilibrium) measured concentration ratio would be biased downward.

An additional, or alternate, hypothesis involves the effect of the growth-concentration interaction on rivalry. In low concentration industries, growth has little likely impact on rivalry, which will remain strong. In high concentration industries, however, rapid growth and the subsequent requirements that firms grow to maintain existing market share may upset the collusion of agreement among firms which is associated with high concentration. Industry growth increases the payoff of competitive strategies which seek to take market share from competitors. Further, high growth adds another element to collusive behavior—firms must agree on sharing additions to sales and capacity. The resulting greater rivalry may lead to lower industry rate of return. Shepherd found that in high concentration industries the growth-concentration relationship was substantially more significant. This reinforces the hypothesis that the growth-concentration interaction occurs primarily in high concentration industries. Of the alternative methodologies for capturing the interaction effect I have adopted a variable which is the simple product of demand growth and the concentration ratio.[63] Other possible techniques were inconsistent with the limited degrees of freedom available.[64]

Equations incorporating the growth-concentration interaction variable in the convenience sample are shown in Table 6–23. Both hypotheses imply that the effect of the growth-concentration interaction on profits is negative, if both concentration and growth are also included in the model. If an interaction variable is excluded, the growth-concentration interaction will bias the concentration coefficient downward. The interaction variable enters with the expected negative sign and is highly significant. The concentration coefficient becomes positive, though it is only moderately significant. The modest significance may be due to the collinearity between the interaction variable and concentration (the

62. See W. G. Shepherd (1964), p. 205, for statistical tests which support this proposition.
63. I am indebted to T. A. Wilson for suggesting this specification.
64. For alternatives, see B. T. Gale (1972), p. 412.

TABLE 6-23. Multiple Regression Equations Explaining Profit Rates: Results Incorporating Interaction of Growth and Concentration

| Intercept | Eight firm concentration ratio | Minimum efficient scale | Advertising/ sales | Growth | Regional dummy | Absolute capital requirements | Growth-concentration interaction variable | Percent non-household | $R^2$ | Corrected $R^2$ |
|---|---|---|---|---|---|---|---|---|---|---|
| | | | | | *Convenience goods* | | | | | |
| -21.67 | .92354 | .016812[b] | .63420[a] | .07642[a] | 14.669 | .001687[a] | -.001199[b] | | .912[a] | .856 |
| (.500) | (1.219) | (1.940) | (6.167) | (2.888) | (1.182) | (2.910) | (2.138) | | | |
| -24.02 | .91018[c] | .14567[b] | .67554[a] | .07671[a] | 8.6384 | .008931[a] | -.0012068[b] | .94207[b] | .948[a] | .906 |
| (.684) | (1.481) | (2.058) | (7.957) | (3.575) | (.836) | (4.029) | (2.655) | (2.594) | | |

*Note:* Figures in parentheses are *t* values. The significance of the regression coefficients is tested using a one-tail *t* test and the significance of the coefficients of multiple determination is tested using the *F* test.

[a] Coefficient is significant at the 99 percent level.
[b] Coefficient is significant at the 95 percent level.
[c] Coefficient is significant at the 90 percent level.

simple correlation is .76).[65] Comparing the results with those in Tables 6–3 and 6–13, the significance levels of all other included structural variables are improved. In addition, the inclusion of the interaction variable adds importantly to $R^2$ (.81 to .86). The significance of the variable measuring nonhousehold sales is reinforced.[66]

These results strongly suggest that, in convenience goods, the proper specification of the growth-profit and concentration-profit hypotheses must include the interaction between them. The result tends to support Bradley Gale's (1972) view that interaction effects are probably important in industrial organization. In nonconvenience goods, however, the growth-concentration interaction variable was not significant nor did it improve $R^2$ despite the similarity of the variance in growth rates in the two samples and the higher mean growth rate in nonconvenience goods (these results are not reported). Once again the strong differences in the convenience and nonconvenience samples are evident.

**Overview of the Statistical Results**

The results presented above provide substantial support for the implications of the theory presented in Chapters 2 to 5. The nature of the structure-performance link is markedly different in the convenience and nonconvenience bifurcation of industries suggested by the theory. The standard industrial organization model was found to be quite successful for convenience industries, though it was improved by capturing the interaction of growth and concentration and the extent of nonhousehold sales in consumer industries. The model, with the exception of the negative concentration coefficient, supported the appropriateness of the structural variables which have characterized previous work. In the nonconvenience industries, however, the standard model was quite unsatisfactory. Advertising was nonsignificant and the sole variable showing promise was absolute capital requirements. It became apparent, in addition, that the negative relationship of concentration on profits observed by several authors stemmed from the convenience sample.

With regard to this original result, it is clear that previous structure-performance testing involving consumer goods has mixed industries which have very dissimilar characteristics. In many ways the distinction between convenience and nonconvenience goods has sharper implications for

65. If the included growth-concentration interaction variable was irrelevant, the coefficient of the concentration variable would still be unbiased. See Rao and Miller (1971), p. 57. Thus we can reject the hypothesis that the reversal in sign is spurious due to irrelevant variable bias.

66. A growth-concentration interaction variable using adjusted four-firm concentration proved unsuccessful.

the structure-performance model than does the producer goods-consumer goods distinction. On the simplest level, any study including firms in both convenience and nonconvenience industries may yield confusing results for advertising to sales and depressed significance levels and explained variance as a result of the asymmetrical effects of advertising and concentration. The results obtained by Comanor and Wilson, among others, can be seen to be a curious blending of two very different models.

The basic differences between convenience and nonconvenience industries extended beyond the performance of the basic model. Different patterns of residuals were observed and the collinearity among variables was strikingly different in the two groups. The hypothesis advanced by Comanor and Wilson that the partial effect of concentration was minor was seen to hold primarily for nonconvenience goods. Among nonconvenience goods, concentration was explained largely by technical entry barriers and was positively related to industry size. In convenience goods, on the other hand, advertising and growth in demand were most important, although they explained relatively little of the variation in concentration. Parenthetically, my results imply that Shepherd's work relating growth and concentration was the mixture of different relationships among subsamples.[67] This may explain his modest values for $R^2$. Industry size was negatively related to concentration as might be expected. This result, coupled by the persistent and negative concentration coefficient in the model, suggests a more complicated interaction process among structural variables in convenience goods than exists in nonconvenience goods. This is perhaps related to the apparent dominance of advertising as an entry barrier to convenience industries. This entry barrier, unlike scale economies, is not tied to concentration: that is, a large minimum efficient plant scale forces concentration much more directly than the requirement for large advertising outlays does.

In line with the more complex interaction between variables in convenience goods, the negative relation between concentration and profits in convenience goods was reversed when a growth-concentration interaction variable was introduced into the model. The growth-concentration interaction variable proved to be highly significant and greatly improved the fit of the model in convenience goods; it was notably unsuccessful in nonconvenience goods. Other explanations for the negative concentration-profits relation were tested and rejected.

The final major set of empirical results supported my expanded theory of the relationship between advertising and performance and the

67. W. G. Shepherd (1964), pp. 203–208.

appropriate specification of the advertising variable based on this theory. Careful specification of the advertising variable, in addition to the incorporation of a variable measuring nonhousehold sales, greatly improved the performance of the model in nonconvenience industries. The best equation in the nonconvenience sample still falls far short of the convenience results, however. Besides advertising and concentration, substantial differences between the convenience and nonconvenience models have survived all respecifications and were stable throughout all tests. Most notably the growth variable appears to be irrelevant in the nonconvenience sample. Its coefficient is unstable and has consistently low significance; collinearity does not appear to be a valid explanation based on correlation analysis.[68] The other standard structural variables appear to be appropriate, though in quite different ways, in both samples. However, the basic differences in the two industry groups predicted by theory remain.

---

68. This may be due to misspecification as noted above.

# 7

# Strategy Variation, the Structure of Retailing, and Industry Performance

Making the distinction between convenience and nonconvenience industries is only the first step in testing the implications of the theory in Chapters 2–5. In the last chapter I stayed within the confines of the more or less traditional measures of market structure used in previous research in industrial organization. My theory, however, suggests two major areas for improving the structural-performance link outside the confines of the traditional variables. This chapter presents the results of empirical tests which incorporate the presence of variations in marketing strategy within industries and measure the effects of multiple dimensions of the structure of retail distribution for consumer goods. These additional structural characteristics of consumer goods industries will yield further significant improvements in explaining cross-industry variations in rate of return in manufacturing.

## Strategy Variations within Industries

In Chapter 4 I identified the presence of important differences in strategy among firms within industries. A model was developed linking these and industry performance through the operation of their indirect effect on structure and their direct effect on intraindustry rivalry. The model was then specialized to consumer goods industries and focused toward marketing strategy differences.

The model was then applied to the convenience-nonconvenience bifurcation of consumer goods industries. In convenience goods, the indirect effect is potentially important reflecting the likelihood of polar $D$ and $U$ strategies. Their direct effect on rivalry, however, is likely to be weak in view of their large strategic distance and low market interdependence, unless the size of the $U$ group is large. In nonconvenience industries, conversely, the direct effect is likely to be relatively large, reflecting a rich potential for important strategy differences coupled with high market interdependence. The operation of the direct effect is clouded by the presence of powerful retailers who may bargain away manufacturer rate of return in strategies relying on heavy retailer push.

To bridge the gap between theory and empirical tests of the model, one must investigate the question of the measurement of strategy variation. In convenience goods, the retailer is relatively unimportant unless the manufacturer's product is weakly brand identified and in any case can exert little influence on the consumer's purchase decision. Thus in convenience goods, variations in marketing strategy are largely signaled by variations in advertising and the problem of measuring strategic variation is relatively easy. Differences in manufacturer policies toward retailers are likely to be relatively small.

In nonconvenience goods, however, the retailer is important and powerful. Variations in marketing strategy will, therefore, involve variations in the emphasis placed on retailer push versus advertising pull as well as variations in the target level of product differentiation. Thus variations in advertising alone will not capture all important variations in strategy. Firms with the same advertising rates may be following importantly different strategies. A further problem is the power of the retailer to bargain down manufacturer rate of return. Product differentiation by the manufacturer and retailer leads to rate of return which is divided between the two stages based on relative bargaining power. Since varying strategies not only affect structure in manufacturing but retailer power, the indirect effect is complicated. A strategy with high advertising, though implying relatively greater manufacturer power over the retailer, may not ambiguously imply high ultimate product differentiation because of the power of the retailer to build differentiation. High ultimate product differentiation may not necessarily imply high manufacturer return because of retailer bargaining power. A further complication is that retailer structure is likely to be quite important in nonconvenience goods, since it can affect retailer bargaining strength.

Structure of the Test

Measurement of marketing strategy variations across a broad sample of industries involves severe data problems, although in some cases these can be somewhat overcome. Ideally, one would like to have firm specific data measuring the range of dimensions of marketing strategy. Without studying firms in all the industries individually, we cannot achieve this ideal. Given the reality of having to use available cross industry data, the problem becomes one of developing crude proxies for intraindustry strategy variations.

The only consistent data available are data on advertising. Using the *IRS Statistics of Income,* it is possible to compute several measures of the average advertising rates of various size classes of firms within industries. To proxy the variation in marketing strategy I utilized the intraindustry variation in advertising rates. As a measure of the variance in advertising, the advertising behavior of the largest firms accounting for at least 30 percent of industry sales was compared to advertising behavior of the entire industry. Six basic measures of advertising variation were computed. For each of the three advertising variables used in this study (advertising to sales, advertising per firm, and the advertising interaction variable) two strategy variables were constructed. One was the ratio of the advertising variable for large firms to the variable for the entire industry.[1] The second was a dummy variable constructed using these ratios by assigning industries to high variance and low variance groups based on arbitrarily chosen cutoff points.

The measures were introduced as structural variables in the structure-performance models for the convenience and nonconvenience samples of industries developed in the previous chapter.[2] In view of the greatly different character of strategy variations as between convenience and nonconvenience goods, I will discuss the results for each class of consumer goods separately.

Convenience Goods

For convenience goods, advertising is a relatively good proxy for overall marketing strategy. The strength of the indirect effect is likely to be weak. Private label offers the major potential for leading to destabilizing intergroup rivalry. The presence of private label would tend to lower the rate of return of differentiated producers. The benefits of private label accrue primarily to the retailer, however. The indirect effect of structure variation on performance can be quite strong and is accentuated by the shifting power of the retailers in the $D$ and $U$ strategies. For a manufacturer in the $U$ group, not only is the product un-

---

1. For example,

$$\frac{A/S \text{ (largest 30 percent)}}{A/S \text{ (entire industry)}}$$

2. Square roots and squares of these variables were also tested.

differentiated relative to the $D$ group producer, but the retailer is likely to exert further downward pressure on rate of return.

General observation suggests that the differentiated ($D$-group) producers are typically the large firms in convenience goods. This is borne out in the data. Of 19 convenience good industries all but 4 (cigarettes, drugs, books, and perfumes, cosmetics, and toilet preparations) have large firm advertising to sales ratios higher than the industry average.[3] In one other industry (beer) the large firm and industry ratios are quite close.[4] Let us examine these exceptional cases more closely to see how they relate to the model. A moment's reflection suggests that in these industries $U$ group products are rare to nonexistent. In all five cases, the large firm and entire industry ratios are nearly equal, and the result may be explained by economies of scale in advertising which allow large firms following a $D$ strategy to spend proportionally less on advertising than small firms following it. Thus the ratio of large firm advertising to industry advertising is a good proxy for the relative $D$ group–$U$ group split. Since I have argued that the primary impact of strategic variation in performance on convenience goods is through the indirect effect, and empirically the large firms are the $D$ group producers, then the ratio of large firm advertising to entire industry advertising will be a good measure of strategic variation.

The independent variable in the study is the industry average rate of return.[5] In the tests for the effects of strategy variation one must still include a variable measuring the conventional effects of advertising on performance. The advertising variable used thus far has been an industry average advertising to sales ratio. The indirect effect predicts that $D$ group firms will have higher return than $U$ group firms; the indirect effect predicts that those industries with high variation in advertising behavior will show lower returns, other things being equal. In view of the quality of the data, separating the direct and indirect effects will be quite difficult. A large $D$ group will imply higher industry average advertising, which is the sales weighted average of the $D$ group advertising rate and the $U$ group rate. Thus industry average advertising will

---

3. These results are nearly identical to those reported by Comanor and Wilson (1974), pp. 199–200, in their study of advertising and firm size. Their discussion of differences in large firm advertising hypothesizes that firms may be selling to different market segments. This is consistent with the model.

4. In all these industries the variation in advertising per firm is also low.

5. It is highly desirable, in view of the strategy variation model, to examine the distribution of rates of return within the industry. This is done in a later paper which followed from this study. See M. E. Porter, "The Structure within Industries and Market Performance," forthcoming.

move with the size of the $D$ group. Similarly, if $D$ group profits exceed the $U$ groups, then industry average profits will move with the size of the $D$ group as well. Thus using industry average advertising to sales and profits captures at least some of the indirect effect of strategy variation on performance in convenience goods. This coincidence may help further explain the quality of fit of the standard model in the convenience sample and in previous tests in consumer goods industries. But it raises problems for isolating and measuring the direct and indirect effects. It is apparent that one cannot simply append a strategy variable to the model, and one will be forced to devise an alternative testing procedure to isolate strategy effects.

*Results.* Table 7–1 presents a correlation analysis of the measures of variation in advertising (strategy variables) and other structural traits. All the measures of strategy variation are negatively correlated with profits (as predicted by the model) and, curiously, with many other structural variables. An interesting result in the correlation analysis is the relationship of the strategy variables to concentration. All strategy variables are negatively correlated with eight-firm concentration;[6] this correlation becomes much less negative (or even positive) when the adjusted four-firm concentration ratio is substituted. The strategy variables least affected by the switch in concentration ratios are the variables constructed using the advertising to sales ratio. These results appear to support my earlier discussion about the problems of using advertising per firm as a measure of advertising in the convenience sample. Because of the presence of regional industries, advertising per firm may vary because of differences in regionality among firms although each is following a similar marketing strategy in its geographic area. Thus correcting the concentration ratio for regionality would have a relatively large effect on its relationship with advertising per firm.

In view of the problem of regionality which plagues advertising per firm, another strategy variable was constructed. The dummy variable measuring high variation in advertising per firm was adjusted to remove the effect of regionality. Each local or regional industry, not surprisingly, showed high variation in advertising per firm in the data. The adjusted variable was constructed by setting the dummy for regional industries to low variation in advertising per firm, whatever its actual value. Such an adjustment would eliminate any regional industries which might actually have high variation, but such is the price of ensuring that our results are not simply due to regionality. The adjusted dummy variable is negatively correlated with profits as are the other strategy

6. This discussion does not apply to the adjusted variation in $A/F$ variable. See below.

TABLE 7-1. Convenience Goods: Correlation Analysis with Strategy Variables

| Strategy variable | Profit | Eight-firm concentration ratio | Adjusted four-firm concentration ratio | Minimum efficient scale | Advertising/ sales | Large firm advertising/ sales | Growth | Regional dummy | Absolute capital requirements | Percent non-household |
|---|---|---|---|---|---|---|---|---|---|---|
| Variance in advertising/sales | −.324 | −.078 | .055 | .055 | −.387 | −.120 | −.558 | −.063 | −.247 | .274 |
| Square root variance in advertising/sales | −.341 | −.072 | .070 | .066 | −.405 | −.135 | −.572 | −.081 | −.247 | .267 |
| Variance in advertising/firm | −.275 | −.433 | −.095 | .044 | −.236 | −.105 | −.102 | −.549 | −.404 | −.115 |
| Square root variance in advertising/firm | −.285 | −.496 | −.172 | −.045 | −.244 | −.099 | −.060 | −.526 | −.487 | −.106 |

TABLE 7-1. (continued)

| Strategy variable | Profit | Eight-firm concentration ratio | Adjusted four-firm concentration ratio | Minimum efficient scale | Advertising/sales | Large firm advertising/sales | Growth | Regional dummy | Absolute capital requirements | Percent non-household |
|---|---|---|---|---|---|---|---|---|---|---|
| High variance in advertising/sales dummy | −.111 | −.103 | .055 | −.105 | −.261 | −.027 | −.399 | −.077 | −.168 | .344 |
| High variance in advertising/firm dummy | −.372 | −.305 | −.102 | −.142 | −.305 | −.149 | −.095 | −.369 | −.245 | −.214 |
| High variance in interaction | −.276 | −.436 | −.0962 | .039 | −.250 | −.088 | −.175 | −.497 | −.396 | −.038 |
| High variance in interaction dummy | −.247 | −.378 | .001 | .037 | −.186 | −.032 | −.040 | −.508 | −.403 | −.123 |
| Adjusted high variance in advertising per firm | −.278 | .105 | −.177 | −.414 | −.125 | .026 | −.050 | .331 | −.009 | −.081 |

variables. However, the adjusted $A/F$ dummy variable is positively correlated with concentration, the opposite of that of the other strategy variables. This difference suggests that regionality may have been strongly affecting our earlier results.

Table 7–2 presents multiple regression equations incorporating the strategy variables. *A priori,* the meaning of variation in the advertising to sales ratio is somewhat difficult to interpret, following the discussion in Chapter 6. Firms with the identical advertising to sales ratio may, because of size differences, have very different marketing strategies.[7] On the other hand, variation, in advertising per firm is clearly relevant if the effects of regionality are controlled for.

How do we isolate the impact of the direct and indirect effects given the earlier discussion? If the included advertising variable is the industry average advertising to sales ratio, the strategy variables measure the direct effect; the indirect effect is lost in the averaging process. The greater the variation in advertising, the greater the direct effect and hence the lower profits. Thus the sign prediction is negative.

The data, however, also give us the advertising to sales ratio for large firms, which are the $D$ group producers.[8] If the included advertising variable is advertising to sales for the large firms, then high variation in advertising (which implies a large $U$ group) should negatively affect profits through the indirect effect (the sign of the strategy variable should be negative here). Since using average $A/S$ allows us to measure the direct effect and large firm $A/S$ the direct and indirect effects, we are able through this testing procedure to isolate the two.

Equations 1 and 2 in Table 7–2 give results using large firm advertising to sales as the advertising variable without any strategy variables. These results are interesting in their own right. Comparing them to Table 6–16, it is apparent that large firm $A/S$ is a superior measure of advertising as a structural variable for convenience goods. Large firm $A/S$ is more significant itself, improves the significance levels of other included variables, and increases corrected $R^2$ from .82 to .84 in comparable equations. This suggests that advertising barriers and the effect of advertising on rivalry is primarily set by the behavior of large firms, and is consistent with the hypothesis that only limited $D$-$U$ strategic variation is present in convenience goods.

The results with strategy variables follow two patterns; one for the variables constructed using the advertising to sales ratio and another for all the rest. All regression coefficients of the strategy variables com-

---

7. R. E. Caves has suggested that this will be enhanced by the presence of advertising scale economies. It also relates to media segmentability.

8. The largest firms accounting for 30 percent of industry sales.

**TABLE 7-2.** Multiple Regression Equations Explaining Profit Rates in Convenience Goods: Results Incorporating Intra-industry Strategy Measures

| Intercept | Adjusted four-firm concentration ratio | Minimum efficient scale | Advertising/ sales | Large firm advertising/ sales | Growth | Regional dummy | Absolute capital requirements | Percent non-household | Variance in advertising/ sales | Variance advertising/ firm | Variance in advertising/ firm | Square root variance in advertising/ firm | Variance in advertising interaction | High variance in advertising/ sales dummy | High variance in advertising/ firm dummy | High variance advertising interaction dummy | Adjusted high variance in advertising/ firm dummy | $R^2$ | Corrected $R^2$ |
|---|---|---|---|---|---|---|---|---|---|---|---|---|---|---|---|---|---|---|---|
| 51.86c (1.433) | -.74551b (2.361) | .01837b (1.847) | | .55670a (5.168) | .03193b (2.389) | -5.9339 (.427) | .001700b (2.583) | | | | | | | | | | | .870a | .805 |
| 48.72c (1.487) | -.76433b (2.676) | .01642b (1.815) | | .59035a (5.966) | .03265a (2.701) | -12.097 (.933) | .001930a (3.180) | .90291b (1.918) | | | | | | | | | | .903a | .841 |
| 45.87 (.772) | -.75780b (2.371) | .01655c (1.701) | | .58829a (5.372) | .03329b (1.989) | -11.858 (.835) | .001932a (3.032) | .89497c (1.749) | 1.1411 (.059) | | | | | | | | | .903a | .825 |
| -.909 (.016) | -.61310b (2.222) | .01567c (1.779) | .67054a (6.131) | | .03596b (2.440) | -11.110 (.872) | .001881a (3.281) | .72448c (1.590) | | | | | | | | | | .921a | .857 |
| 27.27 (.677) | -.69093b (2.316) | .01925b (2.004) | | .55639a (5.241) | .040037a (2.751) | -7.2501 (.516) | .001860a (3.020) | .71439c (1.385) | | | | | | 7.8576 (.925) | | | | .910a | .839 |
| 26.84 (.824) | -.62602b (2.641) | .01892b (2.406) | .64785a (6.770) | | .03580a (2.967) | -6.3077 (.554) | .0016814a (3.383) | .50316 (1.218) | | | | | | 18.477b (2.814) | | | | .940a | .892 |
| 90.08 (1.953) | -.78000b (1.958) | .01062 (1.029) | .67384a (5.410) | | .01835 (1.228) | -22.491 (1.313) | .001714b (2.623) | .86530c (1.695) | | -.11881 (.684) | | | | | | | | .897a | .815 |
| 91.45b (2.334) | -.90148a (3.273) | .011741c (1.337) | | .60701a (6.613) | .02772b (2.048) | -26.722b (1.825) | .0018523a (3.298) | .84636b (1.944) | | | -.25553c (1.712) | | | | | | | .925a | .865 |
| 107.0b (2.494) | -.94248a (3.431) | .010237 (1.163) | | .61051a (6.789) | .02358b (1.976) | -28.981b (1.963) | .001765a (3.181) | .84061b (1.973) | | | | -3.3308b (1.874) | | | | | | .928a | .870 |
| 98.04b (2.198) | -.78458b (2.586) | .007589 (.701) | .65601a (5.336) | | .016998 (1.168) | -24.501c (1.513) | .001826a (2.875) | .77184c (1.511) | | | | | | | -9.3973 (1.018) | | | .902a | .824 |
| 108.2a (3.199) | -.92852a (3.957) | .005582 (.582) | | .59559a (7.593) | .02066b (1.961) | -30.924b (2.503) | .002103a (4.335) | .68040b (1.782) | | | | | | | -18.832a (2.742) | | | .944a | .900 |

TABLE 7-2. (continued)

| Intercept | Adjusted four-firm concentration ratio | Minimum efficient scale | Advertising/ sales | Large firm advertising/ sales | Growth | Regional dummy | Absolute capital requirements | Percent non-household | Variance in advertising/ sales | Variance in advertising/ firm | Square root variance in advertising/ firm | Variance in advertising interaction | High variance in advertising/ sales dummy | High variance in advertising/ firm dummy | High variance in advertising/ firm dummy | High variance advertising interaction dummy | Adjusted high variance in advertising/ firm dummy | $R^2$ | Corrected $R^2$ |
|---|---|---|---|---|---|---|---|---|---|---|---|---|---|---|---|---|---|---|---|
| 81.26[b] (2.154) | -.75377[b] (2.506) | .009389 (.918) | .66692[a] (5.459) | | .01893[c] (1.334) | -14.936 (1.074) | .001817[a] (2.851) | .81255[c] (1.609) | | | | | | | | | -7.9614 (.971) | .902[a] | .823 |
| 76.00[a] (2.793) | -.87321[a] (3.871) | .008695 (1.153) | | .61642[a] (7.951) | .02424[b] (2.459) | -11.579 (1.148) | .0021036[a] (4.418) | .74955[b] (2.025) | | | | | | | | | -17.346[a] (2.859) | .946[a] | .904 |
| 86.29[c] (1.741) | -.76627[b] (2.359) | .00139 (1.082) | .67843[a] (5.366) | | .01896 (1.209) | -19.753 (1.143) | .001741[b] (2.634) | .89771[c] (1.740) | | | | -.04875 (.399) | | | | | | .894[a] | .809 |
| 93.00[b] (2.261) | -.92897[a] (3.250) | .01167 (1.303) | | .62183[a] (6.580) | .02271[c] (1.764) | -26.367[c] (1.757) | .001891[a] (3.330) | .91616[b] (2.082) | | | | -.17160[c] (1.612) | | | | | | .923[a] | .861 |
| 77.07[b] (1.907) | -.72854[b] (2.341) | .01185 (1.156) | | .67100[a] (5.270) | .02088[c] (1.434) | -18.565 (1.163) | .001711[b] (2.544) | .87844[c] (1.692) | | | | | | | | -3.4863 (.383) | | .894[a] | .809 |
| 71.53[b] (2.093) | -.79421[a] (2.944) | .01320[c] (1.505) | | .59885[a] (6.415) | .02908[b] (2.503) | -22.147[c] (1.602) | .001783[a] (3.076) | .84920[b] (1.910) | | | | | | | | -12.047[a] (1.550) | | .922[a] | .859 |

*Note:* Figures in parentheses are $t$ values. The significance of the regression coefficients is tested using a one-tail $t$ test and the significance of the coefficients of multiple determination is tested using the $F$ test.

[a] Coefficient is significant at the 99 percent level.
[b] Coefficient is significant at the 95 percent level.
[c] Coefficient is significant at the 90 percent level.

puted from the variance in the advertising to sales ratio are positive. Where the included advertising variable is the average $A/S$, the coefficients are significant (especially the dummy variable). Where the included advertising variable is large firm advertising to sales, however, the coefficients are not significant.

In view of the conceptual problems with the use of $A/S$ to construct strategy variables, these results are not surprising. The positive coefficients of the strategy variables when average $A/S$ is included may reflect capture by the strategy variables of the importance of large firm advertising. High $A/S$ variation implies relatively greater large firm $A/S$.[9]

The results with the strategy variables derived from advertising per firm are of more interest. With average $A/S$ as the included advertising variable, strategy variables based on the variation in $A/F$ enter with a negative sign but are not very significant. This result holds for the dummy variable adjusted to remove the effects of regionality. The $t$ statistics for the strategy variable hover, in both cases, near 1.

Where the included advertising variable is large firm $A/S$, the coefficients of the strategy variable remain negative but greatly increase in magnitude and significance.[10] Once again, this result holds for the dummy variable adjusted to remove the effects of regionality. The best fit is in fact obtained using this variable, suggesting the appropriateness of the adjustment. Including the strategy variable yields a large increase in the significance of the advertising variable, improvement in the significant levels of all variables in the model, and a large increase in corrected $R^2$ from .841 to .904.[11]

These results strongly support my theory. Where the included advertising variable is average $A/S$, the strategy variable measures the direct effect. It shows up as exerting a negative influence on profits, as expected, but is not strongly significant, though significant at the 80 percent level. The low significance may be due to measurement errors, but it is consistent with the prediction that the direct effect is not as important in convenience goods. My theory suggests that the indirect effect will dominate in convenience goods and indeed it does here.

---

9. Since $A/S$ is bounded from below (by zero) the mean-variance relation may be positive for statistical reasons as well. I am indebted to R. E. Caves for this point. Equation 5 in Table 7–2 may be due to this. The conceptual problem with the variance of $A/S$ in convenience goods leads me not to put much weight on it.

10. The best results are obtained using dummy variables. This may be due to the fact that the dummy variables further remove the effects of regionality.

11. This pattern holds for the strategy variables constructed from the advertising interaction variable.

With large firm $A/S$ as the included advertising variable, the strategy variables are negative as predicted and highly significant, yield substantial improvements in the fit of the model, and the coefficients of the strategy variables increase greatly in size. Since the direct effect was very weak, this suggests that the indirect effect is indeed powerful and works in the expected direction.

Nonconvenience Goods

The potential for strategy variation to affect rate of return seems far greater in nonconvenience goods. However, while there is a relatively clear theoretical correlation between intraindustry variations in advertising behavior and differences in firm strategy in convenience goods, this relationship blurs for nonconvenience goods. Nonconvenience selling importantly involves the retailer, and hence differences in strategy will likely correspond to different combinations of push and pull. Variations in advertising may reflect this, but only partially. A further complication is that different strategies imply different levels of retailer power and thus potentially different levels of manufacturer rate of return. In addition, the clean $D$-$U$ separation no longer holds. Thus the relationship between large firm and industry-wide advertising is dubiously linked, theoretically, to strategy variation. This is reflected in the data on the relationship of large firm advertising on industry-wide advertising. In contrast to the convenience case, 11 of 23 nonconvenience industries had large firm advertising to sales ratios either below or equal to that of the entire industry.

Tables 7–3 and 7–4 present the results of an analysis of strategy variables in nonconvenience goods. The results confirm my fears that advertising variation may not capture strategy variation. The theoretically appropriate measures of advertising variation in nonconvenience goods are unadjusted advertising per firm and our advertising interaction variable, since there are few problems of regionality. All the variables are positively correlated with profits and enter the multiple regression equations with the expected negative sign. However, significance levels are very low and contribution to explained variance nonexistent.

One interesting result is that the simple correlations between the strategy variables and growth is consistently negative in convenience goods (Table 7–1) while it is consistently positive in nonconvenience goods (Table 7–3). One would expect faster industry growth to be associated with more experimentation in marketing strategies and more widely spread intraindustry expectations. This relation is apparent in numerous case studies of individual industries where early variations in

TABLE 7-3. Nonconvenience Goods: Correlation Analysis with Strategy Variables

| Strategy variable | Profit | Eight-firm concentration ratio | Minimum efficient scale | Advertising interaction | Growth | Absolute capital requirements | Percent non-household |
|---|---|---|---|---|---|---|---|
| Variance in advertising/sales | -.158 | -.444 | -.358 | -.357 | .039 | -.240 | -.186 |
| Variance in advertising/firm | .486 | .363 | -.051 | .490 | .266 | .351 | .228 |
| Variance in advertising interaction | .413 | .258 | -.120 | .410 | .295 | .270 | .158 |
| High variance in advertising/sales dummy | -.244 | -.074 | -.071 | -.184 | .031 | -.205 | -.185 |
| High variance in advertising/firm dummy | .289 | .107 | -.251 | .156 | .201 | .235 | .207 |
| High variance in advertising interaction dummy | .467 | .399 | -.043 | .437 | .234 | .348 | .256 |

TABLE 7-4. Multiple Regression Equations Explaining Profit Rates in Nonconvenience Goods: Results Incorporating Intra-industry Strategy Measures

| Intercept | Eight-firm concentration ratio | Minimum efficient scale | Advertising interaction | Growth | Absolute capital requirements | Percent non-household | Variance in advertising/sales | Variance in advertising/firm | Variance in advertising interaction | High variance in advertising/sales dummy | High variance in advertising/firm dummy | High variance advertising interaction dummy | $R^2$ | Corrected $R^2$ |
|---|---|---|---|---|---|---|---|---|---|---|---|---|---|---|
| 93.42[a] (2.862) | -.48513 (1.009) | -.01875 (.994) | .0001258[a] (3.814) | .004268 (.238) | .0005085[b] (1.923) | .57185[c] (1.466) | 6.0278 (.326) | | | | | | .741[a] | 620 |
| 104.9[a] (3.634) | -.30491 (.556) | -.03234 (1.216) | .0001467[a] (3.290) | .001792 (.101) | .0004490[c] (1.707) | .53728[c] (1.383) | | -.37032 (.723) | | | | | .748[a] | .630 |
| 102.7[a] (3.667) | -.33342 (.640) | -.03129 (1.262) | .0001442[a] (3.507) | .004095 (.243) | .0004277 (1.590) | .53609[c] (1.384) | | | -.32919 (.772) | | | | .749[a] | .632 |
| 98.95[a] (3.497) | -.51641 (1.048) | -.01853 (.968) | .0001245[a] (3.752) | .0061165 (.356) | .0004947[b] (1.760) | .58090[c] (1.454) | | | | .20623 (.022) | | | .739[a] | .617 |
| 99.68[a] (3.515) | -.44382 (.753) | -.002242 (.331) | .0001294[a] (3.132) | .004888 (.269) | .0004788[b] (1.779) | .56875[c] (1.444)[c] | | | | | -2.7251 (.199) | | .740[a] | .618 |
| 100.0[a] (3.574) | -.44772 (.914) | -.02370 (1.101) | .0001297[a] (3.778) | .005686 (.337) | .0004774[b] (1.833) | .59741[c] (1.533)[c] | | | | | | -4.8017 (.486) | .743[a] | .623 |

*Note:* Figures in parentheses are *t* values. The significance of the regression coefficients is tested using a one-tail *t* test and the significance of the coefficients of multiple determination is tested using the *F* test.

[a] Coefficient is significant at the 99 percent level.
[b] Coefficient is significant at the 95 percent level.
[c] Coefficient is significant at the 90 percent level.

strategy among firms become reduced as the industry matures.[12] Hence growth would imply a greater variance of strategies chosen where a wide range of potential strategies exists. In nonconvenience goods, where strategic options are numerous, growth is positively associated with strategy variation (especially for the superior advertising per firm-based variables) which supports this view. In convenience goods, where strategic choice is limited, such a relation would not hold. In addition slow growth may deny firms the windfalls that might be used in attempting to shift from the $U$ to the $D$ group. Hence a negative relation between growth and strategic variation would be predicted, which shows up in the data.

The nonconvenience results, though disappointing in their inability to improve our ability to explain the cross-industry variance in profits, are at least indirectly supportive of the view that the retailer is extremely important in nonconvenience goods. We are left with only the indirect evidence of larger unexplained variance in profits in nonconvenience goods to support the view that strategy variation is important there. Once again the results contrast sharply with those in the convenience sample, in the manner predicted by the theory. The next section explores the effect of several measures of retail structure on manufacturer performance. The results with strategy variables suggest a clear mandate for doing so among nonconvenience industries.

**Retailer Structure**

Chapter 2 presented a series of hypotheses which linked the structure of the retail distribution system for a product to rate of return in manufacturing. This section reports the results of adding measures of retailer structure to our model explaining cross industry variations in rate of return.

Five elements of retailer structure were linked to manufacturer profits:[13] 1. Manufacturing industry return will decrease as the number of retail buyers decreases. 2. Manufacturing return will decrease as the concentration of the retail outlets in their relevant retail markets increases. 3. Manufacturing return will decrease as the number of retail outlet types through which a product is sold decreases. 4. Manufacturing return will decrease as the absolute size of the retail firm increases. 5. Manufacturing return will decrease as the breadth of the retailer's product line increases. In addition to pure effects of retailer structure, the discussion of convenience and nonconvenience goods further suggested

12. For example, see *Note on the Recreational Vehicle Industry,* Harvard Business School, International Case Clearinghouse 9–375–092.

13. All hypotheses carry an assumption of other things being equal.

that retailer structure would interact with the ability of retailers to influence differentiation. The power of retailers to influence differentiation creates the potential for bargaining away manufacturer rents; retailer structure influences the extent to which bargaining will occur. In convenience goods, retailer power to influence differentiation is minimal, and hence the importance of variations in retailer structure in affecting the exercise of that power is limited. Among nonconvenience goods, however, differentiation-related retailer power is high and variations in retailer structure may strongly influence the exercise of that power. Since retailer specialization (narrowness of product line) is positively associated with retailer power to influence differentiation in nonconvenience goods, the tests of the effects of breadth of product line will test the net effect of two offsetting hypotheses. Other measures of retailer structure may also proxy the retailer's power in differentiation.

Measures of retailer structure may further provide an empirical link to intraindustry strategy variation. Fewness of retail firms selling a product, for example, may signal the importance of strategy variations involving the retailer. The presence of multiple retail outlet types selling a product may provide increased potential for strategy variation and hence lower manufacturer return due to enhanced rivalry. Such links may be useful in rationalizing results but are unfortunately not separately testable.

Structure of the Test

The theoretical specification of the retailer structure hypotheses is clear enough. When one begins to translate these into empirical specifications, however, some formidable problems emerge. One problem is the relationship between the aggregate industry-wide distribution arrangements and those of individual manufacturers. Suppose, for example, that a given manufacturing industry sells 50 percent of its sales through one retail outlet class and 50 percent through another. Can we assume that each individual manufacturer sells in this 50/50 ratio, or do some manufacturers specialize in one outlet class and some in another? The answer is crucial to the specification of many of my hypotheses. Another question revolves around whether we should look only at the dominant outlet class through which an industry sells, or all outlet classes? If we look at all outlet classes, the specification of the buyer concentration hypothesis is difficult. Is the relevant number of buyers the sum of all outlets in all the outlet classes an industry sells through, a weighted average of these, or some other measure? Should an outlet class selling a small fraction of an industry's product receive equal weight to the dominant outlet class? These issues will be central to the specifications chosen below.

In struggling with these specification issues, let us examine the nature of the data available on retailing. Data measuring the structure of retailing were obtained primarily from the *Census of Business*. The *Census* divides the retailing sector into categories of retail stores. With modifications, these categories were used as the retail outlet types in the study. The modifications and a full description of the derivation of the retailer data are found in the Technical Appendix.

There are two major types of retailer data available, that relating to the manufacturing industry and that relating to each retail outlet type. With respect to the former, the *Census* gives the distribution of manufacturing industry sales by retail outlet type for each industry in the sample. For example, in the appliance industry 54 percent of sales are made through appliance stores, 41 percent through department stores, and 5 percent through radio and television stores.[14] For two industries in the sample this data was not used: periodicals and medical/optical goods. In both these industries the usefulness of the data was questionable, since periodicals are sold heavily by subscription and the medical/optical goods industry classification encompasses products with widely different retailing characteristics. These industries were omitted from the sample for purposes of the retailer structure analysis, resulting in one less convenience good industry and one less nonconvenience good industry in the sample.

The distribution of industry sales by retail outlet type was used to construct a variable measuring the extent to which multiple outlet types sell each manufacturing industry's product. In specifying the variable, it it useful to review briefly the mechanisms by which multiple outlet types influence the manufacturer. Multiple retail types, except in impulse goods, lowered entry barriers into distribution and enhanced rivalry at the retail level, reducing retailer power vis-à-vis the manufacturer. The effects of these on manufacturer return had opposite sign prediction. The hypotheses imply that both the number and relative sales share of retail outlet types selling a given manufacturing industry's product are relevant. For this reason the extent of multiple type selling was measured with a Herfindahl index calculated as follows:

$$H = \sum_{i=1}^{n} s_i^2$$

where the $s_i$ is the fraction if industry sales sold through the $i^{\text{th}}$ retail outlet type and $n$ is the number of retail outlet types selling the product. As the number of outlet types increases and the relative shares become more equal, the Herfindahl index decreases. Conversely, as the product

14. Store categories are defined by the *Census of Business*. Radio and television stores, for example, sell primarily these items.

is sold more and more through a dominant retail outlet type, the Herfindahl index increases.

The other major type of data in the *Census* related to the characteristics of each category of retail outlet. Using the *Census* and other sources, the following series were obtained for each retail outlet type: number of establishments; number of firms; average firm size; retail advertising to sales ratio; retail profit on equity; breadth of product line.

For number of firms and average firm size two approaches to measurement were used. Data was collected both for all retail firms in the outlet type, and also for the largest firms accounting for 50 percent of retail sales in that outlet type. The latter data was judged to be preferable, since it more accurately recognizes the larger, more important retailers while omitting the many small, less influential retailers. Empirically, however, the two series were highly correlated. Measuring concentration of retail outlet types by looking at the share of the top few firms was deemed inappropriate. Few retail firms sell nationally, and hence looking at the top few firms did not capture the characteristics of the number and size distribution satisfactorily in retailing.

The number of retail establishments was used as a measure of retailer concentration in the relevant retail market. This assumes that the distribution of establishments across SMSA's is uniform, that is, there is approximately the same density of establishments in each outlet type across SMSA's. Thus by comparing the number of establishments across outlets nationally we get a proxy for the comparison in each SMSA. It further assumes that the size of the relevant retail market for all outlet classes is the same. Thus, for example, we can compare the number of food store establishments with the number of drug store establishments without correcting for the fact that the retail market for one differs from that of the other. While this latter assumption at first seems severe, all tests are performed for convenience and nonconvenience goods separately. Within each subsample, the assumption that the relevant retail market is similar is probably quite good and hence variations in the number of establishments is a good measure of variations in their concentration in any given retail market.

Data on retailer advertising to sales and retailer profit on equity were obtained from the *IRS Statistics of Income*. The usefulness of these data was limited by their high level of aggregation and lack of coverage of the retail sector which necessitated some approximation and the use of supplementary data sources (see the Technical Appendix).

The data are designed to measure additional aspects of the bilateral relationship between manufacturer and retailer which are suggested by the theory. Presumably retailer advertising increases retailer power vis-à-vis the manufacturer, since it may enhance the retailer contribution to product differentiation (reputation, store image, and so on). Retail profit also suggests greater retailer bargaining power *ex post,* other things being equal. However, Chapter 2 argues that rate of return extracted from the consumer is the result of the total amount of product differentiation developed by both the manufacturer and the retailer. The distribution of this return is determined by relative bargaining strength between manufacturer and retailer. Thus if retailer advertising increases retailer contribution to product differentiation, total return will increase and the effect on manufacturer return is ambiguous. Similarly, higher retailer return may signal higher ultimate differentiation as well as high relative retailer product differentiation. The direction of these effects on manufacturer return, then, becomes an empirical question.

Breadth of product line of each outlet class was measured with a Herfindahl index of the following form:

$$B = \sum_{j}^{m} sh_j{}^2$$

where *sh* is the percentage of total sales of the outlet class accounted for by product line *j* and *m* the number of product lines. The *Census* gives the percentage distribution of each outlet's sales by broad product line, and additional detail for important product lines. These were used together to disaggregate product lines to approximately IRS industries.[15] As a retail outlet class' product lines become broader, the Herfindahl index declines.

We now come to the most difficult specification problem; namely the translation of the data for each retail outlet type to a series that can be matched to the sample of manufacturing industries to capture the two retailer concentration hypotheses (national concentration and market concentration). The problem arises because more than one outlet type typically sells the product of each manufacturing industry. Four alternatives were used in testing. First, a series was constructed using data for the dominant retail outlet type selling the product of the manufacturing industry. Here the variable measuring buyer concentration was the number of firms (establishments) in the dominant retail type. Second, the total number of retail firms (establishments) selling the product was obtained by adding the number of firms (establishments) in each significant retail outlet type selling it. This would seem to correspond closely to the most simple statement of the buyer concen-

---

15. In a few cases the *Census* did not provide sufficient disaggregation for me to do this, and the measure of breadth understates the true breadth in these cases.

tration hypothesis, if one assumes manufacturers' sales are distributed evenly within each retail outlet type. Third, a weighted average number of firms (establishments) was constructed by weighting the number of firms in each important retail outlet selling the product by its share of manufacturing industry sales.

It is not clear just which measure is appropriate, because the answer depends on the unknown distribution of sales between individual manufacturers and the retail distribution system. The dominant outlet class is important but certainly some importance should be attached to other outlet classes selling the product. The total number of retail sellers for most manufacturing industries includes many sellers which although important in number are unimportant in sales share. In view of this ambiguity about which measure was most important (indeed, the answer could very well vary across industries), a fourth series was constructed using a dummy variable technique. The three series described above were partitioned based on apparent break points into low buyer concentration and high buyer concentration groups (separately for convenience and nonconvenience goods). The series were then arrayed and a dummy variable constructed by assigning the value of 1 to any industry which had high buyer concentration based on any measure, and 0 to all other industries.

The average retail firm size variable was constructed three ways: using the dominant retail outlet type selling the product, and weighted averages of the average size of outlets over all retail outlet types selling the product, both for all outlets and for the largest outlets. The three series were highly correlated (.98), which suggests that secondary outlet types selling a product have similar size characteristics to the dominant type. Therefore, no dummy variable was constructed here. It was possible to construct the retailer advertising to sales and retailer profit series only for the dominant outlet class because of data limitations.[16] The measure of product line breadth was only meaningful for the dominant outlet class. We are left, then, with 12 retailer variables which are defined in summary form in Table 7–5. Of these, 4 are different measures of buyer concentration and 3 are different measures of average retail firm size.

Empirical Results

Before examining the regression analysis it may be instructive to look directly at the summary differences in the retail data for the convenience and nonconvenience retailers. Mean advertising to sales is 1.3 for con-

16. Data was unavailable for several outlet classes which were not dominant for any industry but nevertheless important.

venience retailers and 2.5 for nonconvenience retailers. The average number of convenience outlet establishments in each outlet type is 175,000, as compared with 21,000 for nonconvenience outlets. The mean number of largest firms accounting for 50 percent of sales in the dominant outlet class is 3,789 versus 5,765 in nonconvenience goods,

TABLE 7-5.  Definitions of Retailer Structure Variables

| Variable | Definition |
|---|---|
| Number of establishments | The number of retail establishments in the dominant retail outlet class selling the product |
| Number of firms | The number of largest retail firms accounting for 50 percent of retail sales in the dominant outlet class selling the product |
| Total number of retail buyers | The sum of the number of largest retail firms accounting for 50 percent of retail sales for each retail outlet class selling a significant portion of retail sales of the product |
| Weighted number of firms | The weighted average (using percent of total retail sales of the product) of the number of largest retail firms accounting for 50 percent of retail sales for each retail class selling the product |
| High buyer concentration dummy | A dummy variable sorting industries into high or low buyer concentration based on a composite of the above three measures |
| Average retail firm size | The average firm size of the largest firms accounting for 50 percent of retail sales in the dominant retail outlet class selling the product |
| Weighted average firm size | Same procedure as used in weighted number of firms except for use of firm size; also computed for all retail firms as well as for the largest ones accounting for 50 percent of retail sales of the product |
| Breadth of product line | An index measuring the number and relative shares of merchandise lines carried by the dominant outlet class selling the product |
| Herfindahl index of multiple outlet type selling | An index measuring the number and relative shares of retail outlet classes |
| Retail advertising to sales ratio | The advertising to sales ratio for the dominant retail outlet class selling the product |
| Retail profit on equity | The profit on equity for the dominant retail outlet class selling the product |

suggesting a far greater degree of multiunit or chain development among convenience retailers. The mean of the Herfindahl index measuring the breadth of the retailer product line is .33 in convenience goods and .47 in nonconvenience goods, implying broader lines in convenience goods. Summarizing the major differences between convenience and nonconvenience retailers, the convenience retailer is more intensively located, advertises less, carries a broader product line, and convenience retailing is more amenable to chain store development.

Statistical tests with retailer variables were made separately for convenience and nonconvenience goods in view of the differences in the effect of the retailer variables in the two samples predicted by theory. Additional tests were also made using the entire consumer goods sample. Although the appropriate structural models for the two subsamples are quite different, using the combined sample does not necessarily bias the results with retailer variables whose effect on performance should be similar in the two subsamples unless these retailer variables are correlated with omitted variables which differ in importance for the two subsamples. Such correlation is probably present to some extent. However, the results with the entire sample are of some interest for the retailer variables in view of the scarcity of degrees of freedom due to the sheer number of retailer variables. Results of testing the retailer variables in the entire sample will serve as a check and will be referred to selectively below; they are not reported separately.

*Convenience Goods.* For convenience goods, theory minimizes the importance of the retailer variables. Table 7–6 presents the results of tests on the convenience sample and generally confirms this theoretical prediction. (I emphasize that in the statistical tests the traditional market structure variables were included in all runs but omitted from Tables 7–6 and 7–7 for the sake of brevity.) None of the retailer variables leads to significant improvement in $R^2$. The most successful variable is retailer advertising to sales, which is significant at the 5 percent level and enters with a positive sign. This supports the hypothesis that retailer advertising enhances total return more than it improves retailer bargaining strength in convenience goods. Retailer profit enters with a negative sign which suggests that high retail profits may be at the expense of manufacturing profits—supporting the existence of a bargaining relationship. All the buyer concentration variables enter with perverse signs, but are low on significance. These poor results may be due in part to problems inherent in the data. In the convenience sample, the overall buyer concentration variables are dominated by the somewhat unusual characteristics of grocery stores (relatively few large chains) which are the dominant outlet class in 12 of the 18 convenience indus-

**TABLE 7-6.** Multiple Regression Equations Explaining Manufacturer Profit-Rates in Convenience Goods $(n = 18)$: Results with Retail Structure Variables

| Four firm concentration ratio | Number of establishments (dominant)[d] | Number of firms[e] | Retail advertising/sales | Retail profit/equity | Weighted average retail firm size | Herfindahl index of multiple type selling | Total number retail buyers[e] | Weighted number of firms[e] | Weighted average retail firm size | Breadth of product line | High buyer concentration dummy | $R^2$ | Corrected $R^2$ |
|---|---|---|---|---|---|---|---|---|---|---|---|---|---|
| -.52297 (1.446) | | | | | | | | | | | | .899[a] | .829 |
| -.59249 (1.607) | .00004465 (.994) | | | | | | | | | | | .909[a] | .828 |
| -.60381 (1.798) | | -.0013997[c] (1.685) | | | | | | | | | | .923[a] | .855 |
| -.37114 (1.104) | | | .29101[b] (1.822) | | | | | | | | | .926[a] | .861 |
| -.70534 (1.846) | | | | -.41164 (1.236) | | | | | | | | .914[a] | .837 |
| -.44364 (1.115) | | | | | .001779 (.759) | | | | | | | .905[a] | .821 |
| -.49804 (1.336) | | | | | | -.14859 (.709) | | | | | | .904[a] | .819 |
| -.53101 (1.383) | | | | | | | -.0001277 (.159) | | | | | .899[a] | .810 |
| -.55037 (1.576) | | | | | | | | -.001469 (1.328) | | | | .916[a] | .841 |
| -.41936 (1.132) | | | | | | | | | .0001740 (1.096) | | | .911[a] | .832 |
| -.34040 (.699) | | | .30984 (1.171) | .04723 (.093) | | | | | | | | .926[a] | .844 |

TABLE 7-6.  (continued)

| Four firm concentration ratio | Number of establishments (dominant)[d] | Number of firms[e] | Retail advertising/ sales | Retail profit/ equity | Weighted average retail firm size | Herfindahl index of multiple type selling | Total number retail buyers[e] | Weighted number of firms[e] | Weighted average retail firm size[e] | Breadth of product line | High buyer concentration dummy | $R^2$ | Corrected $R^2$ |
|---|---|---|---|---|---|---|---|---|---|---|---|---|---|
| -.57776 (1.714) | | -.001501[c] (1.793) | | | | -.19028 (.996) | | | | | | .932[a] | .855 |
| -.52274 (1.371) | | | | | | | | | | | .21209 (.023) | .899[a] | .809 |
| -.33298 (.985) | | | .38298[b] (2.086) | | | | | | | | -9.3361 (1.011) | .935[a] | .861 |
| -.73314 (1.983) | | | | | | | | | | | -18.962[c] (1.333) | .926[a] | .842 |
| | | | | | | | | | | .1985 (.285) | | .915[a] | .839 |

Note: Figures in parentheses are $t$ values. The significance of the regression coefficients is tested using a one-tail $t$ test and the significance of the coefficients of multiple determination is tested using the $F$ test.

a Coefficient is significant at the 99 percent level.
b Coefficient is significant at the 95 percent level.
c Coefficient is significant at the 90 percent level.
d In all cases regression equations included the following structural variables in addition to concentration (which is shown): minimum efficient scale, advertising/sales, growth, regional dummy, capital requirements, percent non-household. The inclusion of retailer variables did not significantly affect the values of the coefficients or their significance levels. Hence the values of the coefficients are not shown.
e Largest firms accounting for 50 percent of total sales.

tries.[17] This curtails the variance of the retailer variables for convenience goods and perhaps their significance.

The Herfindahl variable measuring selling by multiple outlet types enters with a negative sign. This suggests that the net effect of multiple outlet types is to increase manufacturer return. The retailer market concentration variable (number of establishments) enters with the expected positive sign. As the number of establishments increases, retailer market concentration decreases and manufacturer return increases.[18] Both variables are somewhat low on significance, but are consistently of the same sign. Anticipating results I will report below, the multiple types Herfindahl index performs similarly in both the convenience and nonconvenience samples. In a series of tests using the full sample, the Herfindahl index was consistently negative and of approximately the same magnitude as it was when tested in the convenience and nonconvenience samples separately (with significance at the 90 percent level when introduced with no retailer variables). These results indicate that the effect of multiple types is quite constant across the entire sample.[19]

The results with retailer variables in the convenience sample confirm the overall prediction that retailer effects will be relatively unimportant in convenience goods. Of the variables tested, only retailer advertising was significant at the 95 percent level. This is perhaps not surprising nor inconsistent with relative lack of retailer power in convenience goods, since the positive sign of the advertising variable indicates that the manufacturer is a net benefactor, and my theory argues that the manufacturer holds the bulk of the power.

Nonconvenience Goods

The theory suggests that retailer variables will be very important in nonconvenience goods. The ability of the retail stage to exercise the bargaining power afforded it by its importance in product differentiation in nonconvenience goods will be enhanced by a concentrated retail structure, though the retailer's power to influence differentiation will likely have a strong independent effect. Multiple regression equations testing the retailer variables in the nonconvenience sample are given in Table 7–7. The results are quite dramatic. In the best runs with retailer variables, corrected $R^2$ increases from .64 to .91. Thus the first impres-

17. One convenience industry was not used in the tests.
18. This variable is less affected by the fewness of firms in grocery retailing.
19. In all tests using retailer variables in the convenience sample, including those not reported, the coefficient of the adjusted four-firm concentration ratio was negative and significant. It appears, then, that the explanation for the negative coefficient result does not lie with retailer variables, at least none of those tested.

sion confirms the hypothesis that much of the greater unexplained variance in nonconvenience goods is due to omitting the effect of the retailer.

In contrast to the convenience sample results, retailer advertising and retailer profit perform very poorly. This is not surprising, since the theoretical prediction of the effect of these variables is ambiguous, and in the case of retailer advertising my theory argues that retailer power in nonconvenience goods is largely derived from in-store selling efforts and not retailer advertising. In convenience goods retailer advertising would be more related to price image and getting buyers to try the store and thus relatively more important to the manufacturer-retailer power balance.

The single most important retailer variable is the Herfindahl measure of the breadth of the dominant retail outlet's product line. It enters with a negative sign, is highly significant, and increases corrected $R^2$ from .68 to .82. As this Herfindahl measure decreases, product line breadth increases, and thus the observed negative sign implies that as the retailer product line narrows, retailer power increases and manufacturer profits decline. While this result is the reverse of that predicted by the structural hypothesis regarding breadth of product line, it is perhaps the most direct confirmation of the overall model. My theory suggests that the retailer's ability to influence differentiation, though always high relative to convenience goods, varies markedly among nonconvenience industries. Narrowness of retailer product line implies greater salesperson expertise as perceived by the buyer and improved store reputation as an information source. Thus narrowness of product line proxies the retailer's power to influence product differentiation. My theory predicts that this source of power will outweigh others, which is strongly supported by the results. Although the net effect of the increased retailer bargaining power is partly an empirical question depending on the strength of the simultaneous increase in overall product differentiation, the inclusion of a measure of retailer power in the model will control for an important additional element of the simultaneous system. Since we would expect the relationship of the increase in total rents to the change in the distribution of rents incident to the increase in retailer power to remain stable across non-convenience industries, the retailer variable should reduce the unexplained variance in the model. In addition, within the nonconvenience sample, narrowness of product line will also serve as a control for the differing effectiveness of advertising among nonconvenience goods.

The variables measuring the average retail firm size are also significant in all specifications, though they are strongly collinear (negatively)

TABLE 7-7. Multiple Regression Equations Explaining Manufacturer Profit Rates in Nonconvenience Goods ($n = 22$): Results with Retail Structure Variables

| Number of establishments[d] | Number of firms | Retailer advertising/ sales | Retailer profit/ equity | Herfindahl index of multiple-type selling | Total number retail buyers[e] | Weighted number of firms[e] | Average retail firm size[e] | Weighted average firm size | Weighted average retail firm size[e] | Breadth of product line | High buyer concentration dummy | $R^2$ | Corrected $R^2$ |
|---|---|---|---|---|---|---|---|---|---|---|---|---|---|
| .0005079 (1.324) | | | | | | | | | | | | .769a | .677 |
| | .42473 (.408) | | | | | | | | | | | .795a | .692 |
| | | .007681 (.161) | | | | | | | | | | .772a | .658 |
| | | | .006103 (.018) | | | | | | | | | .770a | .654 |
| | | | | −.22303 (.803) | | | | | | | | .769a | .654 |
| | | | | | −.0006756b (2.041) | | | | | | | .779a | .669 |
| | | | | | | −.001983b (1.967) | | | | | | .822a | .733 |
| | | | | | | | .00005236c (1.600) | | | | | .819a | .729 |
| | | | | | | | | .002768b (2.159) | | | | .805a | .707 |
| | | | | | | | | | .0001991b (2.575) | | | .827a | .740 |
| | | | | | | | | | | | | .843a | .765 |

TABLE 7-7. (continued)

| Number of establishments[d] | Number of firms | Retailer advertising/sales | Retailer profit/equity | Herfindahl index of multiple-type selling | Total number retail buyers[e] | Weighted number of firms[e] | Average retail firm size[e] | Weighted average firm size | Weighted average retail firm size | Breadth of product line | High buyer concentration dummy | $R^2$ | Corrected $R^2$ |
|---|---|---|---|---|---|---|---|---|---|---|---|---|---|
| | | | | | | | | | | -.42302[a] (3.592) | | .880[a] | .820 |
| | | | | | | | | | | | -7.497 (.747) | .778[a] | .667 |
| .0008336[a] (2.699) | | | | | | | | .003731[a] (3.321) | | | | .889[a] | .821 |
| | | | | | | -.002590[b] (1.950) | | | | | -7.4184 (.719) | .826[a] | .719 |
| | | | | -.56307[b] (2.500) | -.001145[a] (3.642) | -.004686[a] (4.216) | | | | | | .898[a] | .822 |
| | .002116[b] (2.430) | | | -.07270 (.366) | | | | | | | | .913[a] | .849 |
| | .003578[a] (3.599) | | | | | | | .005229[a] (4.453) | | | -28.818[a] (3.552) | .912[a] | .858 |
| | | | | | | | | | | -.44938[a] (3.997) | -11.531[c] (1.636) | .900[a] | .839 |
| | | | | -.26401 (.930) | | | | | | | -9.046 (.885) | .792[a] | .664 |
| | | | | | | | | .0001405 (.090) | | -.41212[b] (2.399) | | .880[a] | .806 |
| .0005026 (1.033) | | | | | | | | | | | -.23528 (.019) | .795[a] | .668 |

TABLE 7-7. (continued)

| Number of establishmentsd | Number of firms | Retailer advertising/ sales | Retailer profit/ equity | Herfindahl index of multiple-type selling | Total number retail buyerse | Weighted number of firmse | Average retail firm sizee | Weighted average firm size | Weighted average retail firm size | Breadth of product line | High buyer concentration dummy | $R^2$ | Corrected $R^2$ |
|---|---|---|---|---|---|---|---|---|---|---|---|---|---|
| .0004566c (1.500) | | | | | | | | .005174a (4.611) | | | -21.996b (2.448) | .926a | .870 |
| .0005008c (1.736) | | | | | | | | .003119b (1.875) | | -.23820c (1.577) | -15.116c (1.586) | .940a | .885 |
| | | | | | | -.003726a (3.011) | | .001964c (1.374) | | | -38.907a (5.403) | .950a | .912 |
| | | | | | | -.003618b (2.436) | | .001852 (1.124) | | -.02454 (.156) | -37.958a (3.928) | .950a | .905 |

*Note*: Figures in parentheses are *t* values. The significance of the regression coefficients is tested using a one-tail *t* test and the significance of the coefficients of multiple determination is tested using the *F* test.

a Coefficient is significant at the 99 percent level.

b Coefficient is significant at the 95 percent level.

c Coefficient is significant at the 90 percent level.

d In all cases regression equations included the following structural variables: minimum efficient scale, advertising interaction, growth, capital requirements, percent nonhousehold. The inclusion of retailer variables did not significantly affect the values of the coefficients or their significance levels. Hence, the values of the coefficients are not shown.

e Largest firms accounting for 50 percent of total sales.

with the breadth of product line measure.[20] The weighted average firm size of all important retail outlet types selling the product performed slightly better. Contrary to the structural bargaining power hypothesis given in Chapter 2, however, the sign of the coefficient is always positive: as the average retail firm size increases, manufacturer return increases. This strong result justifies further discussion.

The answer lies again in the importance of retailer contribution to product differentiation in nonconvenience goods. Average retail firm size is another proxy for the strength of retailer contribution to differentiation. The small retail outlet types are typically specialty outlets such as photographic supply stores or jewelry stores, and these exert a greater influence over the final customer's decision than does a large department store, motor vehicle dealer, or furniture store. The strong negative collinearity $(-.70)$ between narrowness of product line and average firm size strongly supports this view. Thus as the retail firm size increases, retailer contribution to product differentiation decreases and manufacturer rate of return will increase, other things being equal. Large average retailer firm size also, in most cases, is the result of extensive chain store development.[21] The theory in Chapter 3 suggests that one of the key conditions facilitating the development of chains is the lack of importance of personal selling. Where personal selling is important (and the product is typically a large purchase and considered more important by the consumer) the economies of multiunit or chain development are reduced. This reasoning is supported by the extensive developments of chains in convenience goods. In the present context, however, it suggests that those nonconvenience retail outlet classes with important chain development (implying large firms) will tend to be those where the retailer contribution to product differentiation is relatively low (for nonconvenience goods). Examples are shoe stores and to a lesser extent clothing stores. This reinforces the conclusion thata as retail firm size increases, retailer contribution to product differentiation decreases and manufacturer return will increase. The effect seems likely to swamp the structural effect of absolute size discussed in the first section of Chapter 2.

Breadth of product line is the superior measure of retailer power in

20. In the best equation (equation 25), the significance level of weighted average firm size falls. However, comparison with equation 15 in Table 7–7 suggests that the addition of average firm size greatly improves $R^2$. Weighted average firm size is highly correlated with the weighted number of firms $(-.71)$ and the high buyer concentration dummy $(.64)$ which probably explains its lower significance level in equation 25. Breadth of product line is less correlated with these variables.

21. Average firm size is highly correlated with weighted firm size. Nondominant outlet types are therefore similar in size characteristics to the dominant ones.

the tests, which is perhaps not surprising in view of its greater direct-ness. Its collinearity with average size reduces its significance in some runs when both are included; however, its improvement of $R^2$ testifies to its importance even in these runs. The decrease in the coefficient of the breadth measure in these runs is consistent with the collinearity interpretation.

The variables measuring national retail buyer concentration present a somewhat confusing picture, probably because of the specification problems noted above. That is, no one variable adequately measures the theoretical concept of retailer concentration. In Table 7–7 the number of firms in the dominant outlet class has the expected positive sign but is not a significant and important variable unless it is intro-duced in combination with either the total number of retail firms or the weighted average number of retail firms. The latter variables, however, enter with a negative sign which is the opposite of that expected in the simple buyer concentration hypothesis. The coefficient of the weighted average number of firms is always negative and highly significant. The high buyer concentration dummy variable is negative as expected in all speci-fications, but it is not significant when entered alone. When the weighted average number of firms or breadth of product line is included, how-ever, its significance increases dramatically.

These results strongly suggest that the dominant outlet type and the other outlet types selling significant amounts of the product are im-portant elements of retail structure, as was suggested by the theory. The mixed results may well reflect the imperfection of individual variables in measuring both. A rationalization of the unexpected negative sign for the weighted average number of retail firms and total number of firms could be as follows. Increases in the total number of retail buyers or the weighted average number of retail buyers proxies the increasing number and importance of retail types other than the dominant type, especially when the number of firms in the dominant retail outlet class is an included variable in the model. As the importance of nondominant retail outlet types increases, entry barriers into distribution fall, since the manufacturer has more alternative distribution channels (see Chap-ter 2). With lower entry barriers into manufacturing (including distri-bution) manufacturer return falls (hence the observed negative relation). Also, as the number of outlets in nondominant classes increases, the importance of and possibilities for alternative marketing strategies in-volving the retailer seem likely to increase. Through the destabilizing effects of these alternative strategies on rivalry (through the direct effect), manufacturer rate of return will decrease.

This argument goes in the other direction from that implied by the sign of the coefficient of the Herfindahl variable, which attempts to measure nondominant class selling directly. The Herfindahl measuring multiple types, however, is measuring something quite different from the buyer concentration variables, which measure indirectly the relative number of firms in the nondominant retail outlet types. The Herfindahl is derived solely from the relative market shares of the retail outlet classes selling a product and not their numbers. Market shares are important for manufacturer-retailer bargaining. The sign of the Herfindahl suggests that as the market shares of retail outlet types selling a product become more equalized, the bargaining power of the retail stage decreases. The number of firms in nondominant outlet types seems more important for entry, and thus it is not inconsistent that the two results coexist. In fact, the Herfindahl is most significant (and negative) when it is introduced with both the number of firms in the dominant outlet class and the total number of retail buyers.

The dummy variable measuring high buyer concentration, which by-passes some of the specification problems by giving up information, is consistently negative (high buyer concentration leading to low manufacturer return). This result supports the buyer concentration hypothesis. However, the dummy alone is not as significant or powerful as the combination of buyer concentration variables discussed above or the dummy combined with subsets of these variables. This suggests that the effect of multiple outlet types on retailer power is separately quite important, a result consistent with our *a priori* expectations.

To complete the discussion of the retailer variables, retail market (or local) concentration, as proxied by the number of retail establishments, is significant and consistently enters with the expected positive sign. As the number of establishments increases, retail market concentration decreases and manufacturer return increases.

The retailer variable equations yielding the highest proportion of explained variance combine the buyer concentration dummy, the weighted number of firms, and either weighted average firm size or breadth of product line. Slightly less explained variance results from substituting the number of establishments for the weighted number of firms (equation 25) or substituting the unweighted number of firms for the buyer concentration dummy (equation 16). In these equations the significance levels of the structural variable in the standard model (not reported) are generally improved, especially that of the percent of non-household sales and the advertising variable. With respect to nonhousehold sales, this may indicate the great importance of the variable in capturing those cases where a large part of industry sales are in an area where the retail stage is unimportant (or less important), since the buyer is not the household. The inclusion of proxies for retailer power to influence differentiation should improve the significance of advertising by controlling for variations in its effectiveness, and they do.

## Implications

The results presented in this chapter further highlight the differences between convenience and nonconvenience goods apparent in Chapter 6. The variables measuring the breadth of the retailer's product line (and absolute firm size) allow a successful test of the importance of variation in retailer contribution to product differentiation in the nonconvenience sample. The results here also support the influence of retailer structure on manufacturer profits, and the theory of the effect of strategy variations within industries on profits. Among convenience goods, the standard industrial organization model is relatively good, in part because of the limited power of the retailer there. The tests, consistent with my predictions, found very little explanatory power among the retail variables in the convenience sample. In convenience goods the indirect effect of strategy variation on manufacturer profits was expected to be quite important and the tests confirmed this. The results taken together suggest that the importance of the retail stage in convenience goods appears to be primarily due to its impact on manufacturer strategy. Large convenience retailers provide a vehicle both promoting the existence of and forcing $U$ group status on manufacturers; large retailers are able to create, if you will, the indirect effect. Retailer power in convenience goods is derived primarily from the retailer's control of entry into distribution which takes on great importance among convenience goods if the product is not differentiated.

Among nonconvenience goods the retailer takes on much greater importance both directly and through his impact on strategy variations. Our results clearly show the importance of retailer variables in nonconvenience industries, especially breadth of retailer product line, which provides a measure of differences in retailer contribution to product differentiation within the nonconvenience sample. Buyer concentration nationally and locally, as well as the extent of multiple class selling, also yielded quite strong results, although specification problems led to a complicated problem of interpretation. Strategy variation, though expected to be important, was poorly measured using the advertising variables available.

In view of our inability to measure strategy variation accurately in nonconvenience goods, it is not surprising that the strategy variables performed very badly there. Strategy effects may have been captured to a degree in the retailer variables.

We have come a long way from the initial tests of the convenience-nonconvenience partitioning. From an initial result which showed major differences in unexplained variance between convenience and nonconvenience goods, the study concludes with results reflecting models of similar explanatory power in the two samples. The best equation for the convenience sample yielded a corrected $R^2$ of .904 (Table 7–2) while the best equation for the nonconvenience sample yielded an $R^2$ of .912 (Table 7–7). These results greatly exceed in explanatory power all previous work. The mechanism for this improvement was explicit recognition of the structural differences in the two groups of industries and extensions of the theory to include factors both inside and outside the traditional industry. The end result is two very different structure-performance models, with greatly different implications for economic analysis and public policy.[22]

---

22. Several authors have given explanations for the low values of $R^2$ obtained in previous structure performance work which emphasize limitations in data and departures from profit maximization. See, for example, Weiss (1972). My results have shown that the problem may lie in the theory rather than the data. However, the high values of $R^2$ also reflect the modest number of degrees of freedom.

# 8

## Conclusions and Implications

This study began with three basic premises which represented a departure from the mainstream literature of industrial organization. First, I argued that the buyer's process of choice among brands is an important determinant of the manufacturer's selling strategies and in turn his market power. Second, because the retail stage is not perfectly competitive and the buyer's choice process affords it the power to influence product differentiation, it must be incorporated explicitly in the analysis of structure-performance relationships in consumer goods industries. Finally, economically important differences among firms in an industry affect its performance. These premises spawned the theory presented in Chapters 2 through 5.

In Chapters 6 and 7 some of the major implications of the theory were tested empirically and received strong support. These conclusions need no major repetition here. Differences between convenience and nonconvenience goods in the buyer's process of choice and retailer power lead to sharp differences in the structure-performance link. Measures of the retail sector's structure and market power were developed and their influence on manufacturer's profitability affirmed. Proxies for the intraindustry variation in marketing strategy also proved to be significant determinants of rates of return. The results taken as a whole lend considerable support to the three premises.

The thrust of the study was away from the industry as traditionally defined, both inward toward the firm and outward toward vertically related stages of production and distribution. But our work has come full circle. I have shown how the industry, when properly specified as a collection of diverse firms interacting with each other and with adjacent stages, is restored as a more useful unit of analysis than before.

### Implications for Testing Structure-Performance Relationships

The implications of the study for testing structure-performance relations are clear. First, adjacent stages of production and distribution demand simultaneous analysis, both to capture the direct interaction between stages and to gain important leverage on the critical properties of adjacent stages. Although this expansion is perhaps most important in consumer goods, measures to capture the structure of buying markets should be important in producer goods as well.[1] There the more traditional modeling of buyer concentration combined with indices of the threat of vertical integration by buyers into the producer markets should be central.

Second, the convenience-nonconvenience distinction suggests that the structural determinants of performance vary among broad groups of industries. This conclusion is supported by my analysis of the advertising-market power relation, which suggests that the significance of advertising depends on the media used and which supports a role in influencing market power for direct selling by salesmen in some industries. Although most investigators have strived for generality by employing broad samples of industries, my results imply that the important market structure-performance relationships may vary from one group of industries to another. Care in identifying and specifying these differences can pay off handsomely in explaining variations in industry performance. Yet some industry groupings such as the producer goods–consumer goods distinction commonly used in applied research may be unnecessary, reflecting insufficiently general models of buyer choice. Conversely, our results imply that testing across heterogeneous samples of industries is apt to obscure true relationships. My results have indicated how such aggregation clouded the proper specification of the advertising variable in consumer goods industries, produced misleading conclusions about the signs and significance levels of regression coefficients, and imposed a barrier to further refinements in theory.

Third, my results show that the determinants of allocation performance must include interindustry variations in buyers' choice processes,

1. This is affirmed in a recent paper by Lustgarten (1975) for producer goods. Lustgarten treats all sales to retailers as selling to atomistic buyers, and hence his results in consumer good manufacturing industries are unfortunately incomplete.

which in turn influence the manufacturer's selection of selling strategies. Finally, my results suggest that differences in firms' strategies within an industry will affect its average level of profitability and the distribution of its members' rates of return. Measures designed to capture the direct and indirect effects of strategy variations within industries will yield important increases in variance in profits across industries that can be explained.

**Implications for Managers**

The analytical conclusions take as given the process by which manufacturing enterprises react to the constraints and opportunities about them. Yet the selection of a strategy requires sophisticated understanding of the firm's market environment. I briefly sketch here some suggestive implications of the study for the business manager.

On the broadest level, the study illustrates that the structure of its industry is an important determinant of the potential performance of the firm. The model shows how industry structure interacts with the strategy of the firm in determining the firm's profits. As such, it should be more plausible to managers than previous, more structuralist-oriented work in industrial organization which denies the ability of the firm to influence its performance. Since the structure of the industry is crucial to the manager's determination of his firm's strategy, he should have clearly in mind which elements of industry structure he can influence, which he cannot, and which ones may evolve over time.

The model of the effects of strategy variations on profitability reveals the benefits and dangers of strategy choices by the firm. The model identifies what strategic elements are crucial in determining profits and which ones have little effect. It illuminates the long run structural advantages some firms in the industry may have over others, and helps separate these from the tactical gains and losses in competitive rivalry. By highlighting the forces that cause manager's goals to diverge, the model also can aid managers in seeking competitive advantages through understanding competitors' reactions better. Finally, the strategy-variation model suggests that unique strategies may have benefits but that these are sometimes accompanied by risks of inducing destabilizing rivalry.

The manufacturer-retailer interaction model allows us to identify those situations where the retailer is, or is likely to be, a powerful force. Especially in new or developing markets, the ability to predict this may give firms a competitive edge in retailer relations. The model also clearly identifies the sources of retailer power and is suggestive of ways it can be offset, from the manufacturer's viewpoint, or promoted from the retailer's. Finally, the interbrand choice model has direct applicability to marketing, as does the theory of the relation between sales promotion and market power.

### Implications for Public Policy

The study offers a series of implications for public policy toward consumers, manufacturers, and retailers. The first set of implications follows from the proposition that the buyer's process of gathering information and choosing products varies importantly among consumer goods. Many authors have noted that advertising is a biased source of consumer information and have argued for providing the consumer with more objective information on which to base purchase decisions. Holton introduces the concept of the quality of demand, the "nature and extent of the information that the consumer brings to bear on the purchase decision," to distinguish differences in the information that supports the consumer's purchasing decision.[2] Holton suggests the policy goal of striving for the highest possible quality of demand through establishing product standards, educating consumers, providing better consumer information, and so on.[3] Related public policy issues are the socially desirable level of advertising and policy toward product innovations.

My results offer a somewhat mixed prescription for proposals to increase consumer information, because the consumer's demand for information in various forms is determined by the product attributes he ranks highly and the utility costs of gathering information and is bounded by his desire to make an informed choice. Unless the fundamental determinants of the buyers information equilibrium are altered, there is little hope of stimulating more informed choices. The implications of this can be illustrated using the distinction between convenience and nonconvenience goods.

In nonconvenience goods, major gains in the quality of demand do seem possible. The retailer is one source of information; exposed to consumers' complaints and desires, he can provide a conduit for information flowing from consumer to manufacturer. The retailer's power vis-à-vis the manufacturer will enhance the propensity of the manufacturer to listen and respond, while the manufacturer's need to devote sales effort to the retailer provides a ready mechanism for transferring information between them. The powerful retailer enhances the exercise of Albert Hirschman's "voice."[4] Public policy measures designed to increase the retailer's responsibility (as well as the manufacturer's,

2. Holton (1970), p. 103.
3. This position is also implicit in an early paper by Scitovsky (1950).
4. A. D. Hirshman (1970).

usually stressed) for faulty or misrepresented products could greatly expand this role for retailers.

Furthermore, in nonconvenience goods the consumer desires to make an informed choice and is willing to expend effort to inform his purchase decision. He tends to engage in costly research about relatively tangible product attributes such as reliability and technical characteristics. My results imply that he is less influenced by advertising; advertising is only one source of information he uses in conjunction with other and more costly information sources. Although the consumer's responsiveness to advertising apparently still leads to allocative inefficiencies and elevation of the manufacturer's rate of return, the welfare implications of advertising are less noxious in nonconvenience goods. Advertising, because the consumer checks it against other sources of information, is likely to be directed at providing information about product style, operating features and characteristics, and other relatively tangible product characteristics. Thus although advertising leads to elevated rates of return, the informational content of advertising balanced against this allocative distortion would probably be agreed to be socially desirable.

The nature of buyer choice for nonconvenience goods reinforces a favorable appraisal of advertising where product innovation is important. Because the consumer secures extensive information, meaningful product innovation will be rewarded and cosmetic product changes designed solely to elevate market power will be generally ineffective. Furthermore, the retailer provides a mechanism for bringing product innovations to the attention of the buyer and facilitating his recognition of a product's superiority over competing brands (or discounting cosmetic changes). Hence the manufacturer has an incentive to innovate along socially desirable lines.

Because the buyer desires to make an informed choice, increasing consumer information, encouraging the development of product standards, and eliminating false and misleading advertising claims will be effective in nonconvenience goods. Government policy to increase the availability of technical information, subsidize product testing agencies, and the like, will be effective in promoting competition among manufacturers, especially in areas difficult for the buyer to test such as repair and maintenance records. Such public action will assist the consumer to do better what he is already doing, that is, to make a product choice based on careful search.

This picture changes radically in convenience goods. Retailers are a relatively poor mechanism for the exercise of voice because of the retailer's lack of power against the manufacturer or contact with the consumer.

The consumer makes a relatively uninformed choice, and this moves him in the direction of valuing product attributes involving externalities and intangible product characteristics. These are often hard to evaluate even after experience with the product. Advertising, since it is readily available and costless, will be very influential in this choice, as evidenced by its extraordinary impact on rates of return in these industries. The information content of advertising will be lower because of the attributes on which choice is based. Thus the information value of advertising provides little offset against its tendency to enhance market power in convenience goods.

Social measures to provide the consumer with more information about convenience goods' technical and performance characteristics will probably be relatively ineffective. The convenience goods consumer places little value on an informed choice and employs little information unless his utility cost of acquiring it is low. It is difficult to imagine buyers reading technical descriptions of competing cleansers, for example, in the face of entertaining and low cost television ads. If controls on the content of advertising messages remove one nontangible criterion of choice, the consumer will likely shift to another. In addition, the incentive for socially desirable product innovation will be lower in convenience goods (as explained in Chapter 2).

These fundamentally different processes of buyer choice have differing implications for social policy. In convenience goods the case for limiting the quantity of advertising is persuasive, though my theory also suggests that such a ban should depend on the industry and the advertising media employed. Emphasis on the conditions of supply is indicated; lowering entry barriers and increasing the number of producers will be essential to achieving desirable allocative performance and technical progress where the product's and market's characteristics allow advertising. Measures designed to improve the consumer's purchase decisions must promise fundamental changes in the consumer's propensity to make careful choices, or greatly lower the consumer's decision cost. In nonconvenience goods, on the other hand, advertising may be somewhat more justified, and public provision of improved consumer information should be effective. Actions such as these are more useful substitutes for policies directed toward the conditions of supply.

Social policy toward innovation must recognize the differences in manufacturers' incentives between the two groups of industries. In nonconvenience goods, actions facilitating product innovation through research support, streamlining of patent laws, and so on, are likely to meet with good response. In view of the need for heavy promotional efforts to ensure success of innovations in convenience goods, however, such response is not assured. Measures may be needed to discourage superficial product changes, perhaps through strict control of advertising claims. However, in view of the consumer's decision calculus, stronger and more direct measures may be required, such as independent testing of proposed product improvements.

The second major set of implications of this study for public policy concerns the potential use of the retailer in social control of manufacturing and the need for the extension of antitrust policy to encompass the retail stage. In view of the prevalence of market power among retailers, an alternative to antitrust action against the manufacturing industry is regulation of retail markets' structure. The clearest examples are such industries as automobiles and gasoline, in which the manufacturer retains virtually all the power over the retail stage through control over affiliated outlets. Outlawing such retailer structures would lead to a more effective retail check on manufacturer power, especially in automobiles where the retailer's influence over purchase decisions is great.

Similarly, policy measures may capitalize on the retail stage's influence on strategic variation and rivalry in the manufacturing industry. Actions to promote diversity in the retail distribution systems would tend to encourage strategy variations among manufacturers and thereby enhance rivalry. Retail diversity also provides the consumer with a greater variety of product/service combinations. Chains and discount outlets, so long as they do not overrun the retail market, are a powerful source of enhanced rivalry in manufacturing, especially in nonconvenience goods. In convenience goods, chains provide the impetus for private labels which offer the consumer alternatives for choice and lower prices. Other mechanisms for increasing the diversity of retailers include relaxing restrictive licensing requirements, which appear to impede improved performance in alcoholic beverages by freezing the structure of liquor retailing.[5]

Antitrust policy designed to improve manufacturer performance through retailer structure may seem to comprise a second-best solution to the problem of socially undesirable structures in manufacturing industries. However, a realistic appraisal of the antitrust laws suggests that an impasse has been reached in tightly oligopolistic manufacturing industries. There the probability of overt anticompetitive actions subject to prosecution under Section I of the Sherman Act is low, and the monopoly tests of Section II are too stringent to be useful. The chances

5. Against these benefits of chains one must of course weigh the costs of reducing the number of small businesses and the centralizing of economic power which accompanies their development.

that the statutes will be reinterpreted to encompass joint tacit agreements among oligopolists seem to be low in view of the failure of the courts to follow the precedent set in the *American Tobacco* case (1946),[6] and the problems of "compliability" suggested by Brewster (that is, fairness, a clear way for the businessman to perceive wrongdoing, and so on).[7] Action toward retail structures may then represent the only hope of dealing with existing unsatisfactory manufacturing structures.

Another implication of the study is that opportunities for recognition of mutual dependence are rich in retailing and that entry barriers into retailing may be higher than usually imagined. In view of this, social policy should pay more attention to market power in retailing. Concentration in many retail markets is quite high, and Sherman Act tests may usefully be applied to them.

A third set of implications of our results for public policy lies in the area of antitrust policy towards restrictive distribution arrangements and resale price maintenance. These were extensively discussed in Chapter 3 and need no repetition here.

A final set of implications for public policy follows from our model of the effects of strategy variations within industries on profitability. They suggest a role for social policy that encourages strategy variations leading to greater rivalry in the industry. When examining a market for Sherman Act violations, antitrust policy might weigh both a firm's market share and the uniqueness of its strategy in determining its compliance. Also, indirect measures to encourage strategy variation, such as allocation of government purchases to firms with differing strategies and policy toward retailing are suggested.

## Implications for Future Research

The analysis offers numerous suggestions for further research, and I will focus the discussion on several of the most important areas. First, the models presented in Chapters 2 and 4 provide the beginnings of a theory of the link between the structure of retailing and retail performance that heretofore was altogether lacking. The retail stage contributes an enormous share of the economy's value added, which suggests that the payoff to understanding the structure-performance relationship in retailing is high. Models of this relationship must explicitly include the interaction between the retail stage and manufacturing and recognize the facts that retailers sell multiple products, compete not only with other retail outlets of their type but with other types as well, and use sales-promotion media generally restricted to their local area.

6. *American Tobacco Co. v. United States* 328 U.S. 781 (1946).

7. K. Brewster (1956).

This retail structure-performance link will help answer an important welfare question. The criterion of allocative efficiency relevant for consumers' welfare is the total lump of excess profit that is appropriable by the manufacturing and retail stages together. Existing antitrust statutes implicitly assume that these are independent; improving the performance of manufacturing is independent of the effect of such improvement on the manufacturer-retailer relationship and on retailers' rate of return. My theory clouds this interpretation, however. Public policy that weakens the manufacturer's power vis-à-vis the retailer may not reduce the total lump of excess profit if an increase in the retailer's profit offsets any reduction in the manufacturer's. A theory of the link between retail structure and retail performance and empirical verification of that theory are essential prerequisites for reaching a conclusion on this question.

A second major research area suggested by this study is empirical analysis of the variation among products in buyers' choice processes, and extension of modeling of it to identify the central influential product traits, both theoretically and empirically. Factors affecting the buyers' desire for information and utility costs of obtaining it vary over time, and rich empirical possibilities lie in relating these variations to changes in the quantity of information sources provided over time. International comparisons of buyers' choice processes also promise substantial opportunities for empirical leverage on their determinants. In addition, demand theory must be extended to incorporate differences in preferences (attribute rankings) among buyers, and an apparatus must be developed to evaluate the welfare implications of the presence or absence of product variety in light of these differences. And while much of the discussion in this study has centered on consumer goods, it is evident that important empirical implications of buyer choice processes exist in producer goods as well.

A third major research area suggested by this study is a careful examination of the markets for information. The efficiency of information sources and technical changes in the conveyance of information (such as the advent of television) should provide important predictors of their use. The relation between pricing by the information media and rents accruing to the sellers of goods who purchase media services would shed interesting light on the markets for information. The identification of indivisibilities in the supply of information by the various information sources has critical implications for market power and deserves important attention.

Finally, empirical testing of the hypothesis examined in this study can be extended and improved. The first priority is perhaps the compilation of better strategy data. This may require new research methodologies based on a mix of the industry study and the now more usual cross-section statistical methods. Second, breakdown of advertising expenditures by media would allow tests of the propositions advanced about the effects of differing media segmentability on advertising entry barriers.

Beyond improvements in the methodology advanced by this study, it is hoped that the redirection of structure-performance testing proposed will stimulate research in areas yet outside our awareness and lead to greater integration between the research efforts of economists and scholars of business administration. It will almost certainly require delving into the richness and complexity of individual firm strategies and decision-making processes, while maintaining the overall perspective of the stable structural features of market environments. Such research is what real progress in industrial organization will be made of. The initial barriers broken, opportunities for real progress appear to be on the horizon.

# Technical Appendix

This appendix describes the sources of data and construction of variables used in the empirical sections of this study. The description will be organized to follow the major stages of empirical work: structure-performance testing across convenience and nonconvenience industries and tests involving measures of retailer structure. The construction of the strategy variables used in the study is described in the text.

**Convenience-Nonconvenience Testing**

The convenience-nonconvenience tests constitute the core results on which later testing depends. In addition, the data matrix used for these tests serves as the core for subsequent testing.

The Sample

The basic data were obtained through the courtesy of Esposito and Esposito (hereafter Esposito). It consists of a sample of 43 consumer goods industries which was used in conjunction with a sample of producer goods industries in a recent article.[1] Of the 43 consumer goods industries in the Esposito sample, 7 were excluded because they failed to satisfy the important characteristics of a consumer goods industry in the context of this study, that is, goods sold primarily to households.[2] In addition, 6 other industries were included in the sample which had

---

1. Esposito and Esposito (1971).
2. The industries excluded were: 2110 broad woven fabric mills, cotton; 2212 broad woven fabric mills, man made fiber and silk; 2220 broad woven fabric mills,

been excluded by Esposito for lack of import data which were not used in this study.[3] The final sample consisted of 42 consumer goods industries which are listed in Table 6–1 in the text.

For the sample of 42 consumer goods industries the sources of data and definitions of the variables constructed were as follows.

Data Sources

The profit and advertising variables are constructed from data in the 1963, 1964, and 1965 Internal Revenue Service *Sourcebooks* of the *Statistics of Income;* data for the market growth of demand variable are from the 1958–59 and 1965 *Sourcebooks*. The seller concentration and minimum efficient scale variables are based on data from the *1963 Census of Manufacturers*. The capital requirements series is drawn from both sources. The regional dummy variable is constructed using information presented in Kaysen and Turner, *Antitrust Policy*, table 2, pp. 317–321.

The basic industry sample consists of 42 IRS "minor" industries. IRS industry classifications are broader than four-digit industry classifications reported in the *Census of Manufacturers*. The four-digit census industries comprising an IRS minor industry are identified using the Census Link Project, *Enterprise Statistics*, part 3, 1958.

Construction of Variables

*Profits.* The profit variable equals the ratio of net profit less income tax to net worth averaged for the three-year period, 1963–65. These years constituted a full business cycle. Net worth is the aggregate of common and preferred capital stock, paid-in or capital surplus, surplus reserves, and earned surplus and undivided profits. IRS returns with and without net income are used. The profit variable for each industry is computed for only those firms with assets of over $500,000.[4] This eliminates the need for adjusting the profits of the smaller firms where profits may be understated because of the withdrawals for executive salaries.[5]

*Seller concentration.* The *Census of Manufacturers* reports concentration ratios at the SIC four-digit level. An average four-firm con-

---

wool; 2280 yarn and thread mills; 2291 narrow fabrics; 2712 printing, including manifold business forms; 3580 service industry machinery.

3. The industries included were: 2510 household furniture; 2712 periodicals; 2850 paint; 3520 farm machinery and equipment; 3711 motor vehicles; 3830 optical, medical goods.

4. Comanor and Wilson (1967), p. 427; Kilpatrick (1968), pp. 482–487.

5. Stigler (1963), pp. 125–127. See Marcus (1969) for a test which justifies the cutoff firm size used in this study.

centration ratio, weighted by value of shipments, is obtained for those four-digit industries identified as belonging to each sample IRS minor industry. An identical procedure is used to compute an average eight-firm concentration ratio.

*Minimum efficient scale.*   In estimating minimum efficient scale for the component SIC four-digit industries, the procedure followed by Comanor and Wilson was employed.[6]

*Local and regional industries.*   The adjustment for local and regional industries used in the Esposito data was a local/regional dummy variable based on Kayson and Turner as noted above.[7] This study utilized, in addition, another adjustment for local and regional industries which involved the construction of an adjusted four-firm concentration ratio series. The adjusted four-firm concentration ratio was calculated using data contained in an article by Shwartzman and Bodoff.[8] Adjusted four-digit concentration ratios given in Shwartzman and Bodoff were used to compute weighted average three-digit concentration ratios corresponding to the IRS minor industries used in the sample. Unfortunately, only the four-firm concentration ratio series could be adjusted in this manner, since there were no adjusted four-digit eight-firm concentration ratios. The industries for which local or regional adjustments were made and the magnitude of the adjustments are given below:

| Industry[a] | Four-firm concentration ratio | Adjusted four-firm concentration ratio |
|---|---|---|
| 2010 | 27 | 37 |
| 2020 | 27 | 51 |
| 2030 | 32 | 39 |
| 2040 | 35 | 43 |
| 2050 | 30 | 49 |
| 2070 | 36 | 52 |
| 2082 | 35 | 66 |
| 2086 | 25 | 67 |
| 2330 | 10 | 13 |
| 2510 | 14 | 22 |
| 2850 | 26 | 33 |

[a] Industry names are given in Table 6-1.

6. Comanor and Wilson (1967), p. 439.

7. The three local industries are: dairy products (IRS No. 2020), bakery products (IRS No. 2050), soft drinks (IRS No. 2086).

8. Shwartzman and Bodoff (1971).

*Advertising.*   In addition to advertising to sales ratios two additional series were constructed measuring advertising per firm. The first was constructed by taking the largest firms accounting for 30 percent of industry receipts and dividing the total advertising outlays of these firms by the number of firms. In the usual case where the 30 percent cutoff occured within an IRS asset size class, the entire size class sales and number of firms were included. A second advertising per firm series was constructed by computing advertising per firm taking all firms in the industry.

An advertising to sales ratio for the entire industry was constructed in the usual way, omitting firms with assets less than $500,000. In addition, an advertising to sales ratio was constructed for the largest firms accounting for at least 30 percent of sales. In the usual case where the 30 percent cutoff occurred within an asset size class, the entire size was included.

*Industry growth in demand.*   The variable used to measure the industry demand growth was the ratio of 1965 IRS industry shipments to 1958 shipments. This represented dollar growth. Real growth was constructed by deflating dollar growth with industry sales deflators constructed as indicated below.

Wholesale price indexes for the period 1958–65 were estimated from the Bureau of Labor Statistics, *Wholesale Prices and Price Indexes,* January 1966, Final, and February 1966, Preliminary. This issue contained data for the full year 1965. The Bureau of Labor Statistics base period for the commodity indexes was 1957–59. It was assumed that this represented price levels in 1958 with sufficient precision for the purposes of the analysis, hence no adjustments to the published price indexes were made. It was further assumed that wholesale price changes were representative of manufacturer price changes. Since BLS commodity groups in a few cases did not correspond exactly to the industries in the sample, estimates were made of price changes in some industries utilizing data for similar commodities. Real industry sales growth was obtained by dividing the dollar growth by the index obtained.

*Percent industry sales to nonhouseholds.*   This series was estimated using data contained in the 1958 *Census of Manufacturers,* chapter 10. For each industry, sales in the following three categories were added: other manufacturers; industrial, construction, institutional and commercial users, and state and local governments; and federal government. This was done for each product (sometimes less aggregated than three digit) listed which could be classified into an industry in the sample. Then total nonhousehold sales for all the product classes given for each industry were added and related to the total sales for those same product classes.

The data were of somewhat irregular quality. Some industries had missing product classes. In these industries it was assumed that the product classes given were representative of the industry in terms of percent nonhousehold sales. In 8 of 42 industries no data were given. Percentages for these industries were estimated based on industries included in the data where the pattern of nonhousehold sales was judged to be similar. In only one case out of the 8 did the industries with missing data have large potential nonhousehold sales. In view of this, the data were felt to be fairly representative although somewhat crude.

## Retailer Variables

The basic source for the retailer variables was the 1963 *Census of Business, Retail Trade Summary Statistics.* The number of firms and establishments in each retail outlet class was taken from *Retail Trade Summary Statistics,* part 1, chapter 4, table 2. The measure of the breadth of retailer product line was taken from *Retail Trade Summary Statistics,* part 2, table 1. The distribution of product sales by retail outlet class was obtained from *Retail Trade Summary Statistics,* part 2, table 3. Where broad merchandise line categories were too broad or too narrow to correspond to the industries in the sample of 42 consumer goods industries, additional sources were used to estimate the distribution of product sales by retail outlet class. The primary source utilized was *Retail Trade Summary Statistics,* part 2, table 1, which contained detailed breakdowns of merchandise line sales by outlet class. In addition several other specialized sources were utilized.[9]

Raw Data Series

All retailer variables were constructed using several raw data series derived from the sources listed above. These are described as follows. The construction of the actual variables included in the regression equations is described in the text.

*Retail outlet classes.* The basic retail outlet classes used in the study

---

9. These were: *Fairchild Financial Manual of Retail Stores,* New York, Fairchild Publications, 1966; Accounting Corporation of America, *Barometer of Small Business,* San Diego, California, 1966; Shih and Shih, *The American Soft Drink Industry and the Carbonated Beverage Market,* Brookfield, Wisconsin, 1965; *Dairy and Ice Cream Field,* "Third Annual Survey of Milk and Milk Product Trends," June 1970; A. Wolfman, *Wolfman Report on the Photographic Industry in the United States,* New York, Modern Photography, 1966.

were taken from the Bureau of the Census classification scheme. The retail classes used in the study differed in some cases from the Census classification to the extent that the same level of aggregation within the Census retail outlet classification system was not always used. For example, under the broad category "food stores" the Census lists five first level retail store types: grocery stores, meat and fish markets, fruit stores, retail bakeries, and other food stores. Under "other food stores" the Census lists dairy products stores in addition to several others. For purposes of this study, even though dairy product stores were listed as a third level retail outlet class, they were considered comparable to retail bakeries, a second level retail outlet class. The criterion for identifying comparable retail outlet classes was the difference in merchandise line carried by the outlet class and the character of the service provided. The basic level of Census classification used was the second level. Cases where the second level Census classification was superseded were relatively rare. The retail outlet classes used in the study are listed in Table A-1 below.

TABLE A-1. *Retail Outlet Classes*
Lumber and other building materials dealers
Plumbing and heating equipment dealers
Paint, glass, and wallpaper stores
Electrical supply stores
Hardware stores
Farm equipment dealers
Department stores
Variety stores
Miscellaneous general merchandise stores
Grocery stores
Meat and fish (seafood) markets
Fruit stores and vegetable markets
Candy, nut, and confectionery stores
Retail bakeries
Dairy products stores
Egg and poultry dealers
Other miscellaneous food stores
Motor vehicle dealers
Tire, battery, and accessory dealers
Miscellaneous automotive dealers
Gasoline service stations
Women's ready-to-wear stores
Women's accessory and specialty stores

TABLE A-1.   (continued)

Furriers and fur shops
Men's and boys' clothing and furnishing stores
Custom tailors
Family clothing stores
Children's and infants' wear stores
Miscellaneous apparel and accessory stores
Shoe stores
Furniture stores
Floor coverings stores
Drapery, curtain, and upholstery stores
China, glassware, and metalware stores
Miscellaneous home furnishings stores
Household appliance stores
Radio and television stores
Eating places
Drinking places (alcoholic beverages)
Drug stores
Proprietary stores
Liquor stores
Antique stores and secondhand stores
Sporting goods stores
Bicycle shops
Jewelry stores
Fuel oil dealers
Liquefied petroleum gas (bottled gas) dealers
Florists
Cigar stores and stands
Book stores
Stationery stores
Hay, grain, and feed stores
Other farm supply stores
Garden supply stores
News dealers and newsstands
Hobby, toy, and game shops
Camera and photographic supply stores
Gift, novelty, and souvenir shops
Optical goods stores

*Breadth of product line.*   Table 1 in *Retail Trade Summary Statistics* gave the percentage of the total sales of that retail outlet class which the sales of each broad merchandise line represents. In some cases these merchandise lines were coincidental with IRS industries and in some cases they were too broadly defined (for example, alcoholic drinks). However, for the important merchandise lines in each retail outlet class, further detailed breakdowns were provided. These were used to construct percentages of sales for merchandise lines at approximately the IRS industry level of aggregation. This series was then used to construct the breadth of product line measure described in the text. While additional detail was not provided for the smaller product lines of the retail outlet class, this posed few problems, since our breadth of product line measure (as described in the text) is a Herfindahl measure giving low weight to small product lines in percentage terms.

*Industry sales by retail outlet class.*  Where the industry in the sample corresponded with table 3 in *Retail Trade Summary Statistics* the distribution of industry sales by retail outlet class was obtained directly. Each outlet class accounting for more than 1 percent of industry sales and its percent share of industry sales were obtained. For example, the data for footwear were as follows:

| Outlet type | Percent foot-wear sales |
|---|---|
| Department store | 23.5 |
| Limited price variety store | 3.1 |
| General merchandise store | 4.4 |
| Men's and boys' apparel store | 3.1 |
| Women's and children's apparel store | 3.6 |
| Family clothing stores | 6.1 |
| Shoe stores | 51.9 |
| Mail order | 2.5 |

Generally the outlet types listed did not account for 100 percent of industry sales because of the exclusion of retail classes which accounted for a small percentage of product sales. This did not affect the use of the data, however, except where weighted averages were utilized. Retail outlet classes accounting for less than 1 percent of industry sales were felt to be unimportant in terms of the bargaining model presented in Chapters 2–4. Where weighted averages were used, percentage shares of included outlet types were scaled upward so that they totaled 100 percent.

Census data in table 3 did not represent 100 percent coverage of retail outlets in all retail outlet classes. However, the absolute retail sales were not utilized in the study, only the relative product sales within an outlet class. It was felt that the percentage distribution of sales within an outlet class was not seriously affected by the small percentage of retailers not covered (17 percent of total dollar volume).[10]

As noted above, in some cases the broad merchandise lines reported in table 3 did not correspond to the industries in the sample (in all such cases table 3 defined merchandise lines too broadly). In these industries, other techniques were used to estimate the sales distribution. These ranged from assuming that the distribution of sales by retail outlet in the industry were equal to that of a broader merchandise line to estimating using other sources. In most cases the more detailed data in table 1 were used.

As described, table 1 gives sales by merchandise line for each retail outlet class. For the product group that constitutes the majority of the retail outlet class sales, table 1 breaks down product categories to a finer level than that given in the broad merchandise lines. By finding each retail outlet class that is a major seller of a given product, recording the dollar sales volume of the product and summing over all outlet classes it was possible to construct an estimate of the distribution of that product's sales by outlet class. This process involves a degree of judgment. In addition, to the extent that the Census coverage varies across retail outlet classes, such use of dollar sales volumes introduces errors into the analysis. The errors introduced by these shortcomings were felt to be minor, however, not seriously affecting the usefulness of the data. The sensitivity of the retailer variables used in the study to measurement errors of the magnitude which were estimated here is very low.

In a few cases, non-Census sources were used in estimating sales distributions. These sources were by and large trade publications, and were used only where Census data were felt to be inadequate. In two cases retailer data was not obtained. These industries were periodicals (IRS 2712) and medical and optical goods (IRS 3830). In both cases, the meaning of retailer data was questionable. In the case of periodicals a large segment of periodicals is distributed by subscription and hence the hypotheses of my theory do not apply unmodified. In the case of medical and optical goods it was felt that from a distribution standpoint these goods were very different and could not be included with but a single set of retailer variables. In all regressions using retailer variables these two industries were excluded.

Retail Outlet Class Data

For each retail outlet class a series of data points were tabulated. The source of this data was *Census of Business: 1963*, table 2. The data

10. 1963 *Census of Business,* "Merchandise Line Sales," p. *v.*

were as follows: 1. total number of establishments; 2. total number of firms; 3. total number of firms accounting for 50 percent of total sales starting with the largest; 4. average firm size (in terms of dollar sales); 5. average firm size of firms accounting for 50 percent of total sales starting with the largest.

Items 1, 2, and 4 are straightforward. For item 3 the following procedure was utilized. The source of the data was constructed so that establishments, number of firms, and the corresponding sales data were broken out by the size of multiunit firms (the number of establishments in the multiunit firm). Starting with the largest multiunit category, Item 3 was obtained by adding the number of firms and cumulating sales until 50 percent of total sales was reached. Where the 50 percent of sales cutoff occurred within a multiunit category, the entire category was included. Where the 50 percent of sales cutoff fell within the single unit firm category, however, a different technique was used as follows.

The average sales per single unit firm was first calculated. Then the difference between total multiunit sales and 50 percent of total sales was calculated. This number was then divided by the average sales per single unit firm to get the number of single unit firms to be added to the total number of multiunit firms to get the answer.

In both cases, average firm size was obtained by dividing the sales (which in the first case was slightly greater than 50 percent of total sales) by the number of firms calculated above.

# References

Adelman, M. A. *A&P: A Study in Price-Cost Behavior and Public Policy.* Cambridge, Mass.: Harvard University Press, 1959.

—— "Effective Competition and the Anti-Trust Laws." *Harvard Law Review,* 61.8 (September 1948), 1289–1350.

Akerlof, G. A. "The Market for 'Lemons': Qualitative Uncertainty and the Market Mechanism." *Quarterly Journal of Economics,* 84.3 (August 1970), 488–500.

Alchian, A. "Uncertainty, Evolution, and Economic Theory.' *Journal of Political Economy,* 58.8 (1950), 211–221.

Alemson, M. A. "Advertising and the Nature of Competition in Oligopoly over Time: A Case Study." *Economic Journal,* 80.318 (June 1970), 282–305.

Bain, J. S. *Price Theory.* New York: Holt, 1952.

—— *Barriers to New Competition.* Cambridge, Mass.: Harvard University Press, 1956.

—— *Industrial Organization,* 2nd ed. New York: Wiley, 1968.

—— *Essays on Price Theory and Industrial Organization.* Boston: Little, Brown, 1972.

*Bic Pen Corporation,* Harvard Business School. Boston: International Case Clearinghouse 4–374–305, 1974.

Bloch, H. "Advertising, Competition and Market Performance." Ph.D. dissertation, University of Chicago, 1971.

Borden, N. *The Economic Effects of Advertising.* Chicago: Irwin, 1942.

Bowman, W. S. "Resale Price Maintenance—A Monopoly Problem." *Journal of Business,* 25 (July 1952); reprinted in Blumner and Hefner, *Readings in the Regulation of Business,* Scranton, Pa.: International Textbook Co., 1968, pp. 234–268.

Boyer, K. D. "Informative and Goodwill Advertising." *Review of Economics and Statistics,* 56.4 (November 1974), 541–548.

Brewster, K. "Enforceable Competition: Unruly Reason or Reasonable Rules." *American Economic Review*, 46.2 (May 1956), 472–489.

Bucklin, L. P., "Retail Strategy and the Classification of Consumer Goods." *Journal of Marketing*, 27. 1 (January, 1963), 50–55.

Cable, J. "Market Structure, Advertising Policy, and Intermarket Differences in Advertising Intensity." in K. Cowling, ed., *Market Structure and Corporate Behavior*. London: Gray-Mills, 1972.

Caves, R. E. *Air Transport and Its Regulators*. Cambridge, Mass.; Harvard University Press, 1962.

———— "Uncertainty, Market Structure and Performance: Galbraith as Conventional Wisdom," in Markham and Papanek, eds., *Industrial Organization and Economic Development*. New York: Houghton-Mifflin, 1970.

Caves, R. E., and W. F. Murphy, II. "Franchising: Firms, Markets and Intangible Assets." *Southern Economic Journal*, 42.4 (April 1976).

Caves, R. E., and M. E. Porter. "From Entry Barriers to Mobility Barriers: Conjectural Decisions and Contrived Deterrence to Market Power." *Quarterly Journal of Economics*, forthcoming.

Caves, R. E., and B. S. Yamey. "Risk and Corporate Rates of Return: Comment." *Quarterly Journal of Economics*, 85 (August 1971), 513–517.

Chamberlin, E. M. *The Theory of Monopolistic Competition*, 8th ed. Cambridge, Mass.: Harvard University Press, 1962.

Collins, N., and L. Preston. "Price-Cost Margins and Industry Structure." *Review of Economics and Statistics*, 51.3 (August 1969), 271–286.

Comanor, W. S. "Vertical Territorial and Customer Restrictions: White Motor and Its Aftermath." *Harvard Law Review*, 81 (1968), 1419–1438.

Comanor, W. S. and T. Wilson. *Advertising and Market Power*. Cambridge, Mass.: Harvard University Press, 1974.

———— "Advertising and the Advantages of Size." *American Economic Review*, 49.2 (May 1969), 87–98.

———— "Advertising, Market Structure and Performance." *Review of Economics and Statistics*, 49.4 (November 1967), 423–440.

Copeland, M. T. "Consumers' Buying Motives." *Harvard Business Review*, 2.2 (January 1924), 305–318.

———— "Relation of Consumers' Buying Habits to Marketing Methods." *Harvard Business Review*, 1.3 (April 1923), 282–290.

Curran, K. J. "Exclusive Dealing and Public Policy." *Journal of Marketing*. 15 (October 1950). Reprinted in Blumner and Hefner, *Readings in the Regulation of Business*. Scranton, Pa.: International Textbook Co., 1968, pp. 298–312.

Darby, M. R., and Edi Karni, "Free Competition and the Optional Amount of Fraud." *Journal of Law and Economics*, 17 (April 1973), 67–88.

Dirlam, J., and A. E. Kahn. *Fair Competition: The Law and Economics of Antitrust Policy*. Ithaca, N.Y.: Cornell University Press, 1954, pp. 90–140, 173–201.

Dixon, D. F. "The Development of the Sales System of Petroleum Distribution in the United Kingdom, 1950–1960." *Economica*, 39 (February 1962), 40–52.

Dorfman, R., and P. Steiner. "Optimal Advertising and Optimal Quality." *American Economic Review*, 44 (1954), 826–836.

Doyle, P. "Advertising Expenditure and Consumer Demand." *Oxford Economic Papers*, 28 (November 1968), 395–416.

Else, P. K. "The Incidence of Advertising in Manufacturing Industries." *Oxford Economic Papers*, 18 (March 1966), 88–110.

Engel, J., D. Kollat, and R. Blackwell. *Consumer Behavior,* 2nd ed. New York: Holt, Rinehart and Winston, 1973.

Esposito, L., and F. F. Esposito. "Foreign Competition and Domestic Industry Profitability." *Review of Economics and Statistics,* 58.4 (November 1971).

Farley, J. U. "'Brand Loyalty' and the Economics of Information." *Journal of Business,* 37 (October 1964), 370–381.

Fellner, W. J. *Competition among the Few: Oligopoly and Similar Market Structures.* New York: Knopf, 1949.

Ferguson, J. M. *Advertising and Competition: Theory, Management, Fact.* Cambridge, Mass.: Ballinger, 1974.

Fisher, I., and G. Hall. "Risk and Corporate Rates of Return." *Quarterly Journal of Economics,* 83 (February 1969), 79–92.

Galbraith, J. K. *American Capitalism.* New York: Houghton-Mifflin, 1956.

—— "Countervailing Power." *American Economic Review,* 44.2 (May 1954) 1–6, 26–34.

—— "Mr. Hunter on Countervailing Power: A Comment." *Economic Journal,* 69 (March 1959), 168–170.

Gale, B. T. "Market Share and Rate of Return." *Review of Economics and Statistics,* 54.4 (November 1972), 412–423.

Goldfeld, S., and R. E. Quant. "Some Tests for Homoscedasticity." *Journal of the American Statistical Association,* 60 (1965), 538–547.

Greer, D. F. "Advertising and Market Concentration." *Southern Economic Journal,* 38.1 (July 1971), 19–32.

—— "Advertising and Market Concentration: Reply." *Southern Economic Journal,* 39 (January 1973), 451–453.

Hall, M., and L. Weiss, "Firm Size and Profitability." *Review of Economics and Statistics,* 49.3 (August 1967), 319–331.

*Heublein, Inc.,* Harvard Business School. Boston: International Case Clearinghouse 9–373–103, 1973.

Hicks, J. R. "Economic Theory and the Evaluation of Consumers' Wants." *Journal of Business,* 35.3 (July 1962), 256–263.

Hirschman, A. O. *Exit, Voice, and Loyalty.* Cambridge, Mass.: Harvard University Press, 1970.

Holdren, B. R. *The Structure of a Retail Market and the Market Behavior of Retail Units.* Englewood Cliffs, N.J.: Prentice-Hall, 1960.

Holton, R. H. "The Distinction between Convenience Goods, Shopping Goods, and Specialty Goods." *Journal of Marketing,* 23.1 (July 1958), 53–56.

—— "Consumer Behavior, Market Imperfections, and Public Policy," in Markham and Papanek, eds., *Industrial Organization and Economic Development.* New York: Houghton-Mifflin, 1970.

—— "The Role of Competition and Monopoly in Distribution: The Experience in the United States," in J. Perry Miller, ed., *Competition, Cartels and Their Regulation.* Amsterdam: North Holland, 1962.

Hunt, M. S. "Competition in the Major Home Appliance Industry, 1960–1970." Ph.D. dissertation, Business Economics Committee, Harvard University, May 1972.

Hunter, A. "Notes on Countervailing Power." *Economic Journal,* 67 (March 1958), 85–103.

Isaacson, H. L. *Store Choice: A Case Study of Consumer Decision Making,* New York: National Research Institute, 1966.

Johnson, J. *Econometric Methods,* 2nd ed. New York: McGraw-Hill, 1972.

Kaldor, N. "The Economics of Advertising." *Review of Economic Studies,* 18.1 (1949–50), 1–27.

Kaysen, C., and D. F. Turner. *Antitrust Policy.* Cambridge, Mass.: Harvard University Press, 1959.

Kelley, W. H. *Economic Report on the Influence of Market Structure on the Profit Performance of Food Manufacturing Companies,* Washington: U.S. Federal Trade Commission, September 1969.

Kilpatrick, R. W. "Stigler on the Relationship Between Industry Profit Rates and Market Concentration." *Journal of Political Economy,* 76 (May–June 1968).

Lancester, K. J. "A New Approach to Consumer Theory." *Journal of Political Economy,* 74.2 (April 1966), 132–157.

Learned, E. P., C. R. Christensen, K. R. Andrews, and W. Guth. *Business Policy.* Homewood, Ill.: Irwin, 1969.

Lustgarten, S. R. "The Effect of Buyer Concentration in Manufacturing Industries." *Review of Economics and Statistics,* 57.2 (May 1975), 125–132.

Mann, H. M., J. A. Henning and J. W. Meehan, Jr., "Advertising and Concentration: An Empirical Investigation." *Journal of Industrial Economics,* 16 (November 1967), 34–45.

—— "Advertising and Market Concentration: Comment." *Southern Economic Journal,* 39 (January 1973), 448–451.

Marcus, M. "Profitability and Size of Firm." *Review of Economics and Statistics,* 51 (February 1969), 104–107.

Markham, J. W. *The Fertilizer Industry.* Vanderbilt Press, 1958.

Mathewson, G. W. "A Consumer Theory of Demand for the Media." *Journal of Business,* 45, 2 (April 1972), 212–224.

May, F. E. "Buying Behavior: Some Research Findings." *Journal of Political Economy,* 75 (April 1966), 132–157.

McNally, P. *The Economics of the Distribution Trades.* London: George Allen & Unwin, 1971.

Miller, J. P. "Competition and Countervailing Power: Their Roles in the American Economy." *American Economic Review,* 54.2 (May 1954), 16–25.

Miller, R. A. "Marginal Concentration Ratios and Industrial Profit Rates." *Southern Economic Journal,* 34 (October 1967), 259–267.

Nelson, P. "Information and Consumer Behavior." *Journal of Political Economy,* 78 (March–April 1970), 311–329.

Nelson, P. "Advertising as Information." *Journal of Political Economy,* 81.4 (July–August 1974), 729–754.

Nelson, P. "The Economic Consequences of Advertising." *Journal of Business,* 48.2 (April 1975), 213–241.

Newman, H. H. "Strategic Groups and the Structure-Performance Relationship: A Study with Respect to the Chemical Process Industries," Ph.D. dissertation, Harvard University, December, 1973.

*Note on the Light Aircraft Industry,* Harvard Business School, Boston: International Case Clearinghouse 9–370–036, 1970.

*Note on the Recreational Vehicle Industry,* Harvard Business School, Boston: International Case Clearinghouse 9–375–092, 1975.

Palamountain, J. C., Jr. *The Politics of Distribution.* Cambridge, Mass.: Harvard University Press, 1955.

Pashagian, B. P. *The Distribution of Automobiles: An Economic Analysis of the Franchise System.* Englewood Cliffs, N.J.: Prentice-Hall, 1961.

Penrose, E. T. *The Theory of the Growth of the Firm.* Oxford: Blackwell, 1972.

Phillips, Almarin. "A Theory of Interfirm Organization." *Quarterly Journal of Economics,* 74.4 (November 1960), 602–613.

—— *Market Structure, Organization and Performance.* Cambridge, Mass.: Harvard University Press, 1962.

—— "Structure, Conduct and Performance—and Performance, Conduct and Structure?" in Markham and Papanek, eds., *Industrial Organization and Economic Development.* New York: Houghton-Mifflin, 1970, pp. 26–37.

Porter, M. E. "Interbrand Choice, Media Mix and Market Performance." *American Economic Review,* 66.2 (May 1976), 398–406.

Porter, M. E. "The Structure Within Industries and Market Performance," unpublished manuscript.

Preston, L. E. "Restrictive Distribution Arrangements: Economic Analysis and Public Policy Standards." *Law and Contemporary Problems,* 30 (Summer 1965), 506–529.

Rao, P., and R. Miller. *Applied Econometrics.* Belmont, Calif.: Wadsworth Publishing Company, 1971.

Rhoades, S. A. "The Effect of Diversification on Industry Profit Performance in 241 Manufacturing Industries: 1963." *Review of Economics and Statistics,* 55 (May 1973), 146–155.

Roberts, M. J. "How Should the Content of Entertainment Be Determined? Self Regulation and the Alternatives." in R. E. Caves and M. J. Roberts, eds., *Regulating the Product.* Cambridge, Mass.: Ballinger, 1975.

Scherer, F. M. *Industrial Market Structure and Economic Performance.* New York: Rand McNally, 1970.

Schmalensee, R. A. *On the Economics of Advertising.* Amsterdam: North Holland, 1972.

Scitovsky, T. "Ignorance as a Source of Oligopoly Power." *American Economic Review,* 40 (May 1950), 48–53.

Shepherd, W. G. "Trends of Concentration in American Manufacturing Industries, 1947–1958." *Review of Economics and Statistics,* 46.2 (May 1964), 400–412.

Shwartzman, D., and J. Bodoff. "Concentration in Regional and Local Industries." *Southern Economic Journal,* 37.3 (January 1971), 343–348.

Sherman, R., and R. Tollison. "Advertising and Profitability." *Review of Economics and Statistics,* 8 (November 1971), 379–407.

Siegfried, J. L., and L. W. Weiss. "Advertising, Profits, and Corporate Taxes Revisited." *Review of Economics and Statistics,* 56.2 (May 1974), 195–200.

Stigler, G. J. "A Theory of Oligopoly." *Journal of Political Economy,* 62 (February 1964), 44–66.

—— "The Economist Plays with Blocs." *American Economic Review,* 45.2 (May 1954), 7–14.

—— *Organization of Industry.* Homewood, Ill.: Irwin, 1968.

Taylor, L. D., and D. Weiserbs. "Advertising and the Aggregate Consumption Function." *American Economic Review,* 62 (September 1972), 642–655.

Telser, L. "Advertising and Competition." *Journal of Political Economy,* 63 (1964), 2–27.

────── "Another Look at Advertising and Concentration." *Journal of Industrial Economics,* 18 (November 1969), 85–94.

Theil, H. *Principles of Econometrics.* New York: Wiley, 1971.

Vernon, J. M., and R. E. Nourse. "Profit Rates and Market Structure of Advertising Intensive Firms." *Journal of Industrial Economics,* 22 (September 1972), 1–20.

Voorhees, A. M. "Shopping Habits and Travel Patterns." Technical Bulletin no. 24, Urban Land Institute, 1955.

Ward, T. S. *The Distribution of Consumer Goods: Structure and Performance.* London: Cambridge Univ. Press, 1973.

Watkins, M. W., and National Industrial Conference Board. *Public Regulation of Competitive Practices in Business Enterprise,* National Industrial Conference Board, New York, 1940, pp. 85–140, 209–219.

Weiss, L. W. "Advertising, Profits and Corporate Taxes." *Review of Economics and Statistics,* 54.3 (August 1972), 245–257.

────── "Quantative Studies of Industrial Organization," in M. Intriligator, ed., *Frontiers of Quantitative Economics.* Amsterdam: North Holland, 1972.

────── "The Geographic Size of Markets in Manufacturing." *Review of Economics and Statistics,* 54.3 (August 1972), 245–257.

Wenders, J. T. "Collusion and Entry." *Journal of Political Economy,* 79 (November–December 1971), 1258–1277.

White, L. J. *The Automobile Industry since 1945.* Cambridge, Mass.: Harvard University Press, 1971.

Williamson, O. E. "Selling Expense as a Barrier to Entry." *Quarterly Journal of Economics,* 77 (1963), 112–128.

Wolgast, E. "Do Husbands or Wives Make Purchasing Decisions?" *Journal of Marketing,* 23 (October 1958), 151–158.

Worcester, D. A., Jr. *Monopoly, Big Business and Welfare in the Postwar United States.* Seattle, Wash.: University of Washington Press, 1967.

Yamey, B. S., ed. *Resale Price Maintenance.* Chicago: Aldine Publishing, 1966, pp. 3–22. 67–100.

# Index

Access to distribution channels. *See* Entry barriers

Adelman, M. A., 12, 13, 28–29, 51

Advertising, 2, 3; as an asset, 142; as a barrier to entry in manufacturing, 124–132; as a barrier to entry in retailing, 14; content of advertising messages, 29–30; in convenience goods, 26–29; and industry concentration, 121–124; in large firms, 201, 205, 209; and market rivalry, 128–129; as a measure of product differentiation, 35; measurement of, 170–180, 245; in nonconvenience goods, 30–33; in producer goods, 109; and profits, 125–132, 142–148, 170–180; quality of information, 236; by retailers, 47; social desirability of, 124–125, 235–237; social policy toward, 235–237; as a source of product information, 44–45, 101–107; threshold effects of, 126; by wholesalers, 48

Advertising media: and efficiency of information transfer, 117; and entry barriers, 131–132; and profits, 132;

as sources of product information, 101–107

Akerlof, G. A., 97n

Alemson, M. A., 111, 122

American Can Company, 86n

American Home Products, 27

Antitrust Policy, 6, 61–64, 238–239

A&P (Great Atlantic and Pacific Tea Company) 13, 28–29, 49, 51

Attributes. *See* Product attributes

Automobile retailing, 32

Bain, Joe S., 1n, 2, 27, 70, 77n, 122, 125, 127n, 128n, 129n

Barriers to entry. *See* Entry barriers

Bic Pen Corporation, 45

Bloch, Harry, 142n

Bodoff, Joan, and D. Shwartzman, 181–182, 244

Borden, Neil, 103n

Bowman, Ward, 15, 16, 64–65, 67, 140n

Boyer, K. D., 143n

Breadth of product line: in manufacturing, 26n, 47; and profits, 226;

53549

| DATE DUE | | | |
|---|---|---|---|
| MAR 1 1 '81 | | | |
| | | | |
| | | | |
| | | | |
| | | | |
| | | | |
| | | | |
| | | | |
| | | | |
| | | | |
| | | | |
| | | | |
| | | | |